Bavaria
in the German Confederation,
1820-1848

Bavaria
in the German
Confederation,
1820–1848

George S. Werner

Rutherford · Madison · Teaneck
Fairleigh Dickinson University Press
London: Associated University Presses

© 1977 by Associated University Presses, Inc.

Associated University Presses, Inc.
Cranbury, New Jersey 08512

Associated University Presses
Magdalen House
136-148 Tooley Street
London SE1 2TT, England

Library of Congress Cataloging in Publication Data

Werner, George S   1943-
    Bavaria in the German Confederation, 1820-1848.

    Bibliography: p.
    Includes index.
    1.   Bavaria—Politics and government—1777-1918.
2.   German Confederation, 1815-1866.   I.   Title.
DD801.B378W47   320.9′43′307   76–738
ISBN 0-8386-1932-0

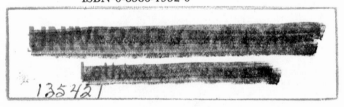
PRINTED IN THE UNITED STATES OF AMERICA

Contents

Preface

Much of modern Bavarian history was marked on the one hand by particularism and the desire to defend local autonomy and, on the other hand, by constant challenges to Bavarian separatism by the larger German powers. As the largest and most powerful of the purely German states, it was important to the proponents of a strong confederation of German states that Bavaria give up elements of her autonomy so that the other, smaller states would also see the futility of resistance. While the spirit of Bavarian independence remained a constant and important factor in German history well into the twentieth century, between 1820 and 1848 particularly strong pressures were placed on the Wittelsbach state for more complete integration into a German state structure ostensibly federal, but one with the potential of becoming, if not the modern nation state, at least something approaching it.

By 1820 the formal constitution of the German Confederation had been established. This had been a victory for the particularist forces in Germany, but procedures had also been established whereby the Confederation could intervene in the internal affairs of the member states. Thus the possibility did exist for the gradual accumulation of power by the Confederation at the expense of its components—a contingency vigorously opposed by the Bavarian government. Indeed, for centralization to have succeeded, Bavaria would either have had to surrender to Austro-Prussian pressure or to have undergone a full psychological reversal. Given Bavarian obstinacy, neither condition could be fulfilled and, as it turned out, external pressures on Bavaria diminished with the disintegration of Austro-Prussian cooperation. As these powers drifted further apart, and as Bavaria failed to develop the desire for leadership in Germany until it was too late, the possibility of a peaceful evolution from federal structure to German national state became increasingly remote. Ultimately it became clear that other means would have to be employed to bring the jealously autonomous states into a more effective union.

By 1834 a working accommodation had apparently been reached between Bavaria and the Confederation. Bavarian autonomy seemed assured, for by that date it was clear that the federal constitution per se would evolve no further. At the same time the federal Diet, generally with Bavaria's cooperation, was able to restore a state of tranquility to Germany. Not until the explosions of 1848 thundered throughout the German states was it again necessary to reconsider the role of the Confederation in German life.

The problem that will be considered here is a study of the techniques and justifications used by Bavaria to influence federal policy in order to maintain her autonomy and to thwart the forces of centralization, and, conversely, the means by which the German Confederation sought to influence Bavarian policy and decisions.

Acknowledgments

First among those to whom I owe a debt of gratitude is Professor George G. Windell of the University of New Orleans. I would also like to thank *Archivrat* Dr. Hans Puchta and the staff of the *Bayerisches Geheimen Staatsarchiv* in Munich for aid and advice. Special thanks are due to Freiherr Rudolph von Lerchenfeld, whose hospitality and assistance are here gratefully acknowledged. Mrs. Joyce Storm of the Interlibrary Loan department of the University of Delaware was especially helpful in quickly obtaining materials that would otherwise not have been available to me. The research was in part made possible by a grant from the University of Delaware. I wish also to thank Professor Lawrence Duggan, who read and criticized the manuscript. Responsibility for all errors is, of course, mine alone.

Introduction

i

The foundations of the medieval *Reich* were severely shaken by the French Revolution, and under the onslaught of Napoleon the edifice finally collapsed, an anachronism in a world caught up in a storm of war and nationalism. The *Reichsdeputations-hauptschluss* of 1803, the final attempt to preserve the empire, served only to limit or abolish those elements, the free ecclesiastical territories and the petty secular rulers, which were its mainstay in order to compensate the larger states for lands on the left bank of the Rhine lost to France. Finally in 1806, the *Reich* was formally acknowledged by its emperor to be defunct; the Holy Roman Empire quietly expired.

Since a Germany composed of several weak and disunited states would invite aggression and annexation by stronger states, as had been the case during the previous centuries, another mode of organizing the German states was needed. The Confederation of the Rhine (*Rheinbund*), the loose federation of sixteen small and middle-sized German states under French protection that replaced the Empire in 1806, was an artificial creation with little possibility for organic development. Accordingly, it could last only as long as Napoleon. When active French support was withdrawn it, too, collapsed, making it obvious that no arrangement which excluded

Austria and Prussia or major foreign powers could exist. Such a body would be too weak to survive in nineteenth-century Europe. Thus, one of the major problems that the statesmen at the Congress of Vienna faced was the reestablishment of order in Germany in light of the alterations in power relationships brought about during the preceding quarter century.

While the organization of Germany was disintegrating, Bavaria used the instability of the revolutionary period to advantage. From the very beginning of his reign, Kurfürst Maximilian IV Joseph (1799–1825) pursued a policy of benevolent neutrality toward France, and, after the Peace of Lunéville of 1801 signified Austrian defeat, he openly supported Napoleon. Consequently, Bavarian claims for territorial compensation on the right bank of the Rhine for lands lost to France on the left bank were supported by Napoleon, and, largely due to French pressure, the *Reichsdeputationshauptschluss* met these demands by granting to Bavaria lands formerly held by ecclesiastical princes.

Franco-Bavarian friendship ripened into an alliance in September 1801, in which Bavaria furnished 28,000 troops to France for war against Austria. The pressure that these soldiers placed on the emperor's northern frontiers facilitated Napoleon's victory over Austria. Accordingly, the Treaty of Pressburg, which ended this phase of the war between France and Austria, rewarded Bavaria with additional territories, increasing her stature and power in Germany. Finally, on January 1, 1806, Kurfürst Maximilian IV declared himself King Maximilian I.

Realizing that he was becoming too dependent on Napoleon, the king attempted to return to a policy of neutrality, albeit one of benevolence toward France. Napoleon, however, would not allow this and forced Bavaria to join with the other *Rheinbund* states in the August 1, 1806 declaration of secession from the Empire. Although, over the seven-year existence of the Confederation of the Rhine, Bavaria grew in strength to become the most powerful of the purely German states, so too did Bavarian dependence on Napoleon increase, depriving Bavaria of her cherished freedom of action. Moreover, her losses in men and treasure erased the immediate value of the gains of territory that friendship with France had brought, and Bavaria soon became disenchanted with the French.

The disaster in Russia provided both the opportunity and the occasion for a change in policy. Given assurances of continued independence and no loss of territory by Austria and Prussia, Bavaria declared her absolute neutrality on April 25, 1813. Three weeks later she concluded an alliance with Austria. Not until the Treaty of Ried on October 8, however, did Bavaria declare her withdrawal from the *Rheinbund* and her adherence to the allies, shifting the balance of power in South Germany away from the French, as Bavarian armies under General Karl von Wrede forced Württemberg and the other southwestern states to join the allies. They did, however, fail in an attempt on October 30 to defeat Napoleon's retreating army at Hanau-am-Main.

When Napoleon proved unwilling or unable to accept the loss of French conquests as the price of peace, the allies concluded the Quadruple Alliance and cautiously but consistently began an invasion of France, entering Paris on March 31, 1814. There the first Peace of Paris was signed on May 30. Despite a brief flurry of activity during Napoleon's short-lived return from exile, the problem of Napoleonic France was settled. To deal with the issues facing the remainder of Europe and to reorganize the German states, a congress was convened in Vienna on November 1. By the positions taken by Bavaria's representatives at the congress, it soon became apparent that Bavaria's chief minister, Maximilian von Montgelas, a proponent of enlightened despotism and of Bavarian autonomy, hoped to raise

Bavaria from the ranks of the territorial princes to that of a European power.[1] He accepted as a temporary necessity the fact that a German Confederation had to be created but wanted sufficient freedom of movement for Bavaria so that when the *Bund* was dissolved, as he fully expected, Bavaria would be strong enough to pursue an independent course in Europe.[2] Montgelas would have been satisfied if the future organization of Germany were based solely on a simple alliance between the states. He would even go so far as to accept a German Confederation, but never another German Empire that might limit Bavaria's freedom of maneuver in her domestic or foreign policies. This attitude formed the foundation on which all Bavarian activities vis-à-vis the Confederation would be based until the Confederation's suspension in 1848.

In Vienna the major German states agreed to the creation of a confederation based exclusively on governments rather than on the German people. The *Bundesakt,* which would serve as the new Confederation's constitution, was embodied in the final treaty of Vienna, thereby creating a guarantee— subject to interpretation—by German and non-German great powers.[3] As finally agreed upon, the *Bundesakt* was a compromise: concessions were made to Bavaria and other states by the great powers, yet no one was fully satisfied. Some states, notably Prussia and Württemberg, saw it as a basis for further discussion, which would lead to a more fully integrated structure; Bavaria saw it as her final concession to the federal structure and, to prevent further erosion of her autonomy, would oppose all further attempts to strengthen the *Bund.*

The German Confederation as established by the Congress was a federation of sovereign princes and cities, not of peoples, joined in a permanent union to preserve the external and internal security of Germany and the independence and "inviolability" of the individual states.[4] The organ through which the member states were to work was officially known as the

Bundesversammlung (federal Assembly), often called the *Bundestag* (federal Diet), a gathering of the ambassadors of those states. Normally the federal Assembly met in the form of an *Engerer Rat* (Select Council) in which the larger states each had one vote, while the other votes were shared by the smaller states. In all there were a total of seventeen votes distributed among the thirty eight (later thirty nine) members of the Confederation. Most matters were decided by simple majority vote, although it became the custom to postpone decisions until each ambassador had received instructions and had cast his vote.[5]

For matters of grave importance, such as the alteration of the federal constitution, the *Bundestag* met as a *Plenum* (Plenary Council). Then, although the membership remained the same as in the *Engerer Rat,* sixty-nine rather than seventeen votes were distributed among the member states, each having at least one vote and none having more than four. Since a change in the basic laws of the Confederation required unanimous approval, even the smallest state had a veto.[6] Consequently, it proved all but impossible to reform the Confederation within the framework of the federal Diet; major modifications had first to be agreed upon outside the formal constitutional structure before presentation to the federal Assembly for acceptance.

As defined by Article 11 of the *Bundesakt,* all member states had the right to make alliances with other German or foreign states so long as these were not directed against the Confederation or any of its members. Should the *Bund* declare war, all members were obliged to supply soldiers and funds on the basis of the *Kriegs-Verfassung* agreed upon in 1821–22. The Confederation alone could conclude peace in such a case; individual states were not to make independent treaties. Finally, the states obligated themselves to forego war against one another, agreeing to bring all controversies to the federal Diet for mediation, or, that failing, for judgment by an *Austrägal* court.[7]

The German Confederation, then, was not a state, but was rather an association in international law, directed primarily toward guaranteeing security for Germany. Its chief organ was no legislature, but was rather a permanent diplomatic conference; its decrees, in fact, were treaties among the member states and binding on all. Nevertheless, the Confederation was more tightly organized than the old Empire. A military organization did exist, and, as events were to show, the Confederation had the means to force compliance with its decrees. At the same time, however, it lacked the ability and energy to fulfill many of the promises made in the *Bundesakt.*

One such promise was contained in Article 13, which stated that each state was to have a constitution. The terminology, "there will be a *landständische* constitution in all states of the Confederation," however, had been made intentionally vague to maintain the power of the princes at the expense of the estates (*Stände*). While an obligation for each state to create a constitution was established, no date was set for compliance and the federal Assembly did not press the issue. Moreover, *landständische* could easily be interpreted to mean the traditional corporations (*Stände* or *Korporationen*) rather than a popular representative assembly.

The relatively liberal Bavarian constitution of 1818 broke with this conservative interpretation. As early as 1815 Maximilian I had ordered a commission to prepare a revision of the conservative 1808 constitution, but this work could proceed with rapidity only after the dismissal of the conservative Montgelas in 1817. The final document, promulgated on May 27, 1818, established a two-chamber Diet, the *Ständeversammlung* or *Landtag*, although power remained primarily in the hands of the king. The *Landtag* was, for example, denied the right to initiate legislation. Most disconcerting to German conservatives, however, was the third Edict appended to the constitution, which granted partial freedom of the press; only political or statistical matter was subject to prepublication censorship.

Baden and Württemberg soon followed with moderately liberal constitutions of their own, but this trend did not continue. Prince Klemens von Metternich, chancellor of the Austrian Empire, seeing a clear danger to his system in liberal constitutions and in the "licentious behavior" of the press, moved to nullify the effect of the new South German constitutions. He used the opportunity afforded by the Wartburg festival and the subsequent assassination of the author August von Kotzebue on March 23, 1819 by a young Bavarian, Karl Ludwig Sand, to push through the federal Assembly measures to suppress movements and ideas inimical to the Confederation. He began by inviting representatives of ten presumably conservative German states to a conference at Karlsbad. One week before the conference opened Metternich met with the Prussian chief minister, Karl August von Hardenberg, at Teplitz to formulate a common policy on the matter. The subsequent Punctation of August 1 provided a basis for the later Karlsbad decrees by interpreting Article 2 of the *Bundesakt,* maintaining the internal and external security of Germany, in a manner designed to open the internal affairs of the individual states to federal interference.

Meanwhile, Bavaria's first *Landtag* had met on February 4, 1819. The delegates in the lower house had been elected on the basis of the formula outlined in Section VI of the Bavarian constitution, [8] whereby each of the newly defined estates elected a percentage of those delegates (nobility and clergy each 1/8 of the delegates, cities and market towns 1/4, peasants and other landowners 1/2, and, in addition, the three universities each had one delegate). The result was a mixture of traditional conservative and liberal parliamentary elements. [9] There were, however, no political parties in the modern sense: those of similar political convictions worked together only on specific issues rather than with any degree of constancy. [10] As a rule, political groupings tended to follow a geographical and historical rather than an ideological division. Although the constitution spoke of a unitary kingdom, Bavaria was still composed of various districts with distinct dialects and customs. Thus it is more accurate to speak of a Frankish or old-Bavarian faction than liberal or conservative parties in the *Landtag*. [11]

Nevertheless, in the session of 1819 a liberal opposition led by Franz Ludwig von Hornthal, a lawyer and mayor of Bamberg, and Wilhelm Josef Behr, a law professor and mayor of Würtzburg, did exist. Although the *Landtag* assumed full responsibility for the government debt, the opposition immediately tried to gain for the *Landtag* the right to initiate legislation. To circumvent the constitutional prohibition to this, the liberals sent their legislative proposals to the king in the form of petitions, requesting the government to place these before the Bavarian Diet. This attempt to transform the right of petition into the right of legislative initiation failed because of the king's resistance. [12]

The liberal opposition, however, did not abandon its quest for power. Its leaders now proposed that royal ministers be excluded from secret sessions of the lower chamber and that the army be required to swear an oath to the constitution. These demands served to turn the king against the constitution and he began to think of a coup d'etat. He requested Prussia's assistance, but received only the advice to repress excesses while working within the framework of his constitution. Since he had received little encouragement from either Prussia or Austria, the Bavarian king was forced to give up his plan to overthrow the constitution he had granted. [13]

It was in this context that Metternich obtained in Karlsbad the firm support of the Bavarian foreign minister, Alois Graf von Rechberg und Rothenlöwen, who acted with the full approval of his king. The conference finally accepted decrees dealing with the universities, with the press, with the creation of an investigatory commission for "anti-federal" movements, and with the establishment of an *Exekutions-Ordnung*, and sent them to the federal Assembly for acceptance. On September 16, 1819, the *Präsidium* of the *Bundestag*, Austria's ambassador Johann Graf von Buol-Schauenstein, introduced the proposals that were unanimously accepted four days later. This approval, however, was of doubtful validity, for several ambassadors were forced to vote without benefit of discussion or instructions as required by the federal Diet's 1816 rules of procedure.

Opposition to the Karlsbad decrees quickly arose in the Bavarian Ministerial Council where Rechberg faced the combined hostility of Crown Prince Ludwig, President of the upper *Landtag* chamber General Wrede, Finance Minister Maximilian Freiherr von Lerchenfeld, and *Generaldirektor* Georg Friedrich von Zentner of the Ministry of the Interior. Those associated with the crown prince felt that the decrees constituted an attack on the Bavarian constitution. Specifically, Ludwig wrote to Lerchenfeld, this could not be tolerated because he had sworn an oath to uphold that constitution. Nothing contrary to that document could be permitted since the "smallest violation would be a breach of faith." [14]

Ludwig's view prevailed and the Karsbad decrees were finally published in Bavaria on October 16, 1819, with one significant reservation: they were not acknowledged to be federal decrees; rather, they were treated as the "common disposition of the member states" [15] and were to be followed only as far as "the sovereignty, the constitution and the standing laws [of Bavaria] are not contravened." [16] Thus the decrees would, for the moment at least, have only limited application in Bavaria.

Metternich had intended the Karlsbad decrees to become

integral parts of the federal constitution. Now Bavaria's action forced him to call the ministers of all the German states to a new conference in Vienna to discuss the further development of the Confederation. The conference began on November 25, 1819, and concluded its work with the signing of the *Wiener Schlussakt* (hereafter cited as *Schlussakt*) on May 16, 1820. Although Metternich had opposed seeking the approval of the federal Assembly for the *Schlussakt* to avoid modifications, he again had to retreat from this stand when the other states supported Württemberg's argument that matters dealing with the German Confederation "should emanate" solely from the *Bundesversammlung* if it were to continue to be "the organ of the Confederation." [17] In order to secure unanimity in Frankfurt, however, Metternich insisted that each ambassador sign the document, [18] and consequently the *Bundestag* accepted the *Schlussakt* without change on June 8. As in the case of the Karlsbad decrees, the proposal had been presented to the federal Assembly as a fait accompli and automatic approval resulted.

On June 20 Frederic Lamb, the British ambassador to the Confederation, accurately reported to his government that the German states were able to work together only because of their fear of losing strength to the revolutionary movements. Only a "common and imminent danger," he felt, would unite them in a "common course of action"; under normal circumstances to "keep them to this as a habit" was a problem that apparently was incapable of solution. Nevertheless, he continued, the Vienna Conference had been able to "reassure the timid" and "flatter the weak." [19] Indeed, to most minds the conference had been a success. With the forging of the *Schlussakt*, most of the ministers left the Austrian capital secure in the belief that they had erected a barrier against revolution without surrendering the sovereignty of their states in the process.

Their creation partially fulfilled ideas contained in embryonic form in the *Bundesakt* and partially added new elements that had not been considered in 1815. The Confederation was now defined as an indissoluble union from which secession was impossible. Ambassadors of the member states in the *Bundestag* were designated as plenipotentiaries, holding all privileges and dignities commensurate with this dignity, but they were described as absolutely dependent on the instructions from their governments by Article 8. Machinery was erected to deal with conflicts *between* member states, but responsibility for the maintenance of order *within* a state rested solely on that state's government. The federal Diet would consider intervention within a state only when intervention was requested by that state or when a matter involved the entire Confederation. Indeed, it was only through such intervention that the *Bund* could act directly on the subjects of the states since there were no federal subjects as such; normally the federal Assembly dealt only with member governments. [20]

While the *Bundesakt* had devoted only one brief article to constitutions, the *Schlussakt* dealt with the topic at length in Articles 54–62. Metternich had intended to secure a reinterpretation of Article 13 of the *Bundesakt*, which required a constitution in each member state, in a strictly conservative fashion at the Vienna Conference. He had hoped to obtain a definition of *landständische* that would clearly mean the traditional corporations and thus invalidate the South German constitutions already in existence. [21] The Bavarians, however, took the position that their constitution was founded on a historical rather than a theoretical basis, and that it therefore satisfied Article 13. Maximilian I, moreover, now refused to tolerate outside interference, stating that he felt obliged to preserve the existing constitution to which he had sworn an oath. [22] Consequently the articles of the *Schlussakt* dealing with constitutions had to be part of a compromise. They acknowledged that while the federal Assembly was to oversee the promulgation of a constitution in each member state, those already existing could be altered only by constitutional means. [23] On the other hand, no constitution could prevent a state from fulfilling its obligations to the Confederation nor could the monarchical principle be abrogated.

The *Schlussakt* also empowered the Confederation to guarantee the integrity of a state's constitution. Whereas Bavaria felt neither the need nor the desire for the Confederation to guarantee her constitution since she believed that such a guarantee would invariably lead to interference in her internal affairs, smaller states saw a guarantee as a device to maintain the monarchical principle and conservative or reactionary constitutions. On the basis of Article 60 of the *Schlussakt,* these states could request that the Confederation guarantee their constitutions based on the traditional *Stände.* Action on such a request carried more weight than the general federal guarantee as provided in Article 2 of the *Bundesakt,* which automatically applied to all members of the Confederation. Article 60 of the *Schlussakt* provided for a special positive guarantee that gave the *Bundesversammlung* the right to decide on the "interpretation of the constitution" [24] in time of conflict, if requested to do so either by the government or by the governed.

Bavaria, as was to be expected, took great care to limit the potential power of the federal Diet to give such a guarantee. Lerchenfeld noted that the *Bundesversammlung* was *"empowered, but not obligated"* to assume the guarantee of a member of the Confederation "for the constitution promulgated in its state." [25] In the case of the Sachsen-Coburg-Saalfeld constitution, promulgated in August 1821, a guarantee was requested from the federal Diet in December of that year. The *Präsidium* wanted to deal with the matter immediately, seeming to attach little importance to it. However, Johann Adam Freiherr von Aretin, Bavaria's ambassador until his death in

1822, was able to delay a decision until he could send a copy of the constitution to his government and receive instructions. In his request he made it clear that "if the guarantee is to be given, it will be given by the *Bund,* not the *Bundestag.*"[26] Here he was representing the firm Bavarian belief that the federal Assembly was to be prevented from acting as an organic political body or as a federal legislature. Rather, it was to remain simply a diplomatic congress with all political decisions to be made by the Confederation, that is, by the member governments. Not until the end of February did Bavaria announce that she would not object to a federal guarantee of that constitution.

The guarantee was not the only means whereby the Confederation could involve itself in local affairs. Article 26 of the *Schlussakt* granted the federal Diet the right to intervene in the internal affairs of a state when its government requested assistance, or when a disturbance in a state prevented its government from requesting assistance, or when a disturbance threatened several states or the Confederation as such. A *Bundesintervention* provided the means by which the federal Diet could assist a member menaced by antifederal or anticonstitutional threats.[27] When a majority of the ambassadors in the *Bundestag* approved an *Intervention*, one or more member states would be designated to act in the name of the federal Assembly, since the Confederation lacked forces of its own. The state placed under *Intervention* could then be occupied militarily and ruled under martial law by a federal commissioner until "normal constitutional conditions" had been restored. Once the Confederation had intervened, only the *Bundestag* could determine what methods were applied and for how long: the state government had no voice in the matter.[28]

More ominously, the *Schlussakt* also empowered the federal Assembly to force a member state to work within the framework of the federal constitution and to carry out federal decrees. First provisionally established in the Karlsbad decrees,

the *Exekutions-Ordnung* was made permanent by Article 31 of
the *Schlussakt* and by a decree on August 3, 1820. Whereas
Intervention meant assistance *to* a member state by the Confederation, *Exekution* was defined as the intervention of the
Confederation *against* a member state. [29] According to the
ordinance, the federal Assembly was to select semiannually a
committee from its members that was charged with deciding
whether states were fulfilling their obligations to the Confederation. Should this committee find a state derelict, the
ambassador of that state was to be given a brief period in which
to report to the *Bundestag* that the matter had been disposed of
or to explain why it had not been. If the state's response were
deemed insufficient, the *Bundesversammlung* was to invite it to
fulfill its obligations, and if this proved unsuccessful, a
mandate of *Exekution* would be issued against the government
of the recalcitrant state, requesting that another member state
or states not involved prepare soldiers for use by a commissioner named by the Diet to execute the decree. After one last
warning the offending government would be placed under the
rule of the commissioner, supported by federal soldiers, until
the offense was corrected. [30] In 1834, for example, the Senate of
Frankfurt-am-Main refused to place the city's army under
Austro-Prussian commanders as demanded by a federal
decree. Accordingly, the government of Frankfurt was placed
under a decree of *Exekution*, and the Senate was forced to accede
to the wishes of the Confederation.

ii

The *Bundesakt* as modified by the *Wiener Schlussakt* would
remain the constitution of the German Confederation until the
collapse of the *Bund* in 1866. In general, the final arrangement
represented a victory of particularism over centralism in

Germany, for the emphasis was placed on the independent sovereignty of the member governments rather than on the authority of the Confederation as a whole. There were, however, clauses in the federal constitution that opened the way for creating a more cohesive federation by allowing the federal Assembly to intervene in the internal affairs of its members and to apply pressure to achieve conformity. Bavaria conceded the existence of the Confederation but would not accept limitations on her sovereign rights. Although willing to allow the Confederation to impose on other governments, Bavaria fought continually to exempt herself from intrusion and to prevent further development of federal power. Insofar as she succeeded, the potential for expanding the scope of the Confederation remained only an unfulfilled possibility.

Although Bavaria chose the *Bundesversammlung* as the primary battleground in the struggle to preserve her autonomy, the *Bundesakt* and the *Wiener Schlussakt*, as well as the Karlsbad decrees, had been approved outside that body. Only after the major German courts had accepted these measures were the federal ambassadors in Frankfurt empowered to make them federal decrees. In fact, during the first years of the federal Diet's existence, that body was preoccupied with establishing its own rules of procedure and determining the extent to which the ambassadors could act independently of their instructions, or, alternately, the extent to which they were dependent on the *Bundesversammlung* itself. Only when this problem was resolved did the federal Assembly begin to involve itself in the affairs of the German states and of Germany as a whole.

Bavaria
in the German Confederation,
1820–1848

Part I

Establishing the System
1820–1829

1

The Isolation of the
Bundestag from Germany

i

While the representatives of the German courts were deciding
the fate and direction of the Confederation in Karlsbad and
Vienna, the federal Assembly was occupied with establishing its
rules of procedure. Although the *Bundestag* was intended to have
no existence independent of the member governments, certain
ambassadors attempted to infuse it with a life of its own,
transcending the restrictions imposed by the princes in order to
avoid the influence of the Austrian and Prussian courts. The
first years of the federal Assembly's existence were thus spent in
combating and eventually purging itself of all traces of open
opposition. By the end of 1823 it appeared that this campaign
had been successful, that the *Bundesversammlung,* although
no pliant tool for Austro-Prussian hegemony, had become
docile and manageable. As is usually the case in diplomatic
negotiations, in the last accounting the ambassadors remained
fully dependent on their own government's instructions.

On October 1, 1816, the *Bundesversammlung* met for the first
time in the Thurn und Taxis palace on the Eschenheimergasse
in Frankfurt-am-Main. At a round table in the main hall were
seated the Austrian ambassador, then to his left the Prussian
ambassador, the Saxon, the Bavarian, and so forth, in order of

31

their right to speak and to vote. The director of the presidial chancery, von Handel, sat across from the *Präsidium* and acted as recorder for the Diet. The rooms off the main hall served as places of business for the committees, the chancery, *Registratur,* and the like. [1]

The *Präsidium* (presiding ambassador) was either the Austrian ambassador by virtue of Article 5 of the *Bundesakt,* or, in his absence, another ambassador acting as his substitute; a privilege that Prussia tended to claim for herself "as a matter of right," a right that the other states were "by no means" prepared to accept. [2] Although each ambassador had the right to make proposals, the presiding ambassador could control the direction, emphasis, and timing of the federal Assembly's business. This, however, required a firm hand, for several ambassadors were wont to usurp this authority.

Austria's first ambassador, Johann Graf von Buol-Schauenstein, previously Austria's ambassador to the Netherlands, was unable to exercise the degree of control over the Diet that was necessary for effective and concerted action. The fault did not lie entirely with him, for several states were either unable or unwilling to restrain their ambassadors. Indeed, until Buol's recall in 1822 and the subsequent effort by the states to impose order, the *Bundestag* meetings frequently approached a state of anarchy. Frederic Lamb, the British ambassador, reported that the federal Diet was split into two wings: those supporting Austria and Prussia, and those supporting the "liberal party" led by Karl August Wangenheim, Württemberg's ambassador to the German Confederation and reformer of Württemberg's constitution. Lamb reported that Austria and Prussia could do little more than prevent the liberals from adopting decrees in "direct opposition" to their interests. The sessions, he wrote,

were habitually turbulent, gross insults passed between the members, and the best disposed were ashamed of voting with

Austria from the ridicule which her ambassador had contrived to attach to all his proceedings. [3]

With the arrival of Joachim Graf von Münch-Bellinghausen, who remained presiding ambassador until his recall in 1847, order came to the *Bundesversammlung*. Lamb reported that Münch's arrival brought a complete change in the manner of the Assembly's proceedings. It meant, he wrote, the establishment "of the sole and exclusive supremacy" of Austria in that body and the "putting down of the Liberal party." [4] Although the other ambassadors considered Münch "only as an equal," [5] he was able to convert the potential power of his office into an effective managing authority that he used to direct the actions of the *Bundesversammlung*. Yet how far he could actively control that body and impose Austrian policy was challenged by Bavaria through her ambassadors in the *Bundestag* and by the fact that the Bavarian government on numerous occasions chose to act itself on matters while they were under consideration by the Diet, and sometimes even after that body presumably had resolved them.

According to its constitution, the Confederation was one of sovereign rulers whose control over their subjects was limited solely by the constitutions that they granted and by Article 18 of the *Bundesakt*, which guaranteed certain rights to all Germans. [6] The *Bund* itself, as indicated above, had no direct jurisdiction over the German population, having rather to work through the state governments. In a speech to the Diet in August 1824, Christian Hubert von Pfeffel, Bavarian ambassador to the Confederation from 1822 to 1825 and later ambassador to France and Great Britain, outlined Bavaria's position on this matter. In a confederation like the *Bund*, "independent states" could recognize "only sovereigns and states, such as are all members of the Confederation," and the Confederation as a whole could recognize "only a relationship to its members," who alone had "obligations to the Confederation." Under no circumstances could there be a relationship between the Confederation and the subjects of the individual states, since "for these" there were "obligations only to their sovereign and state." To place federal obligations on such subjects would make them "half-federal subjects" who would then "only half belong to the specific states." This would then turn the Confederation "against its nature and its constitution" into a "federal state" (*Bundesstaat*). "According to the spirit of the Confederation" the ambassadors were "in every respect, the only legitimate organ" for all communication and relationships "between the whole and the parts." [7]

The Confederation could therefore expect to exert an effect on the subjects of a member state only after a federal decree had been enacted and published by that state. There was, however, no federal law obliging a state to publish federal decrees. On the other hand, Article 1 of the *Exekutions-Ordnung* gave the federal Assembly the right to provide for the execution (*Vollziehung*) of its decrees. Thus the question of the relationship of federal to state law naturally produced conflict. In a letter to Lerchenfeld, Ludwig Graf Armansperg, the Bavarian minister of the interior, noted that Münch's basic position was that the "legislation" of the Confederation "superseded" that of the individual states and that "the latter must give way to the former." [8]

Bavaria, of course, would not accept that principle. Indeed, throughout the entire period of the formation of the Confederation Bavaria had constantly opposed all attempts to create any strong central authority that would limit her own freedom of action. Ludwig I (1825–1848), for example, both as crown prince and later as king, wanted no strong federal state in Germany, rather a loose "harmonious federation" of German states, [9] thereby leaving Bavaria ample scope to pursue her own policies.

To those who favored federal supremacy, the 1818 Bavarian constitution proved to be one of the greatest hindrances. Although hardly liberal in the modern sense, it gave to the Bavarian *Landtag* considerable power and also granted relative freedom of the press in that only newspapers and periodicals were subject to prior censorship. Moreover, whenever it seemed convenient, the Bavarian government claimed that it could not carry out a federal decree. on the grounds that it could not contradict its own constitution. This argument was constitutionally specious, for Article 58 of the *Schlussakt* specifically stated that no state might be hindered or prevented from fulfilling federal obligations by its constitution. Bavaria conveniently overlooked this provision or, when challenged, noted that the Bavarian constitution preceded the *Schlussakt* by two years and therefore the latter did not apply.

The Bavarian monarchs, moreover, sincerely felt obligated by oath to maintain their constitution, and, although there were brief periods when they felt frustrated by that document and thought of amending it drastically, they generally chose to protect it from foreign assault. In 1832, for example, Wrede wrote Metternich that the king would gladly fulfill his federal obligations were he not bound by the constitution. However, he wrote, if the constitution of 1818 was then acknowledged as legitimate by the Confederation, why should "defects" be found in it that threatened "subversion or dissolution of the Confederation" in 1832? [10]

This resistence to the primacy of federal decrees represented a continuation of the policies of Montgelas, although the emphasis had now shifted. Under Montgelas the goal of Bavarian policy had been to join the ranks of the European great powers as an equal and to take over the leadership of the purely German states (i.e., a Germany without Austria and Prussia and their non-German populations). The post-Montgelas government realistically rejected great power pretensions as well as isolationism, yet Bavaria remained concerned with maintaining her independence and the power that she had gained since 1805. Thus on one occasion the Prussian ambassador in Munich reported to Frederick William III that Ludwig I would "limit himself to the mien which becomes a second rank power" and would take care to keep Austrian and Prussian friendship, but without surrendering any Bavarian rights. [11]

Indeed, through 1848 there was little change in the Bavarian attitude. In an instruction to the new Prussian ambassador in Munich in 1833, the Prussian Foreign Ministry noted that Bavaria was "undoubtedly" the strongest among the "states surrounded by the Confederation," and that those moments in her history when Bavaria had been able to play a large role in European affairs had not been forgotten. There was a chance, it continued, that under "special circumstances" Bavaria would act contrary to the interests of the Confederation, but "for the moment" such a worry remained "only in the background." [12] This meant, of course, that Bavaria could never be taken for granted, that Bavarian interests would always have to be considered before the Confederation could act.

ii

The decade of the twenties, which saw Bavaria striving to keep herself free from domination by the German Confederation, also witnessed the gradual isolation of the federal Assembly from the individual German. At no time had the Diet been conceived as a popular organ; from its inception it was to be solely a congress of German ambassadors representing their sovereigns. In the first years after 1816, however, the literate population kept itself quite well informed about the discussions and decrees of the *Bundesversammlung*, for the minutes of that body were a matter of public record and newspapers, governmental and private, published excerpts from and commentaries on those minutes.

The ambassadors also demonstrated a capacity for relative independence during the early years of the Confederation. This had been one of the reasons for the calling of the Vienna Conference in 1819, and the resultant *Schlussakt* sharply limited the scope of the ambassadors in Frankfurt. Over the course of the 1820s they evolved into mere spokesmen for their governments, confining themselves to the reading of prepared statements to the federal Assembly, while the amount of information concerning their activities made available to the German public was severely curtailed.

Already in 1820 Metternich's close friend, the German translator of Burke and archconservative, Friedrich von Gentz, was producing critical but accurate analyses of the lack of discipline in the federal Diet, for within the framework of the *Bundesakt*, reinforced by the *Schlussakt*, that body was indeed acting contrary to its original purpose. Gentz argued that such attempts to alter the nature of the *Bundesversammlung* would result in the "immediate beginning of the dissolution of the Confederation." All attempts to present individual points of view, all discussions serving the "satisfaction of personality," digressions into abstract theories, or "popular lectures and grandstand speeches" (*Tribünenberedsamkeit*), ought to be banned from the Diet, for the competence of that body did not extend to those areas. Those questions within its scope, he concluded, ought to be dealt with solely through written instructions from the courts to their ambassadors. [13]

Although instructions were the only bases on which decisions could legitimately be made in the federal Assembly, the ambassador was often forced to ask his court repeatedly for instructions on specific topics before he could cast his vote. Even the presiding ambassador was not immune, Aretin wrote, "as Graf von Buol bitterly complained" to him since he had had no message from Metternich "for quite some time." [14]

Once instructions were obtained the ambassador knew how he was to vote, what he was to propose, and so on. Instructions, therefore, were an integral part of the federal machinery. But at the same time, as is normal in diplomatic transactions, instructions were treated as secret communications between a sovereign government and its ambassador. This often led to difficulties. On one occasion Württemberg's ambassador complained that Alexander Graf von Goltz, the Prussian ambassador, had charged him of acting arbitrarily and independently of his instructions. Although Wangenheim, "like all ambassadors at the federal Assembly, [was] responsible solely to his court," he wanted to justify his actions to the *Bundesversammlung* by placing his instructions concerning the matter under discussion before the other ambassadors in order to demonstrate that the charge was without foundation. Aretin interrupted him with the observation that Goltz had in no way attacked him. Furthermore, since by the laws of the Confederation an ambassador was responsible solely to his government, he could not be permitted to show his instructions, for these were to be "transacted solely between his government and himself." Moreover, no one had a right to ask for an accounting of his actions. As long as an ambassador was not repudiated by his sovereign, it had to be assumed that he had acted according to instruction. Goltz seconded Aretin's remarks and declared that he had intended no specific attack against Wangenheim, who was induced to retract his entire speech. [15] As was usual with spontaneous discussions in matters of this type, no mention was made in the official protocol of the session.

Two months later Buol raised the question of how an ambassador might use his instructions. Aretin again strongly asserted an ambassador's right to maintain secrecy, since the matter under discussion was an affair solely between the ambassador and his government. An ambassador, he argued, could vote on an issue either on the basis of specific instructions or on the basis of a general directive given him by his government. It was to be left "solely to his discretion" how far the ambassador found it "suitable" to request more specific instructions from his government. One could not order a government how and to whom it was to send its instructions, or present a government with a series of questions, as Buol had proposed, which were to be answered before an issue might be fully discussed. Only through the development of discussions in which opposing views were aired, Aretin believed, could a government know how to respond to an issue. [16]

It was thus necessary, he continued, that the ambassadors maintain their right of free debate, for only then could a question be seen in all of its ramifications. [17] "It is good," he had previously written, "when a topic is illuminated from several sides, for the matter can only thusly be resolved."[18] To demand that instructions be shown to the *Bundesversammlung* would serve no purpose, he argued; rather, the *Präsidium* ought to welcome full and free discussion of an issue. Once a question in which there was a difference of opinion had been raised the ambassadors could either request new and more specific instructions from their governments, or agree to proceed with the vote. [19]

This time Aretin's view prevailed. However, Gentz and Metternich were not alone in the view that individualism and independence of action had no place in the federal Diet. In 1822, in an instruction to its new ambassador, Christian Hubert von Pfeffel, the Bavarian court outlined its view of the ambassador's function in Frankfurt. Contrary to prior practice, namely that of Aretin, ambassadors were not to speak or vote independent of specific instructions from their governments, for when an ambassador acted other than directed, the

Confederation lost the power to "smooth over the differences" between member states. However, following Aretin's example, Pfeffel was above all to be "intent on gaining and keeping" the trust of the "collective membership" of the *Bundestag* in order to act successfully for the "common good of the association of German states." The government, it continued, had no doubt that Pfeffel would "contribute to this foundation of trust" that Aretin "had enjoyed in particular degree," especially since the signing of the *Schlussakt*. Bavaria, it was noted, had proven her "sincere and open ties" to the Confederation "in the most unequivocal manner." All that Bavaria had promised to do through the federal Assembly had been fulfilled; at the same time there was complete agreement with Austria and Prussia regarding the necessity to "counter with firmness" the "revolutionary spirit of political innovations and radical transformations" in the *Bundesversammlung*. Pfeffel was to adhere strictly to this guideline. [20]

The importance that the Bavarian government attached to this instruction and the continuity of the Bavarian outlook was emphasized when Ludwig I saw fit to send precisely the same instruction to Lerchenfeld (1831) and to Mieg (1834). The instruction sent to Lerchenfeld directed him to find the 1822 draft or to request that a copy be sent to him. A summary of the philosophy underlying the 1822 version was enclosed for his edification. There had been and was, it stated, a clear danger of a "transformation of the German *Staatenbund* into a *Bundesstaat*." In order to prevent this from occurring, the ambassador must remain within the bounds established by the written instructions from his court, a restriction that had been agreed upon during the 1819–20 Vienna Conference and that was still to be observed. [21] In this way the *Bundestag* would remain a congress of ambassadors and would not evolve into something approaching a parliamentary body. Clearly Bavaria understood the hierarchy of sovereignty in the organization of Germany to be headed by the individual states, downward to the Confederation, concluding with the *Bundesversammlung* at the lowest possible level.

As Lerchenfeld well knew, the instruction continued, directives were forwarded as soon as possible after examination of his "general and special reports." Although Lerchenfeld had argued that the other federal ambassadors held plenipotentiary powers from their sovereigns, and had insisted that the basic laws of the Confederation and the practices of the federal Assembly favored an all-encompassing instruction, he was ordered instead to request specific royal decisions on each important matter. The rule, he was reminded, had been established by Article 8 of the *Schlussakt*, confirming the "unqualified dependence" of the ambassadors on their courts and the instructions sent by them. Thus the federal Diet had no "unqualified right" to decide by majority vote whether or not a request for instructions was necessary. It could not be "a matter of indifference" to the Bavarian government that its "organ" at the federal Assembly cooperated in the "founding of an unheard of (*fremd*) authority." [22]

This limitation on the independence of the federal ambassadors was followed, upon Metternich's insistence in some cases, by most of the German courts. Under the tight rein of the *Präsidium* much of the spontaneity of the earlier sessions vanished. Throughout Pfeffel's reports there was an all but total lack of the interjections ("I interrupted," "he objected," etc.) that filled those of his predecessors. Lerchenfeld, who was given to exercising a bit of autonomy at Frankfurt, received periodic reminders that he was to follow instructions, whereas Arnold von Mieg's years in the Diet (1833–42) demonstrate that the discussions were basically limited to the reading of prepared statements. Thus within the span of a few years, the *Bundesversammlung* became what its designers had intended it to be.

In order to limit better the federal ambassadors to their role of representing only their sovereigns and to prevent them from appealing to or influencing public opinion, Gentz had proposed that the minutes of the discussions be kept secret, that only those protocols which the federal Assembly felt necessary to be published be made available to the general public. [23] The state governments, however, were to be kept fully informed of all transactions in the Diet by ambassadorial reports and the official minutes distributed to each court by its ambassador. Open sessions were covered in the protocols, whereas reports of confidential sessions were published in a *Registratur*. Although special topics were dealt with in the same session as that covered by a regular protocol, a *Separat-Protocol* was published under the heading *in loco dictaturae*, meaning that it was not to be opened to the general public. Eventually all protocols would bear this phrase unless the federal Diet decided it to be beneficial to make the protocol available to the public.

At first, however, the opposite was the rule: all minutes were published except those few which the federal Diet decided to keep confidential. Pfeffel gave one explanation for the withholding of minutes when he wrote that since his statement given to the *Bundesversammlung* was to be considered only as "introductory and thus confidential," it was to be printed solely for the use of the ambassadors and their courts, thus keeping the transactions from the public until they were concluded. In this way the matter would not become a "topic of criticism for interested authors and publishers." [24]

In a federal decree of February 5, 1824, the governments were given the right to censor protocols. The federal Assembly ruled that each government might decide how much of the official minutes was to appear in their newspapers. Such minutes as were not decreed secret could be published in full or excerpted; under no circumstances, however, was more to be printed than appeared in the open protocols.

Publication of the protocols was even more sharply edited when a Prussian proposal, seconded by Hannover and Baden, was adopted on July 1, 1824. The *Bundesversammlung* decreed that public minutes were to contain only the decisions of that body, not discussions or committee reports. Such matters were to be printed solely for the use of the states, not their subjects. Moreover, a number of matters—military topics and disputes between members, among others—were to be excluded entirely from the open protocols.

Pfeffel agreed that the "unfitting publicity of the Diet's transactions" made it "suitable and advantageous" that there be some limitation on what ought to be published. He believed, however, that the definition of what was proper for publication embodied in the decree was "unsuitable, limiting and offensive," and that the federal Assembly ought to return to the original practice of leaving to the ambassadors the right to decide each time what ought to be published. He promised to work for the "resolution of [the question] in that sense." [25] How unsuccessful he was can be seen by comparing the public protocols of 1823 with those of 1825. In the first year there was a total of 195 sections covering 757 pages. Two years later only 93 sections were open to the public; the bulk of the 546 pages was taken up with *Separat-Protocole* printed *in loco dictaturae*. Finally, beginning in 1828, all protocols were printed solely for official use; the public protocol all but disappeared. It now required a special vote of the Diet for the decisions of that body to be published.

In the same year the question of the accuracy of the protocols was raised when the Prussian ambassador, Nagler, implied that it had been the prevailing practice for an ambassador to enter supplements to his comment, or to propose changes in the minutes before they were closed and signed. Lerchenfeld argued that although the rules of procedure were silent on this point, the protocol ought to contain an "accurate picture of each session's proceedings." He acknowledged, however, that there was a tacit understanding that an abstention might be supplementally explained, and that the leaving open of the protocol formed a basis for the "right of supplemental declarations" as well as for the possibility of such a declaration in a future protocol. [26]

Nagler then asked that a definition be given on this question in order to prevent potential confusion. Münch, however, did not want a discussion of the matter. He stated that the prevailing practice ought to be continued: briefly given comments could be purged from the minutes in "their main features or at least in their tendency" by the ambassador involved. In other areas, he concluded, the federal Assembly had to decide each time whether a supplemental comment or explanation was to be included in the minutes before they were signed. Lerchenfeld objected on the grounds that if this were to be a determination of principle, the question ought to be studied by the committee named to revise the rules of procedure, which, he noted, had been fruitlessly engaged in this task for eight years. [27]

Here the matter ended, for after more than an hour's discussion it was decided to send the question to that committee and to leave the whole matter out of the minutes. Since the committee never offered a proposal for reforming the rules of procedure, the question of the accuracy of the minutes was never officially decided. On the other hand, it appears that the protocols continued to reflect accurately the sense of the discussions of each session. Rarely is there mention in the reports of the Bavarian ambassadors that a protocol contained falsifications or inaccuracies. At worst, one can say that the minutes did not contain the spontaneous comments of the ambassadors; they were confined to prepared statements, reports, votes, and decrees accepted.

Thus, of the three main avenues connecting the federal

Assembly with the German public, two, the independent action of the ambassadors and the public minutes of the transactions of the *Bundesversammlung*, were closed. The last remaining link was also soon severed. It had been common practice to dedicate or address books and other printed matter to the federal Diet, which often made note of those actions by commending the author and decreeing that the volume be placed in the federal archives or, alternately, condemning the author and refusing acceptance. Moreover, the federal Assembly was mistakenly taken for a court of last resort or as a vehicle to promote German unification by elements of the population who on occasion petitioned that body for redress of grievances. On July 3, 1823, the *Bundestag* put an end to all such occurrences when it decreed that all printed matter addressed to it had first to go to the author's government for censorship. Otherwise, it was decreed, it would not be acknowledged. The same provision was applied to petitions on January 15, 1824.

Thus the federal Assembly had decreed its own isolation from the German public with no Bavarian opposition of note. As the designers had intended, the federal Diet was not to be a parliamentary body representing the German people, but was to be solely a diplomatic congress representing sovereign governments. Bavaria worked to guarantee that this distinction would be followed at all times. All that was needed to complete the process was the enforcement of a rigid censorship over the nongovernmental press.

2

Censorship and Trias

i

Between 1822 and 1825 the main arena for the battle between federal authority and Bavarian autonomy was the question of censorship of the press. Theoretically this had been answered by the federal press decree of September 20, 1819, which had subjected all newspapers and periodicals to censorship and which had been the first step in insulating the federal Diet from the states' subjects. Bavaria, however, chose to ignore this decree, choosing rather to proceed within the framework of her own constitution.

As part of the compromise required to win approval of the press decree from the German courts, Metternich had conceded that the decree was to be provisional and to be of only five years duration. By 1822 it appeared to him that the time had come to strengthen and make permanent this temporary measure. Bavaria's Foreign Minister Rechberg shared that opinion because, as he noted to the Austrian representative in Munich, the German states singly were too weak to resist the "pressures of their revolutionaries." Only through a union of the states would resistence be effective. [1] A renewed federal press decree would be a step in the right direction.

46

These and similar sentiments elsewhere led Metternich to believe that a new Vienna Conference might be used to make the Karlsbad decrees permanent. In a letter to Crown Prince Ludwig, Lerchenfeld made note of Metternich's intent and wrote that the Austrian was coming to Munich to discuss a new congress "concerning German affairs." [2] However, three days later Lerchenfeld had to write that Metternich had abandoned his idea of a conference and now intended to propose directly to the federal Assembly measures concerned with the abuse of freedom of the press. [3] The Austrian minister obviously believed that, once purged of all dissident elements, the *Bundesversammlung* would prove the most effective instrument for preventing revolutionary activities in Germany.

During the first years of the Confederation there had been no unanimity of opinion concerning the meaning of the concept "Germany." The various ideas expressed covered the full spectrum—from a democratic nation state to the loosest of federations composed of independent sovereign rulers. It gradually became evident, however, that the German governments no longer doubted that their states would have to work within the context of the guidelines established for the Confederation in Vienna in 1815 and 1820. What now received attention was the question of whether the preponderance of Austria and Prussia ought to be accepted. Few other states could withstand the pressure exerted by either because of their sheer size; no state acting along could defy the two German great powers when they cooperated.

But there appeared to be an alternative to the overwhelming authority of Austria and Prussia with their large non-German populations. This entailed the creation of a third force, a purely German power, whereby the major purely German states would act in concert for common goals. This policy of the so-called Trias, the three Germanies, originated not in Bavaria, the largest of the purely German states, but in the kingdom of

Württemberg. Too weak itself to oppose Austria and Prussia, Württemberg proposed to achieve that goal by promoting closer cooperation between herself and Baden, the two Hesses and Bavaria. [4]

Metternich feared that such a project might be brought to fruition, for, as he wrote early in 1820, Bavaria, Württemberg, and the other South German states sought to isolate Austria within the Confederation. If Austria, Prussia, and Russia were to go to war with one another, or should Austria become involved in any war, Metternich believed that Bavaria would place herself at the head of a "purely German federation," and that her first act would be to declare the "neutrality of her army." [5] The Austrian minister, however, had not clearly understood the sentiments of the Bavarian court. Rather than continuing the traditional anti-Austrian policy of the Wittelsbachs, Maximilian I spent his last years laboring to regain the confidence of the two German great powers, and he would not surrender that friendship for what he saw as fantasy. Furthermore, Maximilian I considered exorbitant the price that Bavaria would have had to pay in entering a purely German confederation. Bavaria had claims on lands held by Baden and Württemberg, and these would have to be abandoned if there were to be harmony among the South German states. As it was, these territorial claims poisoned relations between the South German states throughout the 1820s. Gentz reported to Metternich that Maximilian I "did not express himself favorably" about the king of Württemberg, nor did he appear "to be especially fascinated" by the Grand-duke of Baden. [6] This personal animosity all but guaranteed that the Trias would remain an unfulfillable dream.

Since the *Rheinbund* period Bavaria had rejected all overtures seeking her entry into a purely German federation. Montgelas had preferred to keep free of all entangling alliances that might have prevented Bavaria from becoming an independent European power. Moreover, like his king, Montgelas would not accept closer ties with Württemberg or Baden until Bavarian territorial claims had been settled. Rechberg continued his predecessor's policy with the major modification that he now sought closer ties with Austria. As Rechberg confided to Gentz in 1820, "Bavaria can stand or fall only with Austria." [7] On another occasion Wrede noted to the Austrian chargé d'affaires, Wolff, that "as a neighboring state" Bavaria had "the greatest interest in adhering" to Austria. No longer did Bavaria wish to "stand in the ranks of the great powers"; Bavaria now felt "her worth as a German state." [8]

Still, Bavaria's opposition did not prevent Württemberg from pursuing the matter further. On December 14, 1820, Lamb reported that there appeared to be the "beginning of a union of the constitutional powers" of South Germany directed against those states "that are purely monarchical." Only fears of Bavarian predominance, he concluded, had prevented such a federation in the past. [9] Two weeks later Lamb wrote that although there was as yet no agreement among the South German states, they were drawing closer together and were "coming to a better understanding every day." The only court that proved reticent in acceding to the system was Bavaria, but the other states were hopeful of her eventual approval. [10]

Württemberg continued her efforts, and Metternich was informed that discussions were proceeding with Bavaria to "retie old friendly relations" and to conclude closer ties among all the South German governments. Rechberg, however, continued to oppose such ties and told Wolff that while his government desired good relations with all its neighbors, they could best be achieved within the framework of the Confederation. [11] Moreover, the Prussian ambassador informed his king that while the liberals in Bavaria, including several ministers, wanted the constitutional states to conclude a union to "protect their autonomy" in order to "avoid dependence on the greater powers," Rechberg and the king were opposed to any such arrangement. [12]

While it was true, as these reports correctly observed, that a political foundation for Trias proved impossible to erect, it was just as true that an economic basis for a third Germany did exist. The continental system proclaimed by Napoleon in 1806 had cut off the German states from British goods and markets, resulting in the rapid growth of substitution industries in Germany. With Napoleon's defeat, however, these industries collapsed in the face of a flood of British goods more efficiently produced due to her technological and capital-amassing preponderance. The effect of renewed British competition on the German market was aggravated by the sudden and rapid demobilization of the German armies, together resulting in deflation and unemployment. [13] By 1819 conditions had grown so bad that German businessmen began to organize to put pressure on their governments and on the German Confederation to alleviate the misery.

There was little that an individual state could do on its own other than to erect protective tariffs on its frontiers and to create a free-trade zone for its own products within those frontiers—something that Bavaria had already done in 1807 and that Prussia did in 1818. This could provide only limited relief, however, since most of the German states were too small and too industrially underdeveloped to create a sustainable, self-contained market. A real solution could only be found through agreement between the states, and the federal Assembly could have provided the framework for negotiations since Article 19 of the *Bundesakt* empowered it to treat questions of interstate trade and navigation.

It was against this background that the members of the Confederation met at Karlsbad and Vienna. It is quite clear that these conferences were to deal primarily with political

problems, and that economic questions received only secon-
dary consideration. Nonetheless, an effort was made to arrive
at some resolution applicable to the whole of Germany.
Bavaria and Baden played key roles in convincing the 1819–20
Vienna Conference to consider the question even over Metternich's objections. But the committee chosen to recommend
action on fulfilling Article·19 was able to resolve nothing. Its
report to the full conference on March 4, 1820, advised only
that the matter be referred to the federal Assembly for
study—a suggestion greeted by the near unanimous laughter of
the ministers. [14] At this point, practical federal activity
concerning German economic unity ended; it was again
necessary to bypass the *Bundesversammlung*.

This had been anticipated in Munich where the arguments
of those favoring economic unity prevailed over Rechberg's
skepticism. Aretin, although expressing doubts as to whether a
German customs union could be created, encouraged the king
to continue discussions with the other states since this might
lead to a "closer accord" among the "purely German states." [15]
Lerchenfeld, then Bavarian finance minister, argued in favor
of a South German customs union on the grounds that it would
restore Bavarian economic prosperity. Protective tariffs, he felt,
only hurt Bavaria, especially the Bavarian Rhineland (Rheinkreis) separated from the remainder of the state by Baden and
Hesse-Darmstadt. A customers union with those states, he
believed, would reverse the "decline of prosperity" in that
province, which contained roughly twelve percent of the
population of Bavaria. He realized that only through a
customs union between Bavaria and either Baden or Hesse-
Darmstadt could the Rhineland be joined to Bavaria proper. [16]

Prodded by Aretin, Lerchenfeld, and the crown prince, the
king instructed Zentner, his representative at the Vienna
Conference, to deal secretly with the ministers of the South and
Central German states about the erection of a purely German

customs union. [17] An agreement was finally signed on May 19, 1820, among Bavaria, Württemberg, Baden, and five smaller central German states consenting to discuss mutual freedom of trade and traffic at a conference to be held in Darmstadt. [18] That this and the subsequent conference in Stuttgart in 1825 failed was due to a combination of the economic differences and political ambitions of the individual states and of Rechberg's continued opposition to a South German customs union.

While Lerchenfeld and the crown prince, supported in the main by the Bavarian *Landtag,* pressed for an economic union, Rechberg and Friedrich Graf zu Thürheim, then minister of the interior and later Rechberg's successor as foreign minister, were in strong opposition to it. In particular, Rechberg feared that by entering into such a union Bavaria would lose her political independence. Bavaria, he argued, was not a state large enough to play an independent European role but was of sufficient size to be a "welcome ally" for any great power. If Bavaria were tied to the smaller states by a customs union, then those powers would look to the union rather than to Bavaria. In the process Bavaria would lose her freedom of decision to those smaller states. Moreover, he noted, Bavaria could act independently in the German Confederation, and by joining neither the large nor the small states she exerted a great deal of influence—something that would be lost by the creation of a "*Bund* within a *Bund*." [19]

While he remained steadfast in his opposition, Rechberg was forced to continue negotiations at Darmstadt (although he frequently left Bavaria's representative there without instructions for long periods). The conference, which began in September 1820 and lasted through July 1823, almost immediately split into two factions: Bavaria and Württemberg on one hand, Baden and the remainder on the other. This division was partially based on technical questions, such as whether to collect duties solely at the frontiers of the customs union and whether each state would have one vote in determining policy or if the votes should be apportioned according to population size, and partially on political differences, especially between Baden and Bavaria. Since these problems proved unbridgeable, the conference collapsed.

In February 1825 another attempt was made when, on the initiative of Bavaria and Württemberg, Baden, Hesse-Darmstadt, and Nassau were invited to a conference meeting in Stuttgart. This also failed, for the differences between Bavaria and Baden were too great to be bridged by Württemberg's mediation. The only course remaining open to Bavaria was to create a customs union with Württemberg, a matter discussed in Munich at an October 1824 session of the royal ministerial council. Lerchenfeld argued that talks with Württemberg were necessary so as to prevent that state from joining with Hesse-Darmstadt and Baden, thereby "completely isolating" Bavaria, "hemming her in" with "foreign customs houses." Thürheim and Wrede, however, warned that the more advanced industries of Württemberg might destroy the welfare of the Bavarian craftsmen and industries.[20] Nevertheless, Lerchenfeld's counsel prevailed and the discussions already begun early in 1824 were continued.

Even though Württemberg proposed a treaty on tariffs and trade in April 1825, the talks remained fruitless until Ludwig's accession to the Bavarian throne. In a personal letter to the new monarch, Württemberg's King William I complained of the protective tariff system newly enacted in 1826 and requested that negotiations for a customs union be renewed.[21] On his ministers' advice, Ludwig responded positively[22] and the discussions were resumed early in 1827. With amazing speed for such matters, a preliminary treaty was completed on April 12 and the final treaty was signed on January 18, 1828. This was, as M. Doeberl noted,[23] the first German customs union enacted on a basis of equality between the members and, as such, would provide the model for the future German *Zollverein*.

Ludwig had accepted the idea of a Bavarian-Württemberg customs union in the hope that other states, especially Baden and Hesse-Darmstadt, could be induced to join it. In this way a bridge could have been constructed between the Bavarian Rhineland and Bavaria proper. That this would not happen was due largely to two facts: the bulk of Baden's and Hesse's commerce traveled north rather than toward the new South German customs union and, as long as Bavaria refused to surrender her claims to part of Baden's territory, no economic agreement was possible. Hope of bypassing Baden and joining the Rheinkreis to Bavaria through Hesse-Darmstadt ended when that state joined Prussia in a customs union in February 1828.

One last attempt came in 1829 when Baden declared her readiness to join with Bavaria in a commercial agreement if Bavaria would surrender her claim to the duchy of Sponheim [24] and make no subsequent claims. Bavaria would not agree, insisting instead on territorial compensation and indemnification. Since Baden rejected this, this last attempt at closer cooperation among the South German courts also failed. An alternative to the German Confederation and Austro-Prussian preponderance was not to come from a third Germany led by Bavaria or any other southern state.

As long as the Trias had seemed possible, its foremost proponent was Karl August von Wangenheim, Württemberg's ambassador to the *Bundesversammlung*. With the tacit approval of his king, William I, Wangenheim often led the Middle and South German ambassadors in opposing Metternich's policy in the Diet, but, although a personal friend of Aretin, he received Bavarian support only when such support suited the policy of the Bavarian government. [25] In February 1823 Metternich moved to erase all such independence from the federal Assembly by calling the representatives of the "restoration states" (Prussia, Bavaria, Baden, Mecklenburg, etc.) to purge the federal Assembly of dissident ambassadors, limit its sessions, and halt publication of its protocols. Although the conference resulted in no firm decision, Metternich later seized upon a speech by Wangenheim to force a "cleansing" of the *Bundestag*.[26]

As reported by Lamb on May 3, 1823, diplomatic relations with Württemberg were to be broken by Austria, Prussia, and Russia unless the king replaced his ambassador at Frankfurt.[27] This threat was carried out two weeks later. Finally, in July 1823, Württemberg's monarch conceded defeat and removed Wangenheim. At the same time the governments of Hesse-Darmstadt and Kurhesse were forced to recall their ambassadors since they had been working closely with Wangenheim in Frankfurt. In a futile gesture of dissatisfaction, Württemberg named no replacement for eight months. Eventually, however, she sent an ambassador acceptable to Metternich. The purge was complete.

Although initially unsuccessful, Metternich had been able to use the February Vienna conference as an instrument to prevent the coming to fruition of the revolutionary threat. He feared that the "so-called representative system" would threaten *landständische* institutions, which Article 13 of the *Bundesakt* "incontestably sanctioned," if action were not quickly taken. Continuing to act according to this archconservative interpretation, he especially condemned the "implanted democratic elements" in the South German constitutions, which, if left unchecked, would reduce the monarchical form of government to a shadow. He damned the "arrogance" of the "constitutional and ultra-constitutional opposition" that made it increasingly difficult for the German governments to maintain their rights and guarantee the "welfare of their people" against the "disturbing influence" of the "revolutionary spirit." Since, he argued, it could not be expected that the South German states would act without an "external impulse," it remained for the federal Assembly to set a limit to this evil.

The federal Assembly, Metternich observed, was a "permanent congress of ministers, composed of the representatives of the sovereign princes." Any attempt to impart another character to that body would result in the "immediate beginning of the dissolution of the Confederation." Accordingly, everything incompatible with the structure of the federal Diet had to be kept away from it. Referring then to Württemberg and Wangenheim, he argued "that the idea of an opposition could arise" in the federal Assembly "adequately" proved how far it had "deviated from its original functions and definitions." Therefore, ambassadors had to be chosen through uniform and firm principles so that the federal Assembly might be an "effective and beneficial tool" of the German princes. As soon as all ambassadors demonstrated "reciprocal trust and loyal cooperation," it would be possible to complete the measures necessary to maintain the Confederation.

Metternich accordingly proposed a revision of the Diet's rules of procedure in order to expedite and simplify its business. [28] This, however, like earlier proposals to the same effect, would languish in the federal Assembly's committees until the Revolution of 1848 made the issue moot. Metternich could also see no benefit in the publication of the Diet's minutes, finding it rather a "definite drawback" because of some ambassadors' greater concern with their public image than their obligations to their governments. He therefore proposed that only those minutes which needed to be brought to the public's attention be published. This, of course, was accomplished by 1828. Finally, he proposed that the federal Assembly meet only four months each year, a proposal that found no positive response among the other states.

Turning his attention to the states' constitutions, Metternich raised the question whether, in light of Article 61 of the *Schlussakt*, federal decrees were to be regarded as absolutely superior to state legislation. This article, which forbade the federal Assembly from interfering in "local parliamentary matters" or in conflicts between the *Stände* and the ruler, was not, Metternich argued, to be understood as hindering any state government from acting against its own parliament. Thus, if a state government determined that its constitution needed modification for the "maintenance of the monarchical principle" or for the "public order," there could be no doubt that, with the unanimous approval of the federal Assembly, it could accomplish the revision with the "total influence and strength" of the Confederation. Indeed, he argued, if federal legislation was to exist at all, federal competence to deal with the "abuse of parliamentary prerogative" had to be established. In emergency cases, the Confederation possessed the legal authority to offer "every kind of assistance." Metternich noted that, contrary to a decree of September 20, 1819, which stated that federal decrees were binding on the states and could not be supplanted by local legislation, some states not only tolerated, but used as a basis for their opposition, the published opinions of scholars and academics who denied federal authority. The time for such "errors," he observed, was "hopefully past." It was in the "highest interest" of the German governments to honor the "supreme authority" of the Confederation and its legislation. Once convinced of that, no state would allow such slander to continue to be published or uttered by public speakers.

Equally important, he concluded, was the form in which the transactions of the parliaments were distributed to the "entire German reading public." Observing that Article 59 of the *Schlussakt* allowed publication of these transactions only in such a way as not to disturb the peace of the individual states or of Germany, Metternich argued that publication in "dialogue or dramatic forms" did not follow the sense of the article. He saw a true danger when citizens of one state were exposed daily to the "abuse of all authority from the highest to the lowest" in a neighboring state that was lax in its responsibilities. There could be no objection to a federal decree designed to eliminate such abuses.

Finally, Metternich turned to the abuse of the press. The Karlsbad decrees had signaled the first attempt to "exert the authority and legislative might" of the Confederation against "frivolous injury" to the general peace and security of Germany. Although incomplete, the decrees had assured the authority of the Confederation against "open opposition." The greatest danger in an "agitated and stormy period" such as the one then facing the German rulers was an unfettered press. In the absence of a uniform system for controlling the press, Metternich could see no chance for "internal peace," not even security for the Confederation's continued existence. This, he noted, had been the basis for the 1819 press decree, but that "salutary law" was frustrated because so few states enforced it strictly. The result was a licentiousness not believed possible in 1819.

Although the individual governments had remained inactive, he continued, the Karlsbad decrees had given the federal Diet the right to suppress any publication that attacked the dignity of the Confederation, threatened the security of the individual states, or disturbed the peace and quiet of Germany as a whole. Once invoked, there could be no appeal; each state was obligated to execute the decree of suppression. Metternich regretfully observed that even this course of action had proven as ineffective as censorship by the states. He therefore proposed that the commission named in 1819 to watch over the press be revived and charged immediately with the task of singling out newspapers to be suppressed by the federal Diet. Since the Karlsbad decrees were to expire in 1824, Metternich concluded with the recommendation that they be renewed for an indefinite period until a permanent decree would be agreed upon. [29]

Although the February conference ended with no action to renew the Karlsbad decrees, Metternich pursued his discussions of the proposals with Prussia and Bavaria outside the framework of the federal Assembly. He succeeded in inducing Bavaria to propose a measure calling for the suppression of publication of the proceedings of the *Stände*.[30] This failed, however, when Rechberg proved incapable of convincing the Bavarian Ministerial Council to accept the idea. Metternich, moreover, had to postpone his plan for expanding the censorship to include works of more than twenty pages, the limit imposed in 1819, for, as Austria's ambassador to Bavaria, Joseph Graf von Trauttmansdorff-Weinsberg, reported, Rechberg doubted whether this would prove acceptable to the Bavarian government since the Bavarian constitution placed periodicals alone under censorship. Trauttmansdorff found the entire Bavarian attitude to be improper: if one were to consider "the system" that Bavaria followed in her internal administration, it would be observed how opinions, utterances, and so on were "observed here" that elsewhere, "where the monarchical principle" was "better observed," would be "labeled criminal."[31]

Another matter, however, demonstrated that the Bavarian position was still flexible and that the government was hardly truly liberal. The federal Assembly's committee for supervising the press decree, which Metternich had now succeeded in reviving, presented a report on May 30, 1823, that argued that the *Teutscher Beobachter*, a newspaper appearing in Stuttgart, ought to be suppressed by the federal Assembly. The paper was accused of endangering the Confederation, presenting it as a "bloodless silhouette" and as an abject failure. Moreover, the committee charged that the newspaper alternately decried federal decrees as tyrannical or praised them as useful in order to "divide the opinion of the members of the federal Diet." If this tactic were to prove successful, the *Bundesversammlung* would no longer represent the entire Confederation, but only the separate opinions of the individual member governments.[32]

Since the influence of Lerchenfeld and the crown prince, which had limited Bavarian enforcement of the Karlsbad decrees in 1819, had now been supplanted by that of a more conservative group led by Rechberg, it came as no surprise that, along with Austria and Prussia, the Bavarian ambassador declared himself to be "in perfect agreement with the committee's report," and voted with the majority to suppress the *Teutscher Beobachter* on the basis of the decree of September 20, 1819. The government of Württemberg was requested to execute the measure.[33]

The *Teutscher Beobachter* thus achieved the unique distinction of being the first newspaper to be suppressed by the German Confederation. Its suppression marked the beginning of a more repressive policy on the part of the Confederation and some of the states. Bavaria, Lamb reported to London, increased the severity of the censorship, and other states also became more restrictive. The suppression of that newspaper, he felt, was the start of a greater watchfulness over the press and the beginning of a "greater state of repose" in Germany than had existed since the German Confederation's organization.[34]

One year later, in 1824, Metternich again moved to make the Karlsbad decrees permanent, for the press law was due to expire in that year. On his instructions Münch argued that an indefinite extension of the decrees could be effected by a simple majority vote of the federal Assembly. However, since both Bavaria and Prussia demanded that any such action required the unanimous approval of the German governments, Metternich once again had to proceed outside the framework of the federal Assembly to win the consent of the German sovereigns. He first reached agreement with Prussia over the form of the proposal, then turned to the courts of Bavaria and Württemberg. He then called a conference of the major German states to begin on June 22 at his estate on the Johannisberg near the Tegernsee. In the course of the conference's sessions he was able to win over the Bavarian representatives, Wrede and Zentner.

Metternich was especially delighted with Zentner, whose proposals for the renewal of the Karlsbad decrees went much further than the prince had anticipated. In a letter to Gentz, Metternich wrote that he had accepted Zentner's idea for a presidial proposal to the federal Assembly and had instructed Münch to rephrase his own proposal, "retaining as many of Zentner's words as possible." [35] The reason for this was revealed in a letter from Metternich to the Emperor Francis I. The prince wanted to employ the Bavarian suggestions and phraseology in order to "compromise Bavaria deeply in the matter," thereby preventing that state "from retreating in the application (*Anwendung*) of the decree." [36]

Metternich had every reason to feel satisfied. When the conference ended on July 19, all of the representatives present appeared to have agreed on all points concerning the renewal of the decrees, especially those which involved censorship of the press. Moreover, as early as June 26 instructions had been forwarded to Pfeffel outlining the position that he was to take in Frankfurt. The instructions noted that while the Bavarian constitutional edict of May 1818 limited censorship solely to political papers and periodicals with statistical content, certain bookstores in Bavaria also fell under the edict because of the theme of the publications that they sold, "especially the type of pamphlet designated" in 1819. Strong police measures had filled in the gaps left by the previous form of censorship. "As experience on this point" showed, those measures had fulfilled their purpose. Thus "it follows" that Bavaria had no need for a renewal of the Karlsbad decrees for her own needs, but she had "no objection" to such a renewal if the other states felt it necessary. In such a case, the renewal should be expressed "by

unanimous decree" in the interest "of the entire Confederation."[37]

Metternich's optimism, however, proved premature, for at
the last moment Bavaria began to raise objections. At first only
a change in the wording was requested: the substitution of
"measures" (*Massregeln*) for "laws" (*Gesetze*) since Bavaria
could not grant the federal Assembly the right of legislation.
Then the July 29 meeting of the Bavarian Ministerial Council
questioned the proposed indefinite term of the press law. It was
no longer acceptable to the Bavarian government that the 1819
press decree be indefinitely prolonged; rather it ought to be
renewed "for a further definite number of years." Moreover,
the Council approved Lerchenfeld's proposal that the acceptance of any decree be qualified with the phrase: "as formerly,"
thereby continuing and extending the limits that Bavaria had
placed on the press decree in 1819. [38] Instructions to this effect
were sent to Frankfurt.

On August 16 the *Präsidium* delivered an address to the
federal Assembly outlining the Austrian point of view, then
proceeded to offer the proposals that had been agreed upon on
the Johannisberg. The decree of 1819 was to be extended until
such time as the federal Assembly created a permanent law.
When the vote came the proposal surprisingly was accepted by
the Bavarian ambassador and that of Württemburg, who a
week earlier had supported Bavarian modifications. Pfeffel's
acceptance, however, was conditional. He voted for the
measure in the hope that the Confederation would enact a
permanent decree as soon as possible; in the meantime, "the
measures taken in 1819 . . . would [be managed] as before." [39]

In 1819 the Karlsbad decrees were capable of being interpreted as extraordinary measures of a provisional nature to be
retained only for the duration of an emergency. With their
indefinite extension, however, they became part of the legislation of the *Bundesversammlung* and thus part of the normal order

of things. [40] Both the intent of the decrees and the extraconstitutional means used to gain their acceptance signified that the German Confederation planned to follow the path of eighteenth century autocracy rather than that of nineteenth century constitutionalism. Any hope that the Confederation might evolve into a liberal unified Germany with the Diet as its representative legislative organ had firmly been laid to rest.

ii

After the renewal of the Karlsbad decrees the pace of activity noticeably slackened. The federal Assembly entered into a period of quiet development of the federal constitution and appeared to be all but exclusively occupied with private claims and petitions [41] that often dealt with unresolved problems which had their origins in the revolutionary era. Bavaria too turned inward. Her government expended its energies in combating encroachments by the *Landtag* on governmental prerogatives. Although Bavaria continued to follow her own interpretation of the Karlsbad press decree, censorship was expanded to cover most published matter, including *Landtag* debates. The government imposed new rules on the *Landtag* of 1824, limiting attendance at public sessions and forbidding the representatives from attacking ministers, other German governments, or the Confederation. All right of legislative initiation was withdrawn, and, after the budget had been accepted, the third legislative session was ended. [42]

It appeared that the Bavarian government would go even further toward repression of liberalism, but on October 12, 1825, Bavaria's first king died quietly in his sleep. His son and successor, Ludwig I, had been noted for his liberal point of view in regard to the *Landtag* and freedom of the press. On November 24, 1825, shortly after his accession to the throne, he issued an edict that modified the censorship, leaving only periodicals, political newspapers, and pamphlets under the control of the censor. He saw no contradiction between his action and the federal decrees of 1824, for with the phrase, "as formerly," Bavaria had accepted those decrees only in so far as they did not contradict her constitution. [43] With his royal edict King Ludwig I effectively emasculated the principal item of the Karlsbad decrees. [44]

By 1827, when the *Landtag* had reassembled, Ludwig had already begun the task of reforming the government. He had replaced his father's conservative ministers with men more in harmony with his own moderate liberalism. The new minister of justice was Georg Friedrich von Zentner, a former professor of law and one of the creators of the Bavarian constitution, and the new minister of the interior and of finance was Ludwig Graf Armansperg, who proved especially adept at cutting government expenses and streamlining the Bavarian bureaucracy. All this proved a good omen for relations between the Bavarian monarch and the members of his *Landtag*.

3

Conflict Resolution

i

So far only those measures that dealt with the development and internal security of the German Confederation, and the Bavarian response to them during the first fourten years of the Confederation's existence, have been considered. The Confederation, however, also played a second role: it had to preserve the peace in Germany and the security of the German states, for the conflicts and disputes among or involving the member states also had to be resolved. In the event of dispute between a state and the federal Assembly over fulfillment of a federal decree, the members generally attempted to arrange an equitable compromise; only as a last resort did they initiate the procedure established by the *Exekutions-Ordnung* to compel the recalcitrant state to fulfill its obligations. [1] A majority of the disputes brought to the federal Assembly involved demands of one state on another for territory or money, or on the Confederation itself. These disputes generally had their origin in the revolutionary period when, due to the rapid transfer of lands and allegiances within Germany, difficulties arose as to which state should be held responsible for pensions or debts or whether territorial claims were justified. The federal Diet considered individual requests for redress only if more than one state were involved.

Although it was no court in the proper sense, the Diet was the body to which "each and every" controversy between members of the Confederation had to be brought. [2] Its quasi-juridical functions were based on the *Bundesakt* and the *Schlussakt*. Article 11 of the former forbade the states to engage in war to resolve inter-German conflicts. They were obliged to bring irreconcilable differences to the federal Assembly for settlement. Article 30 of the *Schlussakt* empowered the Diet to deal with private claims that could otherwise not be satisfactorily resolved because of divided or contested jurisdiction. Should the federal Assembly be unable to reach a mutually agreeable arrangement, and if all interested parties consented, the matter would be placed before an *Austrägal-Gericht* for adjudication. [3]

A federal decree of June 16, 1817, the *Austrägal-Ordnung*, established the procedure by which a judicial settlement might be reached. The federal Assembly, upon request, was to select a committee to investigate the circumstances surrounding a dispute and to make a report, including all relevant observations and documents, as quickly as possible. If mediation by the *Bundesversammlung* proved unsuccessful, the interested parties were to select a disinterested federal state whose highest court would then act as the *Austrägal Instanz* in the name of the federal Diet. Unless excused by that body the chosen state was obligated to allow its supreme court, required of each state by the *Bundesakt*, to accept jurisdiction. Upon reaching a verdict, the court was to forward its decision to the federal Diet. Since the judgment now had the force of a federal decree, that body assumed responsibility for its execution. Cases could be reopened if new evidence were presented; after a four-year period had elapsed, the state deemed liable could be forced to carry out the court's decision via the *Exekutions-Ordnung*. [4]

As part of its campaign to limit the scope of the Confederation, the Bavarian government opposed the establishment of a
permanent *Austrägal-Gericht* or any other federal court independent of the states. When the federal Assembly promulgated Articles 21–24 of the *Schlussakt* on August 3, 1820, the
Saxon ambassador expressed his regret that no permanent
Austrägal-Gericht had been created. Aretin argued that no such
action was permissible by a federal decree. Since the *Schlussakt*
had been arrived at by the agreement of all the German courts,
the federal Assembly was empowered only to declare its
"acceptance and approval" of articles concerning these
matters. [5]

A committee that included Aretin, however, had been
selected by the ambassadors to study the matter and to propose
a revision of the 1817 *Austrägal-Ordnung*. Aretin wrote to
Munich in December 1820 that in repeated sessions the
committee had more or less completed its task. The committee
report noted, however, that there was no individual court to
deal with all *Austrägal* matters through "generally valid and
uniform formulae" and that there probably could be none. [6]

The committee's proposal, which attempted to strengthen
the *Austrägal-Ordnung* and to clarify that court's procedures, was
often discussed over the next decade, but nothing came of it. In
1831, however, Bavaria proposed a modification to the 1817
decree to assure complete fairness in the proceedings of the
Austrägal courts. The highest court of each state was to create a
special senate that might then be requested to act as the
Austrägal-Instanz. Each senate would contain some thirty judges
who would vote secretly to choose from among their number
the ten or twelve voting members of that court. [7] This would
have secured equitable treatment for all while allowing the
courts to remain under the jurisdiction of the states.

To examine Bavaria's proposal, the federal Assembly elected
a committee that on September 22 reported its disapproval.

Not until November 21, 1833, however, did the *Präsidium* declare that the Bavarian proposal was defeated by majority vote. Thus the decree of June 16, 1817, remained in force unchanged; and it was under the procedures outlined in that decree that the long and complex case of Elisabeth, Princess Berkeley was handled.

On April 25, 1825, the Private Claims Committee of the federal Assembly received a request for aid from Princess Berkeley in obtaining a pension she claimed was rightfully hers. The princess was the second wife and widow of Markgraf Alexander of Ansbach and Bayreuth who, on June 1, 1791, had concluded a secret agreement with Frederick William II, king of Prussia, transferring his lands to Prussia. The Markgraf then published a patent to that effect in 1792, abdicated, and moved to England. In return, the Prussian king wrote:

> we assure . . . to Madame Elisabeth, his wife, a pension of 20,000 Fl [yearly], for her use in case of the death. . of the Markgraf.[8]

In 1801 Kaiser Francis II elevated the Markgraf's wife into the German *Reichsfürstenstand* under the name of Berkeley. Five years later, on January 5, 1806, the Markgraf died, making the princess eligible for her yearly 20,000 Fl. In the next month, however, Prussia, after negotiations with Napoleon, ceded Ansbach to France, and on May 20 the French transferred it to Bavarian sovereignty. Moreover, Bayreuth was occupied by French soldiers during the 1806 war between France and Prussia, and on February 28, 1810, Prussia was forced to officially cede this territory to Napoleon. On June 10 of the same year Bavaria was again rewarded for her support of France, this time with Bayreuth. But at no time since the death of the Markgraf had his widow received her pension, and the matter was further complicated by the fact that no specific mention of the pension had been made in any of the treaties transferring the sovereignty of Ansbach and Bayreuth first to France then to Bavaria.

With the final defeat of Napoleonic France, Princess Berkeley sought to claim her due. She wrote to the Prussian government requesting her pension, but Prussia referred her to the Bavarian court, to which she then forwarded her claim. Not until 1818 was a reply sent by the Bavarians. They denied all responsibility in the matter. Once again, in 1823, she petitioned Prussia, then in 1824 Bavaria, again with no success. Since neither Prussia, which had originally agreed to the pension, nor Bavaria, which now held the territories of Ansbach and Bayreuth, would accept responsibility for the payment of the princess's pension, Article 30 of the *Schlussakt* went into effect.

The princess's lawyer argued that only the federal Diet, on the basis of that article, could resolve the issue. The Private Claims Committee agreed, and on May 13 the question was brought before the full federal Assembly, which decided that the ambassadors of Prussia and Bavaria should request their governments to explain the situation. Pfeffel, however, was ordered to hold private discussions with Nagler, the Prussian ambassador, who also felt that the resolution of the princess's claim should take place outside the framework of the federal Assembly. [9] These talks proved fruitless, however, and the unresolved claim languished without action by the Confederation.

In April 1826 the princess's lawyer sent a printed reminder [10] to the *Bundestag*, which, on May 5, requested both Bavaria and Prussia to report their positions on the matter within six weeks. On June 22 the ambassadors of Austria, Baden, and Hannover were named as a committee to investigate the claim and to propose a solution to the federal Assembly.

One year later this committee presented its report in which the history of the claim was outlined. It also noted that there was no dispute over the validity of the claim, but only over which state ought to pay the pension. Prussia had privately agreed to pay one-half if Bavaria would pay the remainder, while Bavaria countered with a proposal to place the dispute before the legal faculty of either the University of Leipzig or the University of Göttingen. Bavaria, however, also stipulated that the princess would have to accept a maximum payment of 300,000 Fl instead of the more than 400,000 Fl she claimed as a settlement of the debt and in lieu of any future pension. Since Prussia rejected this plan, the committee recommended that the matter go to an *Austrägal-Gericht*. [11]

Meanwhile, on March 2, before the committee had reported its findings, Lerchenfeld received instructions from his government noting that since it was important for Bavaria to avoid any appearance of delay, he was to acknowledge that the talks with Prussia had been fruitless and to request that an *Austrägal-Instanz* be chosen. [12] Accordingly, the federal Diet decreed that since both states were in agreement, the *Oberappellationsgericht* of the Free Cities at Lübeck would act as the *Austrägal* court to decide whether Bavaria or Prussia was obliged to pay the pension, or, if both were responsible, what proportion was due from each. [13]

Finally, after a long delay, on May 18, 1830, a judgment was handed down and published in a rare public *Bundestag* protocol. [14] The court had ruled that Bavaria alone was responsible and ought to pay the widow's pension "in its full extent and including the ·.. . arrears," a sum of about 500,000 Fl. Since the princess had died in the meantime, the court ruled that this sum was to be paid to Richard Keppel-Craven, her son by her first marriage. Bavaria, however, rejected the decision, arguing that the claim had expired with the death of the princess. [16] The matter was returned to the Bavarian courts for adjustment since, as Bavaria would later argue, her courts alone could treat appeals from a decision of the Bavarian government.

Now began a new series of attempts by Princess Berkeley's son to obtain his inheritance. In 1835 Arnold von Mieg, Bavarian ambassador to the Confederation from 1833 to 1842, was notified that after careful examination of the claim and of a proposal for settlement that had been submitted, the Bavarian Ministry of Finance had concluded that no compromise was possible. [16] The suit was pressed in the Bavarian courts where, on May 28, 1839, the superior court of appeals decided that the claim was without merit. [17] This judgment was the basis for the Finance Ministry's contention that the matter was now extinct.

Following his mother's path, Keppel-Craven appealed directly to the federal Assembly for assistance, noting that the judgment of 1830 had been specifically in his favor. Bavaria, however, argued that the court at Lübeck had "decided and intended to decide nothing more than the preliminary question," namely whether the matter should proceed through the Prussian or Bavarian court system. Bavaria argued that she had followed this ruling and that her courts had found in favor of the government. As far as Bavaria was concerned, the federal Assembly had no further role in the matter. [18]

This severe limitation by a single state on the effect of a judgment by an *Austrägal-Gericht* was accepted by the *Bundesversammlung*, which decreed that it was "limited in its competence" and could no longer act. There the matter ended. [19] In effect, the Diet had ruled that the original decision finding Bavaria responsible had overstepped the bounds of the Confederation's competence and that Article 30 of the *Schlussakt* was to be interpreted as narrowly as possible. All contact between the federal Assembly and the German populace was to be avoided; the Confederation would not be permitted to assist individuals. The chance for an expansion of the Confederation's judicial competence had come and gone. For her part, Bavaria had succeeded in evading the responsibilities that ought to have followed her acquisition of territories, but more important to the Bavarian government was the establishment of an effective limitation on the Confederation's power in any matter affecting Bavarian interests.

The use of the *Austrägal-Gericht* to resolve disputes thus proved to be more the exception than the rule. In most cases the federal Assembly was itself able to work out a compromise acceptable to the parties involved. One such case involved a request for redress by the city of Bayreuth to the federal Assembly, which, contrary to normal procedure, was able to reach a workable solution within a few weeks. In 1805-06 Prussian soldiers had been quartered in the then Prussian city with the permission of the municipal government. In return, the Prussian government had promised reimbursement to that city. Although funds had been authorized to pay the expenses of these soldiers, payment had been prevented by the outbreak of war between Prussia and France in 1806 and the subsequent occupation of the city by French armies. In the treaty that ended that phase of the conflict, Bayreuth was ceded to France, which promised to assume responsibility for all debts. When the city was finally transferred to Bavaria she also accepted the obligation for payment. Officials of the Bayreuth treasury, however, found themselves unable to collect these funds, although they utilized all legal means available to them. Finally, in 1827 they appealed to the federal Assembly. [20]

That body voted to request the governments of Bavaria and Prussia to inspect the claim and to report on the results of their examination. In May the Bavarian ambassador acknowledged that his government was at fault and stated that 11,669 Fl 12 Kr would be paid from the royal Bavarian treasury when Bayreuth transferred its claims of allegiance from the Prussian crown to Bavaria as required by the treaty of 1810. Although Prussia, hoping perhaps to regain Bayreuth, asked for more time, the federal Assembly decreed that Bavaria's response had been satisfactory and that the matter was to be considered closed. [21] No doubts could now be raised as to the validity of the transfer of Bayreuth to Bavaria, for the federal decree in effect gave the Confederation's sanction to the 1810 treaty.

ii

Bavaria, however, was not always as successful in defending her interests, for when the Confederation itself was one of the principals it was generally able to resolve major questions in its own favor. One such instance was the fifteen-year debate over possession of the military fortress at the Bavarian town of Landau. As early as 1816 the federal Diet had planned to take control of the three strategic fortresses at Mainz, Luxemburg, and Landau in the name of the Confederation in order to defend Germany in case of a French attack. This arrangement had been agreed upon at the Congress of Vienna, and it was generally believed that the transfer would be accomplished in a relatively short period of time since only the details needed to be worked out.

Landau, the fortress under Bavarian control, had a long history of changing status and allegiance. In 1290 the market town of Landau had received the privilege of becoming a free imperial city from the Habsburg emperor Rudolf. In 1678 the city, then including a fortress, was conquered by the Duke of Lorraine, who lost it to the French in the following year. Under the administration of Sebastian Vauban, the fortifications genius of Louis XIV, Landau was redesigned. It was later used by the French revolutionary armies in the wars against the German states. [22] The fortress and the town came once again under Austrian control during the War of Liberation, and, through the Paris protocol of November 3, 1815, Landau was to become a fortress of the German Confederation, but under Bavarian sovereignty. Its garrison was to be composed entirely of Austrian troops until such time as it was ceded to Bavaria, which would then provide the full peacetime garrison. In time of war Baden was to provide one-third of the garrison, an arrangement unpopular in both Baden and Bavaria. The Austro-Bavarian treaty of April 14, 1816, finally ceded "the district, the town and the fortress Landau" [23] to Bavaria "in all property and sovereignty," [24] a phrase that would form the basis for future Bavarian arguments against federal authority in that fortress.

However, even Bavaria had originally accepted the inevitability of the fortress's change of hands. Indeed, in the early years of the Confederation the Bavarian government had insisted that the transfer be made expeditiously with the reservation that no demands be made that might subtract from or compromise Bavarian sovereignty. As was usual in federal matters of less than pressing importance, there were in this case delays of the transfer of the three fortresses. But it must be stressed that, at this time, Bavaria was not at all opposed to the federal acquisition of Landau or the other two fortresses.

By 1820 it appeared doubtful whether the Confederation would take possession of the fortresses in the near future. Aretin reported to his government that Austria and Prussia wished to hurry federal acquisition of Luxemburg and Mainz, but that they did not seem to desire the rapid transfer of Landau. Therefore, he counceled, Bavaria ought to wait and see how things developed rather than push for the fortress to be taken over. Bavaria, he noted, was receiving no federal money for the maintenance of Landau and should make no demand for recompense at the federal Assembly since this would not be paid in any case. By following this course it would be easier to come to an agreement concerning Landau's status with the North German governments "who wish to pay nothing." Finally, he observed, if the Confederation did not take possession of Landau, which even still appeared possible, and if conditions remained unchanged, Bavaria would lose nothing, for she could retain her sovereignty over the fortress and could avoid the "bothersome influence" of the federal Diet. [25] The Bavarian government, although still willing to allow the Confederation use of the fortress, accepted Aretin's advice.

On October 5, 1820, the federal Assembly, in plenary session, decreed that the three fortresses were to be taken over "on the basis of European treaties to this effect" and that the necessary restoration and repairs to these fortresses were to be carried out. [26] In theory, the Confederation now controlled three fortresses on the French border, a precaution that the experience of the recent past seemed to dictate. In fact, the Confederation would have effective control only of two fortresses before 1830, and those only after a further period of negotiation with the states that possessed them. Landau would not be surrendered to the Confederation for another decade.

Bavaria was still willing to allow the Confederation to use Landau so long as her rights of sovereignty were not questioned. In 1824, however, the problem of an oath to the Confederation was raised in the Diet. The Bavarians, of course, were adamantly opposed, for an oath directly to the Confederation was tantamount to a Bavarian surrender of all claims to the fortress. Pfeffel argued in Frankfurt that since Landau had been given to Bavaria by international treaty, and that since Bavaria's only obligation was to use the fortress for the defense of the Confederation, Bavarian subjects, as such, ought not to be required to take an oath to the Confederation, for this would deprive Bavaria of her just rights and of the full loyalty of all of her subjects. [27]

In a report to Metternich, Trauttmansdorff noted that the Bavarian foreign minister wanted to hear nothing of the "surrender of the fortress Landau" to the Confederation. Rather, the Confederation was to acknowledge that Bavaria possessed the full property rights to both town and fortress. [28]

This argument was based on a literal reading of the Austro-Bavarian treaty, while ignoring the preceding treaties that made Landau a federal fortress.

In February 1825 the Bavarian Ministerial Council met to decide what course of action to follow. It was suggested that the Bavarian ambassador be instructed to request as a tactical move that the question of federal fortresses be voted on in plenary session on the basis of Articles 11–13 of the *Schlussakt*, since the matter was an "organic adjustment" in the Confederation as defined in Article 13, §2. Zentner, however, correctly noted that since the majority of the ambassadors opposed Bavaria's position, the matter would have to be dealt with in the *Engerer Rat*. [29]

Two months later Rechberg told the Ministerial Council that, without exception, the federal ambassadors supported the Austro-Prussian proposal with regard to Landau, thus leaving Bavaria isolated. Zentner then raised the question if, under the circumstances, it was advisable to continue a "useless opposition" to Austria and Prussia, which could only serve to turn them against Bavaria. He observed that the oath to be taken by Landau's commander proposed by the federal Military Commission must contain the "primary obligation of the commander toward the Confederation." He felt, however, that a compromise might be possible and recommended that Bavaria agree to administer the oath to the commander and then send a record of the oath-taking to the federal Assembly. In this way the "obligation of the Confederation" would be satisfied, and the "special relationship" of Landau to Bavaria that was due in part to "Bavaria's control of the land" and in part to "Bavaria's right of occupation" could be saved. [30]

The other personnel of the fortress, he continued, might then be sworn to the Confederation by the commander, and a note of this would be made in the same record. This was deemed acceptable by all, although Wrede asked only that Pfeffel be provided with covering instructions should the compromise be rejected. [31]

Pfeffel had not yet received these instructions when Münch proposed in the federal Assembly that Mainz, Luxemburg, and Landau, when they were taken over, should stand under the "command and special supervision" of the federal Assembly in time of peace, but only in a manner whereby the "administration of the cities and their properties" would remain "undisturbed in every respect" in the hands of the territorial governments. The garrison of Landau, he continued, was to be composed of at least 2,000 Bavarians in time of peace; in time of war, this garrison was to be augmented by an additional 2,000 Bavarians and 2,000 soldiers from Baden. Also in time of war, the federal Diet would turn over its rights in the fortress to the commander of the Confederation's army. Even though this guarantee of Bavarian sovereignty would be unexceptionable, Pfeffel felt it necessary to abstain until he could receive instructions. [32]

In May, having finally received his instructions, Pfeffel proposed a formula for the oath to be given to the fortress commander:

> I---swear to God . . . an oath, that after his majesty the King of Bavaria, my lord, who named me as commander of the fortress of Landau, to act in the interest of the Confederation and its defense . . . . [33]

After several weeks' discussion, however, the federal Diet decided that this formula was unacceptable. Pfeffel then requested that on the basis of the *Schlussakt* the matter be decided by a unanimous vote of the *Plenum*. A majority of the ambassadors, as Zentner had foreseen, refused and voted instead to accept a modification of both the oath and the Austrian proposal of April 21. The oath for all fortress commanders was to read:

I---swear to God . . . an oath, that after his majesty---has
named me as commander of the fortress---, I will conduct this
office in the interest of the Confederation alone . . . and I will
allow myself to be restrained from punctual fulfillment [of
my duties] neither through any consideration of nor any
relationship to a single federal state.

This was embodied in a decree that also contained much the
same regulations delineating federal and state jurisdiction over
the fortresses as those of the original Austrian proposal. The
decree did acknowledge that Bavaria might continue to pay
the full costs for the maintenance of Landau, [34] and that the
treasury officials of the fortress might be Bavarian, although
they were declared to be under the supervision of the governor
and commander. [35]

Bavaria was not yet prepared to surrender to the demands of
the Confederation, for, in the words of Minister of the Interior
Thürheim, "the topic of the federal fortresses . . . and their
surrender" to the Confederation was "one of the most important matters" that had "recently come before the federal
Diet." [36] In the December 19 meeting of the Bavarian Ministerial Council a report was submitted summarizing the matter
for the new king, Ludwig I. It stated that there was no topic of
"such great and substantial importance" before the federal
Assembly, for Landau was a matter touching on the "deepest
questions" concerning the nature of the political and military
position of Bavaria in the Confederation. In 1815, the report
continued, while Landau had been declared a federal fortress,
"the city *and fortress*, with *full property and sovereignty rights*," were
ceded to Bavaria "through the explicit stipulation of treaties."
Moreover, at the 1820 Vienna Conference the Bavarian
delegate had declared that only the fortress itself could be
transferred to the Confederation, all other questions had been
resolved by the then existing treaties. This point of view had
been accepted by the other states; Austria's position, not

Bavaria's, had changed. The Bavarian government, the report concluded, had made its views clear and must now prevent the federal Diet from encroaching into an area where it had no right in order to protect the "rights, dignity and independence" of the Bavarian crown, even if Bavaria were forced to act alone. [37]

To Lerchenfeld, the newly appointed ambassador to the federal Diet and who was attending the Council meeting, the basic question was

> how far a decree formulated by a majority of the members of the Confederation was to be taken as binding, or if it might be considered as not binding on Bavaria.

Lerchenfeld had indeed posed the primary question, for the response could determine not only the relationship of a fortress to the Confederation, but also the relationship of Bavaria to the Confederation. In answer, the Ministerial Council decided that in the unequal relationship between the Confederation and the individual states, it was the state that was superior. The decree, the Council decided, was "not binding in any point" that the Bavarian government had already stated to be incompatible with its own views and with rights derived from European treaties. [38]

The king was thus convinced that he was obligated to continue the policy of limiting federal interference in Bavaria's internal affairs. As the French chargé d'affaires in Munich wrote, Ludwig refused to allow one of his officers to be subordinated to the Confederation. In this the king remained "unshakable." [39] The issue of federal control of Landau had been reduced simply to a question of a mutually agreeable formula for the commander's oath, although the oath was only symbolic of the real question. Here the matter rested for three years.

The question was reopened in July 1828 when Lerchenfeld offered the federal Assembly a way of retreating from its rigid position with no loss of prestige. He observed that his government had acquainted that body with the fortress's special relationship to Bavaria. It was thus clear, he argued, that Landau could not be placed in the same catagory as Mainz and Luxemburg. There was no reason why Landau, in peacetime, should not remain under full Bavarian control since she held complete sovereignty over the property of the city and the fortress. Since, by provisioning the fortress of Landau, the Bavarian king "takes over the obligation" for its care, "there should be no special obligation" of the fortress's commander to the federal Assembly in time of peace. Rather, he continued, "it is sufficient" that he be sworn "by the federal Diet for the duration of a federal war." Moreover, Bavaria was willing to have the commander take a new oath:

> I---swear to God . . . that after his majesty the king of Bavaria, my lord, has named me as commander of the fortress of Landau, I will conduct this office in the interest of the Confederation and its defense, that I will be true to the regulations of the Confederation as far as they relate to . . . this fortress and that I will carry out all instructions with promptness. . . . [40]

The Military Affairs Committee of the federal Assembly was requested to study Lerchenfeld's proposal. In November 1830 it reported that Bavaria's position was not in accord with the decrees of July 28, 1825. "In every case," the report continued,

> the right, with its necessary consequences, remains with the Confederation to maintain and to control Landau as a federal fortress.

The committee found no obstacle in the treaty ceding Landau to Bavaria "in all property and sovereignty," for this applied only to the town and could not be applied to the fortress: Landau "is a federal fortress in peace and war." Therefore the "government of the fortress" had to "act in the interests of the Confederation alone, without regard to" other ties, "namely a single federal state." [41] The federal Assembly, on the basis of this report, refused to make any attempt to compromise with Bavaria.

Finally, in December, Bavaria was forced to concede defeat. The federal Diet now decreed that the Confederation's right of supervision of Landau in peacetime would be given to the Bavarian king "under the superintendence (*Oberaufsicht*) of the Confederation." In November Bavaria had tried to have this wording changed to "supervision" (*Kontrolle*) or "cosupervision" (*Mitaufsicht*) with no success. Moreover, the Confederation was to take formal possession of Landau within four weeks, and the commander would then swear his oath to the German Confederation. The *Bundesversammlung* retained the right of inspection, and the Bavarian ambassador was to present periodic reports to the Diet concerning the condition of the fortress and the progress of repairs. [42] Thus, despite five years of maneuvering, the decree was, in substance, precisely that which the Military Commission had first proposed.

The German Confederation assumed control of the fortress of Landau in a formal ceremony on February 27, 1831. The peacetime garrison remained Bavarian, [43] the territory and the town remained Bavarian, but—in name—the fortress now belonged to the Confederation. Fifteen years of bitter argument and useless maneuvering had occurred. Although Bavaria had been able to postpone the decision and had raised some vital questions as to the scope and purpose of the Confederation in the process, the federal Assembly had been the clear victor in the end. On an issue that Bavaria considered to be of vital importance, involving her right of sovereignty, the federal Assembly proved to be the stronger. Once again,

Bavaria proved unable to win allies to her cause, largely because her interest was selfish, regardless of the principles raised by the Wittelsbach government. Bavaria, acting alone, was not able to dictate to the Confederation.

Thus, as the Confederation matured and the Diet gained strength, it appeared that it might at last become the final arbiter of disputes among the German states. By no means absolute in its authority, the federal Assembly nevertheless was able to resolve conflicts within its sphere of competence, as the above instances demonstrate. Rarely rapid in its decisions, the Diet did offer all parties a fair hearing. Committee reports were paragons of completeness and accuracy. In particular, Bavaria could not legitimately fault the federal Assembly's handling of disputes in which the Wittelsbach government was involved. Bavaria always received a fair hearing, but in the end the federal decision was based less on Bavaria's arguments than on the Confederation's laws and constitution. This, of course, meant little to the average Bavarian or German, for Bavaria was only one of many German states actively working to prevent an expansion of federal authority to the point where the Confederation could act upon the individual German and bypass the state governments. But within this restricted framework the Diet did prove effective at fulfilling its charge: the maintenance of peace among the member states.

iii

The outlines of the Confederation gained substance during the decade of the twenties. The federal Assembly proved useful in resolving conflicts between the member states; it demonstrated that it could enforce its decrees. Acting alone, no state could compel that body to accept its proposals. As long as two of the three most important states in Germany worked in concert, the third, be it Austria, Prussia, or Bavaria, was unable to force its will on the federal Diet, and, as the failure of the Trias amply demonstrated, the German states could not create a counterforce to the Confederation.

Most of the member states were satisfied with the Confederation as constituted, preferring to continue the policies established at Vienna and Karlsbad rather than furthering the evolution of the Confederation. Metternich, for example, had discovered that the Confederation, even after the purge of 1823, would not be a tool for Austrian policies—thus he had no desire to expand its competence. On the other hand, Bavaria was exceedingly jealous of her sovereignty and autonomy and actively attempted to diminish the authority of the Diet. Bavarian arguments were clothed in principles applying to all states; yet she acted alone, primarily because her arguments were founded on motives of self-interest.

To assume that the individual states paid little attention to the demands of the Confederation or that the ambassadors to the Diet were able to act independently and to vote their consciences is to misread the evidence. By 1824 the more independent-minded ambassadors who had come to Frankfurt before procedure and limitations had been firmly established had been replaced either through death or recall. The men who followed them were generally more willing to accept the detailed instructions of their governments, which were now more aware of the tactics that would enable them to pursue their individual policies within the framework of a general federal policy.

Both states and ambassadors could often be kept in line as long as Austria and Prussia worked together; Bavaria alone could succeed only in preventing the Confederation from interfering in the internal affairs of the states. Bavaria, however, proved unwilling or unable to work with other member states to effect positive measures. Addington, the British envoy to the Confederation in 1828, only slightly overstated the matter when he wrote,

Austria and Prussia are the Confederation: but Austria still weighs the heaviest in the scale of influence. [44]

That Bavaria was not even considered by Addington was primarily her own fault.

Addington also reported that as long as Austria and Prussia acted "in tolerable harmony," the Confederation might be considered as secure, although the Confederation itself was "feeble and wanting in the principle of cohesion," which resulted from an "identity of interest or the dread of a common enemy." The Confederation, he continued, had little authority to coerce its members; it acted rather as a "Tribunal of conciliation and prevention." In this role the Diet possessed a "very salutary and by no means inconsiderable influence" on its members. The dissolution of the Confederation would be a "serious and irremiable [sic] calamity" to the smaller states, "especially [those] which are protected and prosper by the due proportion of power" held by Austria and Prussia in the federal Assembly. [45]

The *Bundesversammlung* itself had withdrawn, perhaps dangerously, from the German public. Contemporaries and subsequent historians have condemned it for its lack of initiative and action on the question of the unification of Germany. Treitschke, for example, dismissed it as the "busy idleness of the Eschenheimergasse."[46] That is unfortunate, for it must be understood that at no time was the federal Assembly conceived as a public legislature by the German governments that created it. The federal Assembly was a permanent congress of ambassadors and, as such, performed as it was expected to. In a period of relative stability, the system could and did work. What would happen if the quiet were disturbed?

Part II
Revolution and Reaffirmation
1830–1834

4

1830–31: Repercussions of Revolution

i

As shown earlier, Bavaria and the federal Diet could work together within the framework of the federal constitution during the relatively uneventful decade of the twenties. Moreover, by 1830, the Confederation, like the *Reich* before it, was becoming lethargic and moribund, lessening chances for federal interference in the internal affairs of member states, a development that Bavaria viewed with approval. The calm, however, was soon dispelled, first by the July Revolution in France, then by the spread of revolution to Belgium and Poland, and finally by the outbreak of rebellions in the German states themselves.

The preceding fifteen years had demonstrated that the federal Assembly could act vigorously only in response to stimuli that originated outside the *Bundesversammlung* and the federal structure. The stimulus provided by the disturbances of 1830 and the unrest of the following years revived the Confederation, simultaneously calling into question the effectiveness of the Confederation's particularist constitution and raising again the question of the Confederation's relationship to Bavaria.

The July Revolution was a response to the reactionary

program of the French king, Charles X, and his chief minister, Polignac. Their plans to limit the electorate and to purge the liberal Chamber of Deputies provided the climate for rebellion. Paris was under the control of the revolutionaries by July 29, 1830, and on the 31st the Duc d'Orleans, who had secured the support of the upper middle class and of Lafayette, became king of the French. The doctrine of restoration and legitimacy inherent in the Vienna Settlement was thus shattered in France, and the rulers of the German states feared that the disorder would spread or be brought to Germany.

Within a matter of days preparations were made to combat a possible French invasion. Prussian garrisons on the Rhine were placed on a war footing,[1] while other states brought troops, which they are obligated by the *Kriegsverfassung* to furnish to the Confederation, into a state of readiness. Ludwig I of Bavaria felt that a war with France was probably unavoidable,[2] although he believed that the German constitutional governments had less to fear from France and revolution than did other German princes.[3] The Bavarian Ministerial Council was no less convinced that war with France would come, for it had been reported that the cry "Landau and the Rhine" had been heard repeatedly in Paris.[4] The Bavarian ministers generally approved General Wrede's proposal of a preventive strike by the combined forces of the Confederation and the Quadruple Alliance.

War with France, however, was unpopular with the German populace, and Louis Philippe, in order to insure his newly won throne, made an effort to assure the European states that his intentions were peaceful. In the official notification of his accession to the throne, which he sent to the federal Assembly,[5] the new French king stressed not only the nonaggressive nature of his policies, but also requested assurance from the Confederation of continued Franco-German friendship. With such reassurances, fears of a French attack gradually subsided and with them plans for a federal invasion of that country.

Nevertheless, the July Revolution did provide encouragement for German radicals to rise against their princes. The German governments had good reason to fear that revolutions in states surrounding Germany might lead to similar uprisings in their states. Bavaria in particular feared for her Rhenish provinces (Rheinkreis), especially the Pfalz. Napoleon had given these territories to Bavaria, and, as Thomas Cartwright noted in his report to the British government, the residents of that territory were "perhaps worse disposed" than those in any other German land. The population there was attached to France "by inclination" and by the "natural position" of that province on the French border. They were, moreover, subject not to the laws governing the remainder of Bavaria, but had "preserved the French laws." [6] Since the Napoleonic code then in effect in the Rhine province provided for freedom of the press, that region lived under an arrangement regarding censorship that was more liberal than the rest of Bavaria. The newspapers of the Bavarian Rhineland could therefore libel even their king with impunity. Because of that, from 1830 on the Rheinkreis became a seedbed of revolutionary activity and a hotbed of what conservatives called *Demagogerie*.

It was, consequently, only natural that the Bavarian government would move to curb what it believed was the misuse of the press in that province. Even before the July Revolution Lerchenfeld was notified that the government of the Rheinkreis had been ordered to suppress all disturbances. Accordingly, he was instructed to inform the Diet of the steps taken and to "combat all demands on this government" to yield to federal involvement that might arise in Frankfurt. [7]

The outbreak of revolution in France and the subsequent reverberations in the Pfalz caused Ludwig to change his attitude toward federal intervention. The man who as crown prince had fought against the Karlsbad decrees, whose first act as king had been to repeal all censorship laws that went beyond those permitted explicitly by the Bavarian constitution, and who had struggled to maintain the independence and sovereignty of his state now requested the federal Assembly to work for a comprehensive federal decree against the press.

On September 27 Ludwig sent Lerchenfeld a private letter in which he complained about the negative effect that the "daily newspapers have in these excited times." He now accepted the argument that only the *Bundesversammlung* could end their influence.

> I want the Confederation to put into effect those [measures] which Bavaria refrained from enforcing in the Karlsbad decrees.

However, in order not to "injure Bavaria's independence," Lerchenfeld was ordered to keep the letter secret and to have Prussia initiate the measure.[8]

The ambassador responded that he had been assured by Nagler that if no proposition were offered by the Austrian ambassador, he would introduce the matter at the earliest opportunity. Moreover, Lerchenfeld noted that he had informed Münch that his government would cease its opposition to decrees that dealt with newspapers whose content was limited solely to domestic matters.[9] He also conformed to the king's wishes stated in another letter that Ludwig's name not be mentioned in the transaction. Lerchenfeld was only to assure Münch that Bavaria's constitution did not "stand in the way" of censoring newspapers that dealt with "our internal policies."[10]

Some federal ambassadors procrastinated and events soon took a different turn. *Landtag* elections required by the Bavarian constitution were imminent, and Ludwig, who needed legislative approval for his large budget, began to have second thoughts. He advised Lerchenfeld that discussions of federal censorship decrees must now cease, for he had no desire to face a hostile majority elected in response to this federal threat. [11] Lerchenfeld accordingly acted to halt action on the matter and was soon able to demonstrate to the federal Assembly that Bavaria had no need for a federal decree because a new and more repressive press edict had been instituted by his government one week after the local elections had been held. In accepting Lerchenfeld's remarks the Diet once again abandoned an opportunity to assert its right to intervene in the affairs of a member state in time of disturbance.

Unfortunately for the Bavarian king, however, although he had done nothing to jeopardize the outcome of the election, the liberals were still victorious. Moreover, a student disorder in the streets of Munich, which in retrospect appears to have been little more than the release of pent-up energy, took place on Christmas Eve, probably sparked by the election results. [12] The frightened king responded by closing the university temporarily and moving to limit the constitutional rights of his subjects. He then ordered the press edict that Lerchenfeld announced to his colleagues in Frankfurt. The edict ended the lax enforcement of the censorship and placed all articles of a political nature under prepublication censorship. Although still within the framework of the constitution, it was attacked by the liberals as destructive of freedom of the press and an assault on the basic rights of the Bavarian citizen. [13]

The edict had been countersigned by the minister of the interior, Eduard von Schenk, and was published on December 31, 1830. As the Austrian ambassador to Bavaria, Kasper Graf von Spiegel, reported, the new edict, which was unjustly known as the *Schenk'sche Pressordnung,* placed all newspapers under prepublication censorship and thus filled "an obvious hole" in Bavaria's commitment to the federal decrees of 1819 and 1824. "It was high, it was the highest time" that the

Bavarian government "finally confronted the licentiousness of the press." [14]

One of the first victims of the edict was the newspaper *Der Kosmopolit,* which had been founded on January 1, 1831 by Johann Georg August Wirth. [15] This would not be the last time that Wirth would experience difficulty with press laws in Germany, but the new edict did force the radical editor to leave Bavaria temporarily for a less restrictive atmosphere.

The lower Chamber of the *Landtag* protested the repressive edict and countered the king's action by refusing to consider the royal budget until the edict had been rescinded and Schenk dismissed. The representatives rejected the government's contention that the edict could not be liberalized without prior approval of the federal Assembly on the basis that since Bavaria was an independent state, no other state or organization could interfere in a Bavarian constitutional matter. The argument long used by the Bavarian government in Frankfurt had now become a weapon turned against it at home. On May 16, 1831, the lower Chamber voted 96–29 that the *Schenk' sche Pressordnung* was in violation of the constitution. Although this action found no echo in the upper Chamber, in order to secure approval of his budget Ludwig had to sacrifice both the minister (May 26) and the edict (June 13). [16] In this first example of the dismissal of a minister at the demand of a parliamentary body in a German state, Schenk was replaced by the aristocratic liberal, Ludwig Fürst von Oettingen-Wallerstein (although this was done two days after the dismissal of the *Landtag*). [17]

ii

By mid-September 1830 it was generally acknowledged in the federal Diet that the July Revolution had found an echo in Germany and that some governments appeared unable to deal with the uprisings in their territories. On September 18 the *Präsidium* raised the question whether member states might need the Confederation's assistance in quelling disturbances, a course of action prescribed by Articles 26 and 28 of the *Schlussakt*. Münch accordingly proposed that each state keep a contingent of soldiers ready to assist its neighbors even if no specific decree were adopted to this end. The ambassadors agreed to request the necessary instructions from their governments. [18]

On September 24 Lerchenfeld reported on the session of the 18th, expressing basic agreement with Münch's proposal. The German governments, he wrote, were responsible for aiding neighboring states in the name of the Confederation when those states were unable to cope with a disturbance. Since this assistance had to arrive quickly to be effective, he argued that the contingents owed to the Confederation ought to be put in a state of readiness even before the federal Assembly enacted a decree. Although he realized that this would be expensive, one must "willingly undertake" the necessary efforts for "common reciprocal protection." Since haste was necessary, he continued, each ambassador must be given blanket instructions from his government so that it would be possible to proceed

> in everything that presents itself as urgent and that concerns the external and internal security of the Confederation with the greatest possible saving of time.

He concluded with the observation that this was the best procedure, for if it were necessary to request instructions "in such pressing cases," the entire energy of the Confederation would "be crippled" and all "aid and speedy intervention" would come too late. [19]

The implications contained in Münch's proposal, however, staggered the German courts: Prussia and Württemberg bitterly complained, and Bavaria, despite Lerchenfeld's view, categorically refused to accept the concept of unilateral intervention by one state in the internal affairs of another. Lerchenfeld was ordered to protest against the proposition and to declare that the king would under no circumstances comply with it. He would not acknowledge any obligation to send troops into a neighboring state when they might be needed in Bavaria. [20]

It appeared that Bavarian and Prussian protests would suffice to prevent the Diet from accepting Münch's proposal. On September 24, however, an uprising that threatened to spread to other parts of Germany erupted in the Kurhessian town of Hanau. In the 29th session of the Diet Münch argued that the "entire legal order" in the territories bordering on Kurhesse might "be destroyed" and remained "disturbed and threatened daily." The attacks on the customs houses, he continued, constituted rebellion of the populace against the rights of property (*Gutsherrschaften*), and there was a clear danger that this would spread. Prussia and Bavaria jointly requested an explanation of the local authorities' failure to act in preventing "the outrage" and not combating the rebels. The federal Assembly accordingly decreed that the Kurhessian government declare within three days what measures it would take to restore order and also requested that Prussia, Bavaria, and the other states bordering on Kurhesse station soldiers on their frontiers to prevent a widening of the rebellion. In order to put down excesses, these troops were given federal permission to pursue "disturbers of the peace" across the borders of neighboring states and to "cooperate for the suppression of the uprising." [21]

The matter ought to have ended the next day because the Kurhessian ambassador notified the Diet that order had been restored and that the officials of Hanau had not acted before because they had lacked the authority to arrest or punish the troublemakers. The ministry of the interior, he concluded, had now granted this authority. The Diet's Military Affairs Committee, however, refused to accept this explanation as sufficient and recommended instead that a force of 7,000 soldiers be deployed on the Kurhessian borders. The federal Assembly consequently decreed the creation of such a force from soldiers provided by Bavaria, Baden, Hesse, and Nassau in order "to create a mobile force" and to restore "peace and order to the threatened regions." The Bavarian contingent of 1,700 horse and infantry was to be dispatched to Dettingen on the Kurhessian border, but still on Bavarian territory, and a 4,000 man reserve was to be stationed at Brückenau to safeguard communications between Fulda, where a revolt was expected, and Hanau. Six thousand Bavarians had first been requested, but Lerchenfeld had been able to reduce the number by one-third. All active troops were to be placed under the command of a Nassau general, von Kruse, "a very clever and talented officer" who had taken part in the war in Spain. [22]

In voting to accept this decree, Lerchenfeld had exceeded his authority. The resultant royal displeasure was made known in an instruction through which the ambassador was reprimanded for not requesting instructions as Article 8 of the *Schlussakt* demanded before committing Bavaria to a decree incompatible with her sovereignty. Contrary to Münch's statements, the directive continued, the federal decree was not based on Articles 25, 26, and 28 of the *Schlussakt*, for the Kurhessian government had not requested federal assistance, nor had it exhausted all constitutional means available to it, nor was it prevented by rebellion from requesting federal assistance. Article 28 could be put into force only after discussion and "previous consultation" with the threatened government. Although Kurhesse had been requested to report on the disturbances, the Bavarian government had not been informed of the outcome of that request, nor did it know whether there had indeed been a call for aid. Bavaria, it noted, was ready to fulfill the obligations required by the Confederation's decrees only after all circumstances had been considered. There was, it concluded, no need to request "extraordinary assistance" for the defense of Bavaria's borders since "our military power" could be dispatched "without delay" to each threatened area.

> Since we do not mean to interfere in the internal affairs of a neighboring state of our own accord, we cannot, under present circumstances, accept the federal decree which you reported; rather we must hold it in abeyance. [23]

The following day the Bavarian Ministerial Council met in emergency session to discuss steps to be taken regarding the federal decree of October 1, for it was only now that Lerchenfeld's September 24 and October 1 reports arrived in Munich. Foreign Minister Rechberg offered for the consideration of the king and ministers a proposal that demonstrated that the decree was impractical at best. If, he argued, Bavaria acceded to the request for an "unlimited grant" of aid to each state that requested it, the result would be the "complete debilitation" of Bavaria or other middle-sized states that had common frontiers with several German states. It was conceivable that in times of unrest there could be numerous simultaneous requests, which would exhaust Bavaria's military forces and deprive her of the means for maintaining her own domestic tranquility. Acceptance of the decree's remaining points, Rechberg continued, would serve only to weaken individual states while expanding the competence of the Diet to intervene in the states' internal affairs and administration. In particular, to grant such a "plenary instruction" to the ambassadors would be the same "as if the powers of the German Confederation were transferred" to the ambassadors in Frankfurt, thereby "placing all German sovereigns under tutelage." [24]

Zentner seconded this analysis, noting that the *Schlussakt* had clearly stated the limits to which the federal Assembly was permitted to go and adding that this federal decree gave that body too much freedom. This would weaken the sovereignty of the German princes, "which was ... the basis of the *Schlussakt*," bringing them under the "tutelage of the Confederation." He also noted a gradual tendency to undermine the position of the German sovereigns through "inappropriate" decrees, such as those of Karlsbad, in order to subordinate the princes to the Confederation. Bavarian acceptance of the October 1 decree, he concluded, would constitute submission to the federal Diet. He proposed rather that the Bavarian government bypass the *Bundestag* and discuss with her neighbors arrangements for reciprocal assistance in cases when federal assistance would not come soon enough. [25]

Instructions were accordingly sent to Lerchenfeld informing him that he was to declare to the Diet that Bavaria was prepared to come to terms with each of her neighbors unilaterally on aid in emergency situations when federal assistance would be too late and that Bavaria, on the basis of reciprocal treaties, would give necessary support in a "friendly and neighborly" manner. However, the directive continued, only the government of a federal state could decide the degree to which the federal Assembly was to become involved. This had already been "permanently settled" by the *Schlussakt*. It concluded with the reminder that in the future Lerchenfeld was to request instructions on all important matters. [26]

Had the federal Assembly accepted the Bavarian proposal it would have been excluded from any action in the internal affairs of the German states and would have acknowledged that the Confederation could evolve no further than the position accepted in the federal constitution. The Diet, of course, was not prepared to accept any such limitation, particularly in a time of ferment. Most of the ambassadors concurred with Austria's view that the federal Assembly should preserve its authority to assist actively in suppressing disorders that had the potential to spread to other German states. It was to act immediately rather than wait for the revolution to spill across state boundaries.

On October 7 the Kurhessian ambassador notified the Diet that Kurhessian soldiers were on their way to quell the disturbances in Hanau and gave the Kurfürst's thanks to the federal Assembly for the "assurance of necessary assistance" expressed in the decree of October 1. [27] Lerchenfeld used this declaration to justify his actions to the Bavarian court, explaining that this was not a case of federal interference in Kurhesse's internal affairs, but rather that the Kurfürst's thanks had proven that the federal Assembly's actions had been justified. [28]

His self-defense was premature, however, for the federal Assembly was not yet satisfied that its intervention should cease. The Kurhessian ambassador was requested to give further information before the matter could be considered concluded. In particular, the Diet wanted to know if the authorities had regained effective control, if the concessions obtained through force had been revoked as required by the October 1 decree, if the participants in the uprising had been apprehended, and if Kurhesse could guarantee that there would be no recurrence of rebellion in her lands. [29]

Bavaria too came under scrutiny. Lerchenfeld reported that Münch had begun to apply pressure to ensure Bavarian conformity. He had been informed that unless his government changed its attitude the federal Assembly would reissue the October 1 decree with the addition of the phrase: "all federal governments, with the exception of Bavaria, have agreed to the *Präsidium's* proposal" of reciprocal assistance in the name of the Confederation. Should this in fact occur, Bavaria would then be isolated in "an important and urgent matter," giving all the impression of a division in the Confederation, which, under existing circumstances, ought to be avoided. Lerchenfeld then concluded his report with an observation of his own, noting that the decree ought to be seen as an entity rather than being dissected into individual parts. [30]

On the day this report was written an instruction was sent to Lerchenfeld concerning his report of October 1. He was directed to assure the ambassadors that the king, "according to our well known German-patriotic views," would conform to all that was in accord with "the spirit of the *Bundesakt*" and did not "depart from the basic structure" of the Confederation. Accordingly, since Bavaria was herself not threatened, and since in case of federal intervention to maintain order Bavarian "autonomy in internal matters" must remain undisturbed, Lerchenfeld must reject "firmly and with dignity" all requests that did not specifically follow federal regulations. Therefore he was to insist that it be left to the endangered states to come to an agreement with Bavaria concerning assistance. He was, moreover, to state that it was not useful for the federal Assembly to define specific troop concentrations, but rather that it ought to acknowledge that the state of preparedness of Bavarian soldiers in frontier garrison towns was sufficient to deal with any emergency. Great care was to be taken to prevent the placement of a Bavarian corps under non-Bavarian command should Bavarian troops be needed. Finally, the states requesting military assistance were to bear the full financial burden for such aid. These proposals for reciprocal agreements and the preparations taken on the border of the Untermainkreis were expected to find "favorable recognition everywhere." [31]

Ludwig's annoyance with his ambassador had not yet subsided. He was especially vexed by Lerchenfeld's unwarranted assumption of authority to require Bavarian troops to be sent to the Kurhessian border. As Spiegel reported to Metternich, Lerchenfeld had been reprimanded for acting without authorization: his acceptance of the decree would not be ratified by the Ministerial Council. [32] In particular, as an instruction to Lerchenfeld made clear on October 12, the dispersion of Bavarian soldiers and their placement under non-Bavarian command made an "unfavorable impression" on the king. [33] The royal resolve had not altered, but Lerchenfeld was now informed that Bavaria, taking "local and other circumstances" into consideration, had placed a force stronger than the one requested on her borders to assist other states should aid be requested. [34] Bavaria would do on her own authority what she would not do in response to an order from the federal Assembly.

General von Wolzogen, the Prussian representative to the federal Military Commission, wrote from Frankfurt that in spite of Ludwig's aversion to the federal decree, Bavarian soldiers had indeed been sent to Brückenau and Aschaffenburg and that the king "does in Landau what is to be desired." [35] This was, in fact, a victory for the *Bundesversammlung* because, although Bavaria had not followed the letter of the decree, her actions implied acknowledgment of its spirit: Bavaria had positioned her troops in accord with federal instructions. Whether or not Bavarian soldiers would have crossed the frontier into Kurhesse without that government's direct request cannot be answered with certainty. It does appear, however, that the Bavarian king would have been hard pressed for a legitimate excuse for noncompliance if the federal Assembly had decreed that action. A precedent had been established for expanding the scope of federal competence; in emergency situations it appeared that the Diet could compel a state to surrender a modicum of sovereignty over its own armed forces.

The specific issue that had brought on the conflict between the *Bundesversammlung* and Bavaria, the uprising in Kurhesse, proved to be more easily resolved than the question of Bavarian compliance with the federal decree of October 1.

Federal troops had not been needed because Kurhesse was well able to quell the disturbances using only her own resources. In acknowledgement of that fact the federal Assembly decided that the situation was under control, permitted Bavaria to remove her troops from the frontiers, and concluded that only 5,300 soldiers of the other states need remain on alert. [36] One week later these were also withdrawn.

The question of how far the Diet could go to preserve order in Germany was not yet fully resolved, however. On October 21 the federal Assembly adopted a proposal to strengthen Article 26 of the *Schlussakt*. It provided for direct and immediate military intervention by neighboring states whenever a member government requested such assistance. Federal contingents were accordingly to be kept prepared for action, the federal Assembly was to be kept informed of all disturbances, federal ambassadors were to be given blanket instructions "concerning security and order in Germany," and the provisions of the Karlsbad decrees, as renewed in 1824, were to be strictly enforced. [37]

In voting for this proposal, Lerchenfeld stated that Bavaria was ready to assist a neighboring state if the action were conducted in the Confederation's name. Thus a government that requested Bavaria's aid would be required to report on this assistance to the Diet in accordance with the *Schlussakt*. That meant that any assistance rendered by Bavaria would henceforth be understood as taking place within the provisions of the *Schlussakt* rather than under the principle of one sovereign state aiding another. In other words, Bavaria had dropped her insistence that she would act only on the basis of unilateral agreements that excluded the Confederation in the suppression of rebellion. This attitude was consistent with the harsher policy toward the liberal movement now manifested by the Bavarian government because of the disturbances of the preceding months. However, since Bavaria had not entirely abandoned the concept of state sovereignty, Lerchenfeld also argued in the Diet that the judgment of whether the Confederation ought to intervene in case of a request could only be determined on the basis of the provisions of Article 25 of the *Schlussakt*. The federal Assembly would thus have to decide whether the petitioning state had exhausted all means available to it beforehand. In particular, he continued, in states where there was a constitution, procedures also existed through which grievances could be remedied without the need for federal intervention; all the more reason for the Diet to see that Article 13 of the *Bundesakt*, as expanded by Article 54 of the *Schlussakt*, "does not remain unfulfilled" and that each state promulgate a constitution. In fact, this would all but exclude federal intervention.

On the proposal first offered on October 1 and now renewed, that all concessions granted by a government under duress be considered null and void, Lerchenfeld restated the Bavarian position that it was not advisable for the federal Diet to adopt such a principle "in full generality," since it would be dangerous for a prince to give his word only to take it back later. Finally, in accordance with his previous instructions, the Bavarian ambassador argued that Article 8 of the *Schlussakt* specifically enjoined blanket instructions on matters of such importance, an objection that Münch promised to accept. [38]

The Bavarian position reflected in Lerchenfeld's remarks was essentially that which had been followed since the creation of the German Confederation. Sovereignty lay with the states and could be limited only at the request of a state. Thus the distinction that Bavaria drew between the Confederation as such and the *Bundesversammlung* was an important one. The federal Assembly was only the organ of a federation of sovereign states and could be afforded no recognition that might imply that it had authority independent of those states. Federal action might be taken by the member states in the name of the Confederation, that is, in the name of the sovereign states themselves, not in the name of a body composed of the ambassadors of those states. Thus Bavaria's position had not, in fact, been altered in Lerchenfeld's argument. He had stressed once again the sovereignty of Bavaria and each member state. Power resided with the Confederation and thus with the sovereign princes alone. The federal Assembly was not to be allowed to acquire an independent identity or powers not granted to it in 1815.

In general, however, Lerchenfeld's statement struck a favorable chord among the other ambassadors, producing "cordial trust" in place of the "former coolness and tension" toward Bavaria. [39] His declaration also received the approval of his king, and he was empowered to handle all "provisional preliminary arrangements" should a case for immediate federal assistance arise. Bavaria was now ready to put quickly into effect the measures necessary to assist in the maintenance of "quiet and security" in neighboring states. [40]

Events later proved that the federal decree of October 21 was superfluous. Federal action was needed in no purely German state in response to the July Revolution. The people of Austria and Prussia remained quiet, and those uprisings directly related to the revolution in France were generally small and manageable by the individual governments without external aid. Thus the immediate effect of the July Revolution in Germany as a whole had been to raise once again the question of the relationship between the Confederation and the individual states. But once again the question remained unresolved.

iii

The July Revolution did, however, produce an immediate effect on one member of the Confederation, the Grand Duchy of Luxemburg, and this drew the Confederation into a possible confrontation with other European powers. The Netherlands had been given Luxemburg by the Second Peace of Paris in 1815. Although legally joined to the Dutch kingdom only by personal union, Luxemburg became, in fact, a province of the Netherlands, having neither a separate administration nor a separate constitution. The Grand Duchy, which shared common borders with France and what would become Belgium and was populated both by people who considered themselves German and by French speaking Walloons, was a member of the German Confederation, and the Dutch King thus had an ambassador in the federal Assembly. When revolt broke out in August 1830 in Luxemburg, he requested assistance [41] from the federal Assembly, which, on the basis of Articles 25 and 26 of the *Schlussakt*, it was bound to honor.

Federal military intervention, however, was deemed undesirable by most German governments because, in the accepted view, to intervene in Luxemburg would draw French intervention in response and result in a general European war. Consequently, the federal Assembly temporized: rather than sending troops it requested reports. Meanwhile, the new Belgian state supported the rebels, established a Luxemburg volunteer army and a national guard, and introduced conscription. Finally, on November 18, the federal Assembly acted. It decreed that Austria and Prussia should represent the Confederation at the London Conference called to deal with Luxemburg, an action that made all other federal actions superfluous. [42]

Representatives of Great Britain, France, Russia, Prussia, and Austria gathered in London on November 4 to deal with the Belgian revolt against the Netherlands. The artificial union of the two peoples by the Congress of Vienna had led to immediate friction between the Belgian Catholics and the dominant Dutch Protestants. The July Revolution provided the spark for a revolt by the Belgians who, by early November, had cleared most of Belgium of Dutch control. The London Conference accordingly recognized Belgium's independence and then turned to the question of Luxemburg. The representatives accepted the principle that the Grand Duchy was a part of the German Confederation and decided that it was to remain independent of Belgian control. [43]

However, the only area of the Grand Duchy that had remained undisturbed by the insurrection was the federal fortress and city of Luxemburg, which remained under the firm control of the Prussian garrison. Now that France had demonstrated in London that she would not intervene in this German matter, the Diet decreed that a force from the minor states of Waldeck, Lippe, and Schaumburg-Lippe should reinforce the Prussians at Luxemburg. [44] This action, however, proved to be a farce. Two weeks after their arrival many of these troops mutinied out of sympathy with the rebels, forcing the recall of the federal contingent. The Grand Duchy again requested aid [45] but received no more federal soldiers.

The members of the London Conference had also been signatories of the Treaty of Vienna, which had given Luxemburg to the Netherlands. Moreover, embodied in their guarantee of Belgium's independence was a provision forbidding the new state from interfering in Luxemburg. Thus the members of the London Conference had the legal authority to assist the Dutch if aid against Belgian aggression were requested, and in addition they had a moral obligation to uphold their own decisions. Although the king of the Netherlands asked for no such aid, the members of the London Conference might have taken action to deprive Belgium of the Luxemburg territories she now held illegally. Rather than intervening, they proposed a partition of Luxemburg and thereby accepted the Belgian seizure as a fait accompli. [46] When the Dutch king finally accepted the Confederation's proposals, the federal Assembly again empowered Austria and Prussia to represent the Confederation and to look after "its rights and interests" in London. [47] Finally, on October 15, 1831, an act of separation was approved by the five powers. It awarded the Walloon west to Belgium and the German-speaking east, with the city and fortress of Luxemburg, to the Dutch. The Confederation lost neither territory nor population because the Belgian province of Limburg was given to the Netherlands to become part of the German Confederation as a replacement for the lands lost in Luxemburg. The Belgians, however, continued their occupation of the whole Grand Duchy, except for the fortress and city of Luxemburg, which remained under federal control. Luxemburg would repeatedly bring the Confederation into conflict with other European powers until the Dutch king finally accepted the act of separation in 1839. [48]

No one had acted effectively throughout the entire affair. The Netherlands and the Confederation had lost the western portion of Luxemburg to Belgium because they procrastinated when quick action might have put down the rebellion. The other great powers, which could have intervened, were satisfied with legalizing the status quo after each change: all parties allowed the revolutionary Belgians to dictate the terms of settlement. In particular, the federal Assembly demonstrated by its inaction that the Confederation could not be considered an independent European power. Although in the end the Confederation gained equivalent territory and population in the eighteenth-century sense of "compensation," the exchange had been forced on the Confederation by Belgium's revolutionary aggression. Rather than taking the vigorous action demanded by the *Bundesakt* in such a case, the *Bundesversammlung* temporized, postponing a decision until it was too late. This was not the action of a power demonstrating diplomatic patience in the face of Belgian insolence; this was an indication of the structural weakness of the Confederation in the face of an outside attack on a member state. That the federal Assembly requested Austria and Prussia to represent it in London rather than sending an ambassador of its own is further evidence of the Confederation's doubt of its international standing independent of the two German great powers. Indeed, for all practical purposes, federal foreign policy was determined by Austria in consultation with Prussia. Only once in its entire history, in 1864, was the Confederation represented by its own ambassador. [49]

Clearly it was now questionable whether the Confederation would or could carry out its charge to preserve the territorial integrity and independence of Germany. The Diet had acted decisively and effectively to quell the disturbances generated by the July Revolution *within* Germany. When faced with an attack on federal territory *from outside* the Confederation, the Diet procrastinated. A direct attack on the periphery of the Confederation, as in the case of the Belgian aggression in Luxemburg in 1831, elicited only a verbal response. It was as though the Confederation had expended its energies on internal German matters and had no strength remaining to deal with dangers originating outside the Confederation.

5

1832: Reaction to Revolution

The most visible effect of the July Revolution in Germany was the increasingly strident tone assumed by the liberal press in the German states. Even though the Luxemburg fiasco raised serious questions over the ability of the Confederation to put down rebellion on its periphery, the fact that the federal Assembly had moved rapidly to force the suppression of the Kurhessian disturbances seemed to preclude successful direct action by the German Left. Apparently the only course remaining open to would-be revolutionaries was to arouse the German people and to discredit the federal and state governments by the "spoken and written word." Inflammatory newspaper articles and popular festivals (*Volksfeste*) proliferated throughout the Confederation, especially in the South and Rheinland where French influence had been traditionally the strongest.

Against this background the Confederation served as the dike of reaction against the seemingly all-pervasive liberal tide. In particular, the *Bundesversammlung* was to be used to maintain the monarchical principle against liberal and democratic movements. In a letter to the Austrian ambassador to France,

Metternich complained that Germany was "in dreadful disorder." There were German princes who had "given the appearance" of sharing their powers and sovereignty with democrats, and who had followed "the councils of liberalism," thereby reducing their authority "to zero." "Happily," he noted, "the Confederation exists and we will put it in motion."[1]

Yet there were still some who believed that the Diet would ultimately become a central governing body for a united Germany and, although forbidden to do so by the decrees of 1823 and 1824, continued to send "joint introductions or addresses" concerning "public matters of the German Confederation" to the *Bundesversammlung*. Münch predictably saw such petitions as "dangerous attempts" to destroy the authority of the German governments and "public peace and order." On October 27, 1831, the federal Assembly decreed that all such addresses were to be returned to the sender as inadmissible.[2]

Bavaria, however, refused to implement the decree, for August Freiherr von Gise, former Bavarian ambassador to the Netherlands and to Russia and now foreign minister, believed that it conflicted with the Bavarian constitution. In December Spiegel reported that his attempts to influence the Bavarian government had been fruitless, and the prohibition remained unpublished in that state.[3] The Bavarian Ministry of the Interior examined the matter later in the month and decided that although it was indeed within the competence of the federal Assembly to issue such a prohibition, and that although it did not prejudice any of the king's rights, it would be "purposeless and inadvisable" to publish the decree because under certain circumstances misunderstandings could be raised concerning the "allowability" of such complaints by Bavarian subjects to "foreign powers."[4] Clearly, Bavaria had to have the last word over her own subjects.

Once again, however, Bavaria was forced to retreat. Since most of the other governments published the decree, the Ministerial Council recommended that Bavaria follow suit since continued refusal would "awaken a false opinion" against Bavaria. It recommended, however, that the decree be published with the addition of the clause that had been used in conjunction with the Karlsbad decrees, that is, that Bavaria's constitution and laws not be contravened. This would preserve the Bavarian constitution and the "rights of publication" of the Bavarian subjects within the limits of that constitution. [5] King Ludwig I accepted the advice of his ministers, and the amended decree concerning addresses to the federal Assembly was published in Bavaria on February 17, 1832.

When Lerchenfeld announced this action in Frankfurt, "great excitement" arose among the ambassadors. The addition to the decree was considered by them as a protest against the validity of the federal decree and as "subordination of federal legislation" to the legislation of the states, although Lerchenfeld had argued that the addition was to be understood only as a "corroboration" of the decree. Despite general disagreement with Bavaria's actions, the *Bundesversammlung* proposed no official action, [6] for, by this time, new disturbances caused by the German press had begun to divert its attention.

The occasion for a new attack of the press was provided by the Strassburg newspaper, *Konstitutionelles Deutschland*, which had published articles insulting the Confederation and the member governments. The moribund press commission that had been established in 1819 was revitalized in order to "exercise a sort of general inspection over all journals and publications" in Germany and to report periodically to the Diet with recommendations for action. [7] This commission, after determining the "licentiousness" of *Konstitutionelles Deutschland*, recommended suppression of that newspaper. Münch accordingly offered a proposal to that effect, which, after short debate, was unanimously accepted. In casting his vote, Lerchenfeld stated that Bavaria was willing to join with other member governments to maintain "quiet and the lawful order" in Germany and to suppress "evil enterprises." Because the newspapers had dangerously attacked the individual governments and continued to "prepare the ground for inciting their subjects," Bavaria would vote for its suppression with the provision that "the form" and "the execution" of the measure would "be regulated" in Bavaria "according to its constitutional laws." [8]

On December 7 Baden called the federal Assembly's attention to the fact that the newspaper had resumed publication six days previously under the name *Deutschland*, and that in its new guise it had not been suppressed by Bavaria. Münch proposed that the newspaper be banned "under whatever title it shall appear," and this new decree was accepted by all ambassadors except those of Württemburg, Kurhesse, and Bavaria. [9]

The Bavarian government continued its examination of the matter and prepared its response to the federal Assembly. In a memorandum to the king, Gise observed that both he and the minister of the interior were still studying the implications of the affair and recommended that Lerchenfeld be instructed to delay any federal action that would prejudice Bavarian interests until the government could determine what should be done. [10]

Two days later the foreign minister presented his king with another memorandum that outlined the history of Bavarian press legislation. Bavarian press laws had always been promulgated independently of "external influences." The law of 1803 had been enacted independently of the *Reich*, and the constitutional edict of 1818 had been issued independently of the Confederation. Moreover, the Bavarian government had accepted the Karlsbad decrees only with the proviso that the

Crown's sovereignty would not be impaired, and the renewal of those decrees in 1824 continued that reservation. The *Schlussakt*, Gise observed, had altered nothing: Article 53 guaranteed that the internal affairs of the individual states would be free of federal interference. Consequently, it was not necessary for Bavaria to yield to the Diet's demands; rather, she ought only to maintain and enforce the laws of the kingdom. [11]

Gise had written this "Short Presentation" as a rebuttal to the federal argument in the action that suppressed *Deutschland*, but in the process he had advanced a basic principle: the superiority of Bavarian over federal legislation. The question was whether the federal Assembly, and Austria in particular, would allow this to stand unchallenged. The answer, of course, was that neither could do so, and, after a successful attack on two Württemberg newspapers, the press commission initiated an examination of the *Tribüne des Westbothen* and the *Speyere Zeitung*, both published in Bavaria's Rhine province.

Although Gise was a strong particularist who fought for Bavarian autonomy in the Confederation, he was no friend of an unbridled press. He wanted to check what he considered an evil, but the problem was how to "prepare the remedy" and administer it without injuring the constitution. He joined the Ministry of the Interior in advising a partial change in the administrative personnel of the Rheinkreis, that those newspapers deemed dangerous be prohibited from using the mails for distribution, and that each seditious association be vigorously prosecuted. To make these measures appear satisfactory to the federal press commission, each violation was to be dealt with rapidly by employing the most severe measures available, and precautionary measures had to be carefully thought out. A difficult choice, he concluded, had to be made:

> whether it is advisable to enter the lists with our own means, and in this way at least to secure our sovereignty, or whether

we should dare allow ourselves to be compelled by the federal Diet to take the intended strong measures and to obey foreign interference which, perhaps, can not be completely complied with. [12]

On the following day Gise offered Ludwig a more thorough review of the problem. If the king were to balk at carrying out a federally ordered suppression of Bavarian newspapers, the Confederation would be forced either to initiate *Exekution* proceedings against Bavaria or to accept the fact that its decrees had no effect. The federal Assembly would find the first alternative "distasteful," but would abhor the second, for this would attest to the lack of strength of and cooperation within that body. Therefore, he argued, a way had to be found to bring about a suppression of newspapers in Bavaria by the federal Assembly in a manner compatible with the Bavarian constitution. If this could not be done Bavaria then had to decide whether to remonstrate against such a federal decree or to ignore it. [13] Gise then requested and received permission to instruct Lerchenfeld to inform the Diet that the measures recommended to the king on February 9 had been put into effect.

The legal powers available to the Bavarian government, however, were insufficient to suppress the offending newspapers. Thus the king himself wrote in Lerchenfeld's instructions that he wanted those newspapers that were "maliciously written" and appearing in Bavaria "to be forbidden" by the *Bundestag*. Lerchenfeld was then directed to decide what steps would be necessary to assuage the press commission and, further, to report anything that was said in Frankfurt concerning the steps taken by Bavaria. [14]

Two days later Gise again offered his king an analysis of the situation. He noted that Bavaria was the only German state that asserted the principle that its legislation was superior to that of the Confederation. Basing her argument on her constitution, Bavaria claimed that her sovereignty would be compromised permanently if "surrendered" even for "a very short time" or for "only an individual case." The best way to avoid limitation of Bavarian sovereignty, Gise believed, was to prevent the issue of the relationship between federal and state legislation even from being discussed in Frankfurt. To this end it was essential to avoid anything that might create an opening through which the Confederation would intervene in Bavarian affairs. Bavaria could "in no way concede" that federal legislation or assistance was needed against "misconduct of the press" in Bavaria. Moreover, he concluded, Bavaria had, on her own authority, to create a force that would place legal limits on the "increased abuses." If precautions were not taken she would have to accept federal interference, opening the way to those who wished to place "narrow limits" on the "authority of the princes of the Confederation." [15]

Following instructions, Lerchenfeld informed his colleagues that Bavaria, recognizing the "pernicious effects" on the "Confederation of the sovereign German states" resulting from the heightened misconduct of the press, had directed that all means allowed by her constitution and laws be employed to "limit the licentiousness" of the press. Consequently, he continued, steps were being taken to force those newspapers appearing in the Bavarian Rhineland, with its separate legal code, to observe all regulations defined by the third constitutional edict and to place all newspapers under "legal censorship" as defined by that edict. [16]

Münch was not satisfied by Lerchenfeld's declaration and asserted that the measures taken by Bavaria appeared to be insufficient. On his recommendation that federal action was necessary, the *Bundesversammlung* directed the press commission to examine the Bavarian statement for completeness and to recommend measures to be taken by the Confederation. The commission was also to determine what other newspapers ought to be suppressed. [17]

The press commission was now becoming increasingly concerned with Phillip Jakob Siebenpfeiffer's *Tribüne des Westbothen* and the *Deutsche Tribüne*. The latter paper had been founded by Johann Wirth on July 1, 1831, and it repeatedly attacked the Confederation and the member governments. On February 3 Wirth published a statement that the federal Assembly was the "essence of hostility to the German Fatherland,"[18] and on the 15th he ran an article in which the "glove was thrown down to the collective ruling houses of Germany," threatening them with rebellion.[19] This article insured federal interference in Bavarian affairs. Even Lerchenfeld now asked his king to accept suppression of the two newspapers.[20]

On March 1 a new directive went to Lerchenfeld in which it was assumed that the *Bundesversammlung* would concede that Bavaria had met all possible demands for regulating the press and which reiterated the Bavarian position.[21] Even before this could reach Frankfurt the Diet demonstrated that it was indeed not satisfied with the measures taken in Bavaria. The press commission declared that Bavaria had not acted vigorously enough and that therefore federal action was needed. The Diet accordingly adopted a decree on March 2 to "suppress and generally forbid" the two newspapers on the basis of the 1819 press decree. The editors, moreover, were forbidden to edit any newspaper in Germany for five years.[22]

The purpose of this decree was to prohibit distribution of the two newspapers in all German states simultaneously. It was also intended to serve as a warning to the liberal and radical press, as well as to individual governments, as to what would happen if they failed to heed federal decrees. Since Bavaria once again refused to acknowledge the validity of any decree that interfered with her sovereignty, she disregarded the warning.

On March 8 Lerchenfeld announced to the Diet that both newspapers had been forbidden to appear in Bavaria. The excuse for their suppression was not the federal decree, but rather that the editors, by their refusal to allow prepublication censorship as prescribed by the Bavarian constitution, had violated Bavarian law. Moreover, since the suppression had taken effect one day before the federal decree was issued, he argued that the Diet ought now to acknowledge that Bavaria could manage her own affairs and that the decree was superfluous as far as that state was concerned. In response, acting *Präsidium* Nagler noted only that both newspapers were to be suppressed on the basis of the March 2 decree. [23] In fact, Bavaria's tactics had once again been successful.

In an earlier discussion with Spiegel, Wrede had advanced a second argument against federal interference in Bavaria: namely, that there was no precedent for federal intervention in press matters in that state. The 1824 press decree had never been published in Bavaria and therefore could never have been law in that state. Reporting on this conversation to Metternich, Spiegel characterized this proposition as "completely without content," since the "neglect of publication" was an "offense," at the very least an "omission to be made good." [24]

Two days later, on March 8, the same day on which Lerchenfeld announced suppression of the two newspapers, the Austrian ambassador to Württemberg, Alfred Friedrich Fürst Schönberg-Hartenstein, visited Spiegel and Wrede in Munich. He too found that the Bavarian government drew a firm distinction between the *Bundesakt* and those federal decrees passed after the promulgation of the Bavarian constitution, as well as between the obligation to fulfill those decrees and obligations created by the constitution. Since the Bavarian press edict did not give the government power to suppress newspapers, it was argued, no federal decree could grant that authority to the government. The question, Schönberg noted, of just how far federal decrees superseded Bavarian legislation was still pending in Munich, but the Bavarian government remained resolute in its intent to remain independent of "limiting federal regulations."[25]

This was the heart of Bavaria's opposition to the federal decree. This fundamental philosophy underlay a memorandum to Ludwig from Gise, who outlined the position he believed Bavaria ought to take vis-à-vis the decree of March 2. If the government of the Rheinkreis had carried out the instructions of March 1, then freedom of the press in that district would have been properly limited. That action would have fulfilled Bavaria's obligation to the Confederation of maintaining her own security and that of the Confederation as required by the federal constitution. Simultaneously, he noted, Bavaria would be preserving the "dignity of the Confederation" and the security of the individual states as demanded by the "provisional decree" of 1819. In this regard, if the question of "competence" were neglected, the Confederation's intervention "would then be superfluous," since Bavaria would already have demonstrated that she could act effectively within the bounds of her constitution. However, it would be "morally impossible" for the Bavarian "state government" to carry out a federal decree in "any other than a constitutional way." Therefore, he argued, it was understandable that in 1819 and 1824 Bavaria had had the "moral necessity" to preserve the principles of the constitution regarding the press. Had the decree of 1819 been made fully effective in Bavaria, then the federal Assembly would have taken some action in matters of the press "significantly altering" the Bavarian constitution. Finally, by forcing Bavarian officials to contradict their constitutional oaths, the *Bundesversammlung* would have been proceeding against peace and order in Germany, and thus would itself "invalidate the purpose of the German Confederation."[26]

A few days later Schönberg reported that the Bavarian government felt itself caught in a dilemma: it was required either to act against its own constitution and political system or to renounce its duties to the Confederation. At present, he wrote, a middle course was being sought, for the "decisive will" was lacking to renounce the "old prejudices," yet Bavaria lacked the "strength and power" to withdraw from the Confederation. [27]

The course that Bavaria chose was to open direct negotiations with Austria and Prussia because, as Bavaria argued, the federal Assembly could not appropriately treat "in a moment of general excitement" a question of "such importance upon which the position of the sovereign princes depends." [28] Although the Bavarian ambassadors in Vienna and Berlin were expected to convince Austria and Prussia of the justice and correctness of the Bavarian position, they failed. Metternich refused to accept the argument, responding that Bavaria should speedily publish the March 2 decree without alteration. [29]

All participants realized that at issue in the debate was much more than who had the right to suppress the two newspapers and how it should be done. This struggle against the liberal and radical press had to put to the test the "efficacy" of "federal institutions" and "solve the real question" of whether or not the constitutional governments would "submit on all points to the supremacy" of the federal Diet. [30] There was, as Cartwright accurately saw, a close resemblance between the Germany of 1832 and that of 1819. There was the "same agitation from nearly the same causes," there was the

same thirst after popular institutions, the same hostility to the actual federal system, and the same violences and, in many cases, extravagances on the part of the Journals with a view to excite the population against the legitimate governments.

The Karlsbad and Vienna Conferences had checked this movement in 1819, but it was evident that it had not been suppressed, for the "fermentation of the present day" proved that it had "only slumbered in the interim." The basic difference between 1819 and 1832 was that now France had a government to which the German liberals believed they could turn for aid. Only if the German governments could act in concert, he continued, could the liberals be restrained.

Cartwright also believed that it was questionable whether all the German governments would cooperate, for "great doubts" were entertained as to Bavaria's willingness to work with the Confederation in repressing the liberals. Bavaria had, of course, made no declaration to that effect, but it was "inferred" from her general feelings concerning federal matters, especially "the jealousy she has so often displayed" over the right of the federal Assembly to compel a government to accept decrees that, although "they accord with the most absolute laws" of the Confederation, were not "strictly in unison" with Bavaria's legislation. He further noted that Bavaria had never accepted the supremacy of the Diet and had never carried out a federal decree "without hesitation and seldom in the exact terms and extent" required by that body. Bavaria "usually contrived" to carry out every "obligation which might imply her acknowledgement" of the federal Assembly's competence "in a way to avoid that interpretation."

This issue, he continued, had now come to a head over the suppression of the *Deutsche Tribüne* and the *Westbothe*. Bavaria claimed to have accepted the Karlsbad decrees and the *Schlussakt* only with reservations, an interpretation that the federal Assembly rejected. Since the two newspapers had been suppressed by the Diet on the basis of the 1819 decree, Bavaria had now either to fulfill that decree and thus "set to rest the suspicion" that she fostered "anti-federal notions," or to explain her reasons for "declining to do so." However, if

Bavaria were to accept the superiority of the Confederation, she would thus recognize the "superior power" of Austria and Prussia as long as those powers gave the "sole impulse to the march" of the Confederation, and it was Bavaria's objection to playing a "subordinate part under the direction" of the German great powers that formed "the key of her federal policy."[31]

Bavaria did, in fact, declare that the March 2 decree would be put in force, albeit in modified form.[32] When Lerchenfeld announced this to the Diet, he created a "great sensation" because the action hardly constituted fulfillment of the decree. No mention had been made in the royal edict of suppressing the two newspapers; it simply stated that they would be allowed to appear only if they placed themselves under the required Bavarian censorship. The "conviction" was thus held that the Bavarian edict "in no way" attained the goal of the federal decree, Lerchenfeld wrote, since the *Tribüne* was still appearing secretly and would continue to be circulated "in all possible ways."[33]

The press was indeed the topic that now monopolized the attention of the Diet since it appeared to be the primary cause of the revolutionary excitement in Germany. The actions of the Bavarian government had "given great umbrage" to the federal Assembly and inflicted "a blow in the authority" of that body which would only "with difficulty be repaired." Bavaria had again refused to recognize the authority of the Diet, opening the way for other governments to follow her example.[34]

At the same time, however, in response to a request from the Bavarian foreign minister, the minister of the interior, Ludwig Kraft Ernst Fürst zu Oettingen-Wallerstein, could write that neither Siebenpfeiffer nor Wirth published newspapers in Bavaria. Neither the *Tribüne* nor *Konstitutionelles Deutschland* could appear in Bavaria since the Rheinkreis government had met the newspapers' illegal actions with "the full strength of the law." Moreover, Siebenpfeiffer, the editor of *Konstitutionelles Deutschland,* resided in Mannheim, that is, outside Bavarian jurisdiction. The government, he continued, had taken care to prevent either Siebenpfeiffer or Wirth from undertaking any journalistic enterprise that, as had happened in the past, would compromise the position of Bavaria with the other German states and "especially the two great powers."[35]

Bavaria, Gise wrote to Lerchenfeld, had first to deal with her internal problems before confronting those created by the *Bundesversammlung.* The government had to regain the strength and "popular trust" lost through the actions of the last *Landtag,* which had forced Schenk's dismissal. The government had to "manage the constitution" on the basis of the "monarchical principle" against attempts of a "democratic party wanting foreign institutions." This could be done by preventing the misuse of the press by strong but constitutional measures. "Oppositional papers of mixed content" dealing with both foreign and domestic matters had been placed under censorship with a "beneficial effect." Those "weak state commissioners" who had not enforced the March 1 censorship edict had been removed from their positions and replaced by more active men. Moreover, the strong measures that set in motion the "unremitting activity" of the police against circulation of revolutionary pamphlets had also proved effective in that "demagogic activities" that might have brought Bavaria into "collision" with the "Confederation of federal governments" or with other European governments no longer existed.[36]

It did indeed appear as if the Bavarian government had been successful in dealing with the misuse of the press without the intervention of the federal Assembly, since that body did not insist further that the March 2 decree be put into full effect in that state. The Diet, partially in acknowledgment of Bavaria's successes, turned its attention to other matters, and Bavaria, for her part, did her best to direct the Diet's attention away from matters involving Bavarian rights.

As it was, the federal Assembly found that Baden also had a press law that did not conform to federal standards. But Baden, unlike Bavaria, proved unsuccessful in defending her press law. The death of Grand Duke Ludwig in May 1831 brought to the throne the more liberal Leopold. Moreover, the newly elected *Landtag* was controlled by a liberal majority that requested a change in Baden's restrictive press law. Although bound by the Karlsbad decrees, Baden's new government acceded to this request after the *Landtag* threatened to use its fiscal rights to block the royal budget. A new law that all but abolished censorship was published on January 12, 1832 and immediately produced an uproar in Frankfurt.

Baden's new press law was referred to the standing federal Committee on Press Matters in early February,[37] where it was found to be incompatible with existing federal decrees. Even Bavaria found the law too liberal and was prepared to support a proposal for its temporary suspension.[38] In casting Bavaria's vote, Lerchenfeld declared that Baden was "obligated" to amend her press law in such a way as to make it compatible with the federal decrees of 1819 and 1824.[39] Once again Bavaria had failed to support another German state that was following her example. Bavaria's acknowledgment of the superiority of federal over state legislation in this case ought to have established a precedent that could later undercut Bavaria's arguments against federal interference. That it did not can only be explained by noting that, in this instance, Baden had accepted the Karlsbad decrees unconditionally, whereas Bavaria had accepted them only with reservations intended to preserve her sovereignty.

Finally, on July 5, the federal Assembly decreed that Baden's press law was incompatible with federal law and "ought not to stand." Although it did not itself order suspension of the law, the *Bundesversammlung* stated that it held "the most hopeful expectation" that Baden would suspend the offending law immediately. Her government was given fourteen days in which to comply. [40]

This decision presented Baden's government with a dilemma. It either had to suspend a law "of its own propounding" on the basis of the "incompatibility of its provisions" with the "federal obligations to which Baden is bound," or it had to expose the Grand Duchy to the "immediate chance and consequences" of a military occupation by a federal force carrying out a decree of *Exekution*. [41] Grand Duke Leopold chose to submit to the Diet's decision, albeit with minor modifications. On July 28, without consulting his *Landtag*, an edict rescinding the press law was published in the official newspaper. This procedure in effect acknowledged the superiority of federal over state legislation, for it admitted at least by implication that a state law was automatically void if it were held incompatible with a federal decree. Otherwise the *Landtag* would have had to approve the abrogation of the law. [42] Since the Grand Duke had not followed constitutional procedure and since the federal Assembly had demanded the annulment of the press law, a precedent had been established that might be applied to the other federal states. Once again, however, this would not be applied to Bavaria.

When the Diet's attention shifted again to the Wittelsbach state, it was not the press controversy that bore responsibility. As early as April 12 Lerchenfeld had been instructed to keep the Rheinkreis government informed of rumors that were then circulating in Frankfurt that "many German courts" seemed to believe that a "revolt must break out" in Bavaria's Rhine province. The General Commissioner of the district was to furnish Lerchenfeld with accurate details so that he might correct "each unfounded report" in the *Bundestag*. [43]

The news of the *Volksfest* at Hambach castle near Neustadt

in the Bavarian Rheinpfalz was not so easily explained away. The festival was the most recent in a series of attempts by Wirth and Siebenpfeiffer to gain popular support for a unified, democratic Germany. Both men had tried to agitate through their newspapers, only to have this avenue cut off by the Diet or by individual governments. In January 1832 the two men had founded the *Deutsche Press- und Vaterlandsverein* (Press and Fatherland Society) in Zweibrücken to organize support for a free press. In their view a free press was the single most effective vehicle for the creation of a democractic, unified German state. [44] As with their newspapers, however, the *Verein* too was banned on March 1 by the Bavarian government as a political association dangerous to the state. [45] Thus it appeared to the two radicals that mass meetings would now furnish the only available method for reaching the German people.

The *Hambacherfest*, held on the fourteenth anniversary of the promulgation of the Bavarian constitution (May 27, 1818), had originally been prohibited by the local government. However, the arguments raised by the town and rural councils against the legality of the prohibition and the assurances given that the festival would remain peaceful convinced the district president to reverse his decision. [46] The government still prepared for trouble, but the festival generally involved little more than harmless drinking with a great deal of radical rhetoric. The 15,000–20,000 participants, representing most of the German states and including students and a number of Polish radicals who had fled their country in 1830, succeeded only in presenting the Confederation with another opportunity to suppress political expression and to intervene in Bavarian affairs. [47]

Metternich condemned the festival as the "*Hambacher-Skandal.*" At the same time, he believed that it could provide an excuse for crushing the democratic movement "if properly used." [48] Lerchenfeld reported that news of the festival created the "greatest sensation" in Frankfurt and that the ambassadors "strongly deplored" the revolutionary talks held under the "tricolor flags of the demagogues" without opposition by the police or the local authorities. What the ambassadors could not understand was why the government had lifted the prohibition originally imposed on the gathering. Lerchenfeld, therefore, recommended to Munich that legal proceedings against the leaders, especially Wirth, be brought to a speedy and successful conclusion, for the federal governments had lost their faith in the Bavarian judicial procedure. Some ambassadors, he continued, felt either that Bavarian laws were inadequate to deal with those "disturbing the public security" of Bavaria and her neighbors or that Bavarian courts interpreted the laws too leniently, leaving the "public security" without protection. Because of the lack of "energetic and strong" enforcement of the law in Bavaria, he concluded, it was felt that the "demagogues" had become terribly bold and that through Bavaria's failure to fulfill federal decrees the Confederation's ability to act "was being crippled." [49]

In response, Lerchenfeld received a report about the festival [50] and was directed to give the federal Assembly the "quieting assurance" that Bavaria was using existing laws "with all vigor" to restore order. He was also to announce that Bavaria was reciprocally willing to cooperate with the "united federal governments" to prevent the recurrence of political *Volksfeste*. [51]

Metternich, however, chose to write directly to Gise in order to provoke Bavaria into repressing revolutionary movements. That revolutionary activities were given a "legal playground" in Bavaria could result only in an "incalculable" disadvantage to the forces of order. There were, he felt, two possible courses that Bavaria might take: "the mild and legal, or the strong, namely suppression of all revolutionary uprisings" with military force. If no quick and energetic intervention were forthcoming, "what is yet to come . . . is, sad to say, easy to forecast." [52]

Bavaria needed no such reminder. The government was well aware of the bitter criticism emanating from the Diet, as well as the danger that the festival was indeed the forerunner to revolution. Consequently, several divisions of Bavarian soldiers were sent into the Pfalz to restore order. The commander, Fürst von Wrede, was granted full emergency authority that he effectively used to quell actual and potential disturbances. By June 16 he could write Metternich that Wirth and Siebenpfeiffer were to be arrested and imprisoned in Landau and that he had requested France and the neighboring states to return all those who had fled across the frontiers to escape the troops. Moreover, he had advised the troop commanders to use "force of arms at the slightest opposition." [53]

Wirth and Siebenpfeiffer were indeed arrested and, in 1833, sentenced to two years incarceration. After their release, Siebenpfeiffer decided to leave Germany, but Wirth refused to flee, choosing rather to continue his radical activities.

While Bavaria was restoring order in the Pfalz, there was hectic activity in the federal Assembly. On June 7 Lerchenfeld presented a list of the steps that his government had taken against "demagogues." He concluded his statement with the hope that the Diet was now convinced that Bavaria was taking all measures necessary to "follow the general purpose of the Confederation." Acting *Präsidium* Nagler, however, remained unpersuaded. He noted that the "revolutionary party in the Bavarian Rhineland" and other parts of south-western Germany had openly stated as their goal the "rebirth and transformation" of the "German fatherland," the "restoration" of German unity, and consequently "the dissolution of the *Staatenbund*." To achieve this they demanded a free press buttressed by the Press and Fatherland Society (banned by Bavaria on March 1) and the "living word": speeches to the people through popular societies. Nagler concluded by recommending that the Diet establish a committee, the *Massregeln-Kommission*, to report on antifederal movements. [54] This was unanimously agreed upon.

On July 5 the commission's report became a federal prohibition on all societies meeting for political purposes. Extraordinary popular gatherings and festivals were also forbidden, while those which were permitted were not allowed to schedule political speeches. Since the right of political assembly had never existed in the German states, this decree served to reinforce the historical limitations already in effect. However, it also made the development of mass political parties difficult, if not impossible, leaving secret societies and revolution as the sole means of effecting change. [55]

Of more immediate consequence were the measures prepared during the winter of 1831–32 by Austria and Prussia. As the murder of Kotzebue had made possible the passage of the Karlsbad decrees, so the *Hambacherfest* aided the German great powers in gaining support from the other states for further repressive measures. Only after Austria and Prussia had reached agreement, however, were the governments of Bavaria and Württemberg consulted, and not until apparent accord had been reached among these four was a draft sent to the remaining governments.

As was to be expected, during the negotiations Bavaria demanded assurances that the proposals would not lead to interference in her internal affairs. It appeared that she would stalemate the project, and the other middle states, expecting continued Bavarian opposition, made their acceptance contingent on that of Bavaria. Thus when the Bavarian government, after obtaining firm assurances from Austria and Prussia that her internal sovereignty would remain undiminished, chose to accept the proposals, the other states were forced to accept them as well. This decision disturbed all who saw the federal Assembly "only as a tool" of the German great powers and who feared "measures of force" that tried to control "the intellectual life of Germany." [56]

On June 28 the measures first conceived in Vienna were offered to the *Bundesversammlung* as a joint Austro-Prussian proposal. Their purpose was to devise a method for countering revolutionary movements and the public opinion that supported them. [57] Nevertheless, the Bavarian government, still apprehensive over possible limitations on its authority, became convinced that modifications were necessary to strengthen the individual governments against the encroachments of the Confederation. Bavaria was now persuaded that the constitutional governments ought to combat any decree that might compromise them in carrying out their obligations to the Confederation or to their own constitutions.

Lerchenfeld accordingly proposed alterations in the six-point proposal aiming, in particular, at amending Article 4. As originally worded, that article would have established a commission charged with protecting the dignity and prerogatives of the Confederation and the federal Assembly. The commission was to notify the latter whenever the *Stände* of a state proposed to enact or had enacted measures that would hinder that state in fulfilling its federal obligations, or that would contradict the rights of the state's government, particularly anything opposing the monarchical principle. Moreover, to insure its continued effectiveness, the commission was to serve indefinitely. Lerchenfeld succeeded in getting the commission's term limited to six years, but was unable to secure a change in the definition of its function. He had tried to substitute the wording,

to assist the governments in the administration of their constitutional rights,

for the phrase,

to facilitate the management of the existing constitutional relations between the governments and their *Stände*.

This attempt to prevent the committee from being given the authority to interfere in member states' internal affairs was unsuccessful. [58]

Once the Diet had completed action on the proposed amendments, the ambassadors joined in unanimous acceptance of the Six Articles. The proponents of the decree had argued that there was nothing new in it, that it only reinterpreted certain articles of the *Bundesakt* and *Schlussakt*. Metternich, for example, wrote that "not one new law" had been made, not because the Confederation did "not recognize the right to make them," but because the "existing laws suffice for all needs." [59] However, the question remains: were the Six Articles merely an "interpretation" of old laws or did they effect a change in the federal constitution?

Articles 1, 2, 3, 5, and 6 of the decree only restated Articles 1, 17, and 57–59 of the *Schlussakt* and Article 2 of the *Bundesakt* with the intent to strengthen the princes at the expense of their *Stände* and political expression, the Diet was trying to overthrow the Bavarian constitution by federal decree. Gise feared quite clear, for it provided the means for enforcing the other articles and alone threatened an ever deeper penetration by the Confederation into the affairs of the individual states. As noted above, this article established for a six-year period a commission to watch over the *Stände* and to report any antifederal proposals or resolutions to the Diet. This body, if necessary, would then bring the charge to the attention of the government involved for rectification. Implicit in the article was that if a government did nothing to curb its parliament, the mechanism of the *Exekutions-Ordnung* could be brought into play. [60]

The Six Articles thus constituted a comprehensive frontal assault on the powers of the *Stände*, granting the princes individually and the Confederation collectively an effective means to muzzle opposition to the Confederation and to federal decrees. Moreover, the decree of June 28 was directed not only at the parliaments, but also at the South German constitutions. The Confederation, a union of sovereigns and free cities, now asserted the primacy of federal over state legislation, thereby reaching beyond the princes directly toward the German populace. The *Hambacherfest* had indeed proven useful to the Confederation.

The *Bundestag*, however, was not yet satisfied that it had enacted sufficient legislation to crush the spirit of Hambach. On July 5 it passed another decree, the so-called Ten Articles, [61] which not only banned political associations, but also forbade the "unauthorized" wearing of cockades, flying of flags, and planting of liberty trees. Through this decree the governments were reminded to enforce the provisions of the Karlsbad decrees against the universities and were requested immediately to extradite political fugitives to the state from which they had fled. Moreover, the demand that Baden rescind her press law within fourteen days and the suppression of several newspapers over the next few weeks may be attributed directly to the furor raised by the festival. Little wonder that cries of liberal outrage were heard throughout Germany.

The publication of the Six and Ten Articles produced "the greatest excitement," Gise wrote, and all "constitutionally disposed persons" were "filled with fear" that by limiting the *Stände* and political expression, the Diet was trying to overthrow the Bavarian constitution by federal decree. Gise feared the reaction that the decrees might produce in the Rheinkreis, having often warned Austria and Prussia of the danger involved. "One ought not to be deluded," he wrote, "concerning the true condition of public opinion in the larger part of Germany." [62]

Protests and petitions directed against the new federal

decrees began to appear throughout Germany but were interpreted by the Diet as attempts to coerce the governments to free themselves from the "obligations which they have accepted" and to prevent them from enforcing decrees as required by the basic laws of the Confederation. This would bring the governments "into discord" with the Confederation and "cripple their authority with regard to the Confederation" as guaranteed by the federal constitution. Consequently, the Diet expressed the "hopeful expectation" that the governments of those states where "acts of rebellion" were taking place would immediately start proceedings against the "originators and disseminators" of the addresses and petitions. [63]

In particular, the Diet ordered the suppression of the *Allgemeine politische Annalen*, edited by C. von Rotteck and published by the bookdealer and Bavarian *Reichsrat* Johann Friedrich von Cotta. Once again Bavaria followed her own course, disputing the right of the Confederation to intervene in her internal affairs. Instead of publishing the federal decree suppressing the *Annalen*, the government negotiated a secret agreement with Cotta by which he simply ceased printing the journal. "One can now say," the French ambassador in Munich wrote, "that the federal decree is purposeless since the work no longer appears." [64]

The Bavarian government, the Austrian chargé d'affaires in Munich observed, planned to give proof where possible that it possessed "sufficient means and strength in itself" and the Bavarian constitution to stop the "misconduct of the press" without the need of a federal decree. [65] Documentation of the "effectiveness of the Bavarian system" against "rebellion" was indeed relayed to Lerchenfeld for use against those who continued to insist that Bavaria was not fulfilling her federal obligations vis-à-vis the press. Peace and order, the accompanying directive stated, had been restored by the force employed by the Bavarian authorities against the "pamphlets and papers of revolutionary tendency." The judicial officials, moreover, had justified the trust placed in them by the government, for the court of appeals delivered the "most satisfactory proof" in its judgment against the editors of two revolutionary newspapers. If left alone, the government could deal with the "internal quiet and order" in a "legal manner." The government, therefore, hoped that federal decrees would not vitiate its actions, for this would result in "uncertainty over legal conditions" among Bavarian subjects. [66]

Opposition to the federal decrees, however, came not only from liberal and radical newspapers. Although Metternich had obtained unanimous approval in the Diet, Great Britain, as a signatory of the Treaty of Vienna, [67] protested the decree on the grounds that the federal constitution, which had been guaranteed by Britain, among others, would thereby be altered. The protest came only after Czar Nicholas had declared his support for the decrees as a means of preserving the federal constitution against revolutionary attack. Although the French joined the British in protest, it had no effect. The federal Assembly refused to recognize the right of nonmembers to intervene in federal affairs. [68]

Of greater immediate consequence for the Confederation was the action taken by Bavaria and Prussia. By mid-October the Six Articles had been published by all the federal states, save those two.

> The fact itself proves the disinclination of Bavaria to promulgate acts emanating from the Diet which at all interfere with the internal administration of the country is still the same. [69]

Bavaria did publish the June 28 decree on October 17 but appended a royal explanation that the definitions of the Bavarian constitution were "in no way altered by our acceptance" of the decree. [70]

That this could take place after the unanimous acceptance of the Six Articles in Frankfurt can be explained if it is understood that many governments took one position in Frankfurt and another at home. Thus, although most of the states supported Metternich in the federal Diet, they also had to have a certain respect for the *Stände* and public opinion at home. Consequently, while they unanimously accepted the Six Articles, they hesitated to give the decree legal force by publishing it. [71]

Since the reservations attached to the decree by several states diminished its effectiveness, the *Präsidium* proposed another act to revitalize the decree. The ambassadors then unanimously accepted the proposal that publication of the Six Articles by the member states "with appended explanations" could "in no way" have an effect "on the general obligation" imposed by that decree, [72] thereby apparently accepting the premise that federal decrees were unalterable. With this, the pace of federal activity returned to its normal lethargy. The reinforcing decree remained without practical effect.

The year 1832 had seen the high point of the reaction to the July Revolution. During that year the federal Assembly, still working within the framework of the federal constitution, acted to repress all forms of expression antithetical to the underlying conservative philosophy of the Confederation. That such measures could be passed at all was in no small measure due to the fear of revolution that the German governments derived from such events as the *Hambacherfest*. Even Ludwig I, a strict constitutionalist where Bavarian interests were concerned, became convinced that some limit had to be placed on liberal and democratic expression. Even he was forced to acknowledge that the *Bundesversammlung* had the authority to play a role, if only a limited one. Yet the degree to which the Confederation should impose these restrictions still remained unclear.

1833–34: Reaffirmation of the *Bund*

i

The relative calm restored to Germany by the repression of the *Stände* and the press was soon shattered by a revolt in Frankfurt itself, the home for the *Bundesversammlung*. Although forbidden since 1819, the student political organizations collectively known as the *Burschenschaften* had continued to meet secretly in the major German universities. Early in 1833 a small circle of the Heidelberg *Burschenschaft* plotted to precipitate a revolt in Germany by an attack on the federal Assembly, assuming that a successful revolution in Frankfurt would have an effect in Germany similar to that produced in France in 1789 and 1830 by revolutions in Paris. This assumption, however, was erroneous because Frankfurt was in no way a capital city in the sense that Paris was. [1]

The conspirators, mostly students, academicians, and a few Poles who had fled their country after the Polish revolution had failed, came together in Frankfurt at the end of March 1833. They planned to seize the main guardhouse of the Frankfurt police, then proceed to the Thurn und Taxis palace where they expected to declare a German republic. Surprise, the one element vital to their chances for success, was lost when the authorities received anonymous information of the plot. Although the conspirators knew of their betrayal, they elected to proceed and, on April 3, under the leadership of Ernst von Rauschenplatt, a *Dozent* in law, successfully seized the main guardhouse while other groups attacked other objectives in the city. [2]

Success depended entirely on drawing the population into the rebellion, and when the citizenry remained passive the cause was lost. A small force of Frankfurt soldiers regained full control of the city with only light casualties on both sides. Most of the leaders of the *Wachensturm,* as the uprising was named after the "storming of the guardhouse," fled, while many of the students who had taken part were arrested.

The repercussions of this "local tumult" in the Diet were not so easily dealt with. On the day after the *Wachensturm* the federal Assembly was called into emergency session to deal with the crisis. The acting *Präsidium* noted that it had taken only a short time to restore order and that

> the local citizens took so little part in the uprising that the theater, which lies by the main guardhouse, played peacefully to the end [of the performance].

Prussia and Austria, however, were requested to keep their troops already stationed in the fortress at Mainz ready for speedy action should this be requested by the Diet or its presiding ambassador. Nassau was requested to give standing permission for those soldiers to pass through her territory should they have to march on Frankfurt. [3]

On the 9th the Diet involved itself still deeper into the aftermath of the *Wachensturm* with a decree instructing the governments of Bavaria, Nassau, and the Hesses to cooperate in uncovering the escaped "participants and accessories to the plot" who might have taken refuge within their borders. Moreover, those governments were to "conduct the closest supervision" of all travelers and were to place "a sufficient number" of soldiers on the borders of Frankfurt to "observe, occupy and hold. . . all approaches and roads." [4]

It is evident that the *Bundestag* was deeply disturbed by the events of April 3; between the 4th and the 27th of that month it met eight times rather than the normal four. One session was held on April 10 and, contrary to usual practice, was continued on the 11th. On the next day the session continued on well into the night, again contrary to normal procedures. In the latter session the Frankfurt ambassador declared that the situation was well in hand and that the city was able to preserve order without federal aid. This confident declaration notwithstanding, the Diet accepted the Military Commission's assessment that Frankfurt was, in fact, not capable of maintaining order. As long as the disturbances continued, the Diet decreed, a joint Austro-Prussian force from Mainz was to be transferred to the outskirts of, though not into the city. The headquarters for the force's commanders, however, was to be in Frankfurt. [5] This meant that the city was now surrounded by 2,500 federal soldiers.

No request for assistance had come to the *Bundestag* from Frankfurt; rather, the Senate consistently declared its competence to manage the situation. The federal Assembly, however, justified its decree by adopting the fiction that Frankfurt's government had been prevented from appealing for aid by the *Wachensturm*, although there is no evidence to support this claim. For an extended period, in spite of the Senate's repeated protests, troops were kept in the vicinity of Frankfurt despite the fact that the major disturbance had been suppressed and that there was little chance for a recurrence. The goal of the rebellion, however, had been the overthrow of the federal constitution, not that of the city. Although not warranted constitutionally, the acts of the federal Assembly were politically understandable, since the security of the Confederation had indeed been at stake. [6]

Although Bavaria had acquiesced in the federal decision to enforce order in Frankfurt without an invitation from that city or specific authorization in the federal constitution, she had by no means relinquished her program for preventing the expansion of the Confederation's competence to meddle in the states' internal affairs. In a directive to Arnold von Mieg,[7] Bavaria's new ambassador who had been governor of Ansbach and royal finance minister, the Bavarian government noted that the "manifold disturbances" offered an opportunity to extend the jurisdiction of the Confederation "at the expense" of the individual governments "under the title of the need for collective measures" to maintain the security of the Confederation. Mieg was ordered to defend the "fundamental principle" of the sovereignty of the states. [8]

The *Wachensturm* had thus offered the Confederation one more opportunity to interfere in the domestic affairs of the states. On June 20 the federal Assembly established a committee, the Central Authority for Political Investigations, to search out and expose all plots directed against the Confederation or its constitution. This Frankfurt-based body, composed of lawyers and judges from Bavaria, Austria, Prussia, Württemberg, and Hesse-Darmstadt, was intended to unearth conspiracies against the Confederation, to compile the results of local investigations, and to inform the state authorities of plots against them. [9]

The Bavarian government chose to interpret the purpose of the Central Authority in the most literal sense: to collect memoranda from the state courts of inquiry and produce a "complete picture of each disturbance." This central collection agency had "no other purpose" than to use the gathered data to fill in gaps left by local investigations. The Bavarian ambassador was instructed to see that the Central Authority did not overstep its competence. [10]

Examinations by the Central Authority were to be kept
secret; all material published by or about that body was
subject to rigorous censorship to prevent the appearance of
unofficial reports. [11] Indeed, the final report covering the
investigation of more than 2,000 persons was never
published. [12] It was presented to the *Bundestag* in 1842 by the
Central Authority, which then suspended its activities. The
commissioners returned to their home states, but that body
remained subject to reactivation; not until 1848 was the
Central Authority officially dissolved.

Federal involvement in Frankfurt's affairs did not end even
with the establishment of this investigatory body. In October
1833 one of the imprisoned students managed to escape from
the city's jail, producing renewed charges that security
measures taken by the Senate were insufficient. In a memorandum to Ludwig, Gise explained that as long as Frankfurt
could not offer a sufficient guarantee of the Diet's security, the
Confederation found "itself with the obligation" to provide
that security without otherwise infringing upon that city's
"right of sovereignty." [13]

On November 25 the federal Assembly proposed bringing
federal troops into the city and placing all Frankfurt's soldiers
under federal command. In a marginal note on the draft
instruction to Mieg, Ludwig wrote: "only if the free city of
Frankfurt agrees to this proposal . . . will I obligate myself to
it." Mieg was thus directed to agree to a unified command for
"the duration of the present disturbances" only if Frankfurt
accepted it. The Bavarian government, however, expected that
the city would "freely offer its hand to this," for the measure
was to be only temporary. [14]

But Frankfurt's Senate made known its opposition to the
plan on December 5. The effect, however, was only to delay
passage of the decree until April 3, 1834, at which time all
federal and city troops in Frankfurt were at last put under the

command of General Ludwig von Piret of Austria. The city guard was also to come under Piret's command in case of emergency. [15] Frankfurt again protested, but the *Bundestag* decided to ignore the complaint. When the city refused to place its soldiers under Piret's command, the Diet began the procedure that would lead to a *Bundesexekution* against the Senate. It gave that body until its next session to fulfill the decree of April 3. [16] A renewed protest was rejected as "inimical to the federal constitution," although the basis for the Senate's refusal and its request for the removal of federal soldiers was that "order and quiet" had already been secured and could be maintained by the city alone. [17] Once again the Senate was given a deadline to fulfill the decree.

On May 7 the *Bundesversammlung* learned to its horror that an unsuccessful attempt to free those imprisoned for involvement in the *Wachensturm* had occurred five days earlier. The presiding ambassador proposed that the prisoners be transported to Mainz for security, and there was serious discussion of moving the federal Assembly itself from Frankfurt; at the very least, it was argued, the federal treasuries ought to be transferred to Mainz. [18]

The Senate, however, was not yet ready to accede, declaring again that it could not accept decrees that violated the city's constitution. [19] This argument was also rejected on recommendation of the *Exekutionskommission*, since the *Schlussakt* specifically forbade a state constitution from interfering with the carrying out of a federal decree. The Diet then decreed the continuation of the *Exekution* against the Senate. [20]

Bavaria, too, was concerned with the security of the federal Assembly, but she had not surrendered the concept of the right of state sovereignty. Württemberg's ambassador, acting as a substitute for Mieg, received instructions from Munich noting that the events of May 2 had produced unwarranted demands for strengthened security measures. The Bavarian government believed that the matter could easily be resolved if Frankfurt would extradite "foreign" prisoners to their home states, against some written declaration that through this "voluntary act" there would be no prejudice to the "autonomy and independence" of the city. Bavaria, for her part, was ready to enter into such an arrangement. [21]

This offer notwithstanding, Frankfurt refused to compromise, and on May 28 the federal Diet decreed that Prussia name a civil commissioner who would put the *Exekution* into effect, designating the "*Interventionskorps*" as an "*Exekutionskorps.*"[22] Finally, the Senate of the free city surrendered to federal pressure and, on May 31, allowed its army to be merged with the federal forces then in the city.[23]

With the movement of federal troops into Frankfurt, the *Wachensturm* ceased to be solely an internal German problem. Both Great Britain and France sent notes of protest to the federal Assembly, condemning the federal action. The British note of May 21 remonstrated against a "violent infringement" of the rights of an independent state, since Great Britain, as a signatory of the Vienna treaty, felt obliged to consider as a British interest the "maintenance of the political independence even of the smallest state of Europe." [24] This note, protesting all compulsory measures against Frankfurt, was made known to Gise, who responded that it was strictly an internal matter to be decided by federal law. [25]

Mieg, who was still in Vienna, was notified that Bavaria would approve acceptance of the British and French notes by the *Bundestag* but considered the subject closed since Frankfurt had "voluntarily condescended" to unite its troops with the security force. [26] On the same day, June 12, both Britain and France received answers rejecting their contention that they had a right to demand explanations from the federal Assembly for its actions.

The right to manage its internal affairs without foreign

interference was the Confederation's right for the "preservation of the individual German states" and for the "maintenance of the security of the Confederation." The Diet would "faithfully hold" to its obligations in order to "preserve this right uninjured." [27]

The captured *Wachensturm* conspirators, whose uprising had triggered the federal occupation of Frankfurt and the involvement of Great Britain and France in German affairs, were finally sentenced in October 1836. By January 1837 seven of the prisoners had escaped from the Frankfurt police station in which they had been incarcerated. Finally, the federal Assembly agreed to the four-year-old Prussian proposal that the remaining six be transferred to the more secure facilities in Mainz. Not until September 1, 1842, however, did the federal Diet end the occupation of Frankfurt, reserving the right to reoccupy the city if local authorities failed to maintain order. [28]

Although the most important example, the *Wachensturm* had not provided the only, or even the first occasion on which the western powers had attempted to interfere in federal affairs during 1834. The issue had first arisen when the Belgians, acting contrary to the London agreement, [29] attempted to conscript residents of the federal fortress of Luxemburg, even though this was the "German part" of the province. On February 13, 1834, the prohibition against such conscription was reaffirmed by the fortress commander, but two days later a federal patrol found summonses ordering citizens to a Belgian town for militia duty posted within the fortress perimeter. They bore the signature of the Belgian district commander, Hanno. That night a federal detachment was sent to Bettenburg, a town in Belgium, where it arrested Hanno and brought him back to the fortress for incarceration. As General Dumoulin, the fortress commander who had been a Dutch officer before joining Prussian service in 1806, reported, Belgium demanded Hanno's release before it would begin discussions about conscription. The federal Assembly voted to release Hanno on February 26, [30] and this took place two days later.

The matter became more complicated when, on February 26, the French ambassador presented to the *Bundesversammlung* a strongly worded note of protest, charging that the fortress commander and "his provocateurs" had, "by their intolerable manner," provoked a government that had "great power" and that guaranteed "the common rights of all civil states." Although the Confederation itself, the note continued, had taken no part in the insult offered to Belgium, the federal Assembly would have to accept responsibility if it continued to "tolerate the system" directed by General Dumoulin. The note recommended that the Diet "strongly disapprove" Hanno's imprisonment and stated that if the *Bundestag* would not act, then France would. [31]

The Bavarian king was outraged that the Diet should even accept a note written in such insulting language. He felt that the Confederation ought to have returned the note unanswered in order to "maintain its dignity." He wrote to Mieg that he expected the federal Assembly to defend the "authority and rights" of the Confederation both in the present case and in the future. [32] This note was followed by further instructions informing Mieg of how to deal with the French demands and any similar notes that might "tread upon the dignity" of the German Confederation. Not only were such demands to be rejected, but Mieg was "actively to strive" to insure that the vote returning such notes "be elevated to a federal decree." [33]

Nevertheless, the federal Assembly chose not to overreact to the French note of February 26; it was neither returned nor answered. France's subsequent note of April 8 received an immediate verbal reply from the presiding ambassador, but no official response until May 12. The answer approved on that day by the Diet explained what had happened, defended all

German actions, and blamed Belgium for not upholding her obligations. It was a polite note, but firm and final. As far as the Confederation was concerned, the matter was closed.

France, however, refused to accept this as the last word. France and Great Britain continued to send protests to the federal Assembly about that body's treatment of Frankfurt and made several further references to the Hanno affair. Finally, on September 18, 1834, the *Bundesversammlung* sought to make "clear and permanent" the relationship of the Confederation to the foreign powers. In the interest of unanimity, however, certain terms of the proposal were softened, for Mieg, now back in Frankfurt, had been instructed to stress the "admissibility" of the claim of the western powers to be guarantors of the Vienna treaty and to have the right to protect "suppressed" members of the Confederation. [34] Had Mieg delivered this statement, a foundation might have been laid for strengthening Bavarian ties with France, thereby increasing the weight of Bavaria's claim that she could resist the will of the Confederation. Mieg, however, did not follow through and, with Bavarian objections resolved, the *Bundesversammlung* unanimously accepted the proposal, and the protocol of the session makes no mention of the conflict. [35]

The decree "concerning the inadmissibility of the interference of foreign powers in the internal affairs of the German Confederation" used the very document that France and Great Britain were claiming to protect to demonstrate that those powers had no right of intervention. Noting that the Confederation had been "created exclusively" by the princes and free cities of Germany, the decree argued that although the *Bundesakt* had been incorporated in the Congress Act, that fact granted neither foreign power a right to "supervise the maintenance of the principles sanctioned" in the *Bundesakt*, nor did it create an "obligation" to defend the independence of the individual members of the Confederation for the non-German states who also signed the Congress Act. Rather, "the obligation emerged" from it to "refrain" from any interference in "the internal affairs of the Confederation," since the purpose of the Confederation was itself to maintain the security of Germany and the independence of the member states.

Moreover, it continued, the federal Diet alone had the right to alter the federal constitution and to deal with the "organic order" of the Confederation. All members had promised to defend any single state, as well as Germany as a whole, against attack and to guarantee their collective possessions "without any guarantees by foreign powers." On the basis of the federal constitution Germany had become such a "completely developed" and "strongly based" political body that it, "as a major component of the European state-structure" possessed all the necessary means to guarantee its internal peace and "the inviolate security and autonomy" of the "united sovereign princes and free cities" of the Confederation "without foreign assistance."

The French and British notes were understood only as "foreign interference" in federal affairs and as a demand for powers that "would displace the whole relationship" of the Confederation, endanger its autonomy, and create dependence on foreign powers. Consequently, the Confederation "strongly protests" those notes which contained concepts in "direct contradiction" to the *Bundesakt*. The Confederation, therefore, would "not allow itself" to be disturbed by any attempt at interference "in the quiet and consistent development" of its legislation. This decree was meant to serve as the "guiding principle" for the federal Diet in case of any "similar interferences" in the internal affairs of the Confederation. Copies of the decree were to provide the sole answer to the French and British notes. [36] Later protest notes were simply left unanswered.

From its own point of view the federal Assembly was fully

justified in following this course. Although the *Bundesakt* had been appended to the Congress Act, only the first eleven articles were incorporated into the treaty verbatum; the remainder were only summarized. Yet inclusion of even part of the *Bundesakt* in the treaty could be interpreted as conferring upon the powers the right to guarantee the integrity of the federal constitution. Britain and France chose to so interpret it and argued that there could be no constitutional change without their approval. They reserved the right to intervene if the constitution were violated. This argument had provided the basis for British protests in 1819, 1832, and 1834, although the major revision of the federal constitution in 1820 and the renewal of the Karlsbad decrees in 1824 had elicited no reaction from Great Britain.

At no time, however, had this interpretation been accepted by the German states. The War of Liberation, they held, had been fought to establish German independence, not to place Germany under the tutelage of foreign powers. All the treaties between the allied powers and the German states signed before the Vienna Congress Act maintained that the German states would remain autonomous and free to choose the means for protecting that autonomy. In point of fact, there is no evidence that the signatories of the Congress Act intended anything more than to give collective recognition to the Confederation.[37]

Although Bavaria had succeeded in changing the phraseology of the September 18 decree, the underlying philosophy remained the same. It is improbable that she desired to change that, for she too wanted no foreign interference in either German or Bavarian affairs. The importance of the decree went beyond the stress on noninterference. Although none of the German states would acknowledge that the Confederation had the authority of a national government within Germany, by unanimously accepting the decree they acknowledged that the Confederation was sovereign in international law and ought to be treated as such by the other European states. As was noted in another decree of the same day, the Confederation simply could not accept the right of a foreign state to request an explanation of an internal matter "without giving up a bit of her sovereign position," [38] something no state could afford to do and remain sovereign.

ii

By the middle of 1833 the Confederation still appeared unable to suppress the now openly expressed German radicalism within the framework of existing federal decrees, and the measures taken by the individual states had proven no more effective. [39] Prussia was thus able to convince Austria of the need for a new Vienna Conference to deal with ways for ending revolutionary activity. In August 1833 Friedrich von Ancillon, the Prussian foreign minister, sent a circular to Prussian ambassadors in all German courts, noting that although the actions of 1820 had closed gaps left in 1815, the revolutions of 1830 had created new threats to be dealt with. The ambassadors were to prepare the ground for another meeting of the representatives of the German states to strengthen existing laws. Metternich sent a similar note to all Austrian ambassadors. [40]

On January 3, 1834, representatives of each of the states having votes in the *Engerer Rat* met in Vienna to discuss measures upon which Prussia and Austria had agreed beforehand. Almost immediately, however, the conference split into two groups: the "conservative," led by Metternich and Ancillon, and the "constitutional" which was more concerned with public opinion and potential "encroachments" on the state constitutions. [41] Bavaria, the leader of the latter group, was in a stronger position to block undesirable proposals than in 1832. The government had become more conservative and had repressed radicalism with its own, not federal, edicts. Thus she had neither the need nor the desire for further federal measures. Moreover, Mieg was able to report to the conference that there was no need to attack the state parliaments, in particular the Bavarian *Landtag*, for on March 21, 1834, King Ludwig I had been granted his much-sought-after permanent civil list as well as funds for several of his pet projects. [42]

From the outset the federal Assembly was excluded from knowledge of or participation in these discussions. On request of the Prussian government, ambassadors to the Diet were not to be sent to Vienna. This procedure served to accentuate the fact that any agreement would be extraconstitutional. [43] Of the federal ambassadors, only Münch, as Austria's second delegate rather than in his capacity of *Bundestag Präsidium*, and Mieg, who replaced Gise as chief Bavarian negotiator, attended the conference.

Metternich, in a letter to Wrede with whom he had been conducting a secret correspondence for the preceding four years, explained how he expected the results of the conference to be handled. The protocol of the agreement was to be deposited in the secret archives of the federal Assembly to serve as the "true, government sanctioned interpretation of existing federal laws" and was to remain secret. [44] Unlike the cases of 1819 and 1820, however, Metternich would not accept the idea that the decisions of the conference should be made into a federal decree and requested that Mieg be prevented from asking that they be sent to Frankfurt for discussion. [45]

Finally, on June 12, after five months of reports, proposals, discussions, and modifications, the participating governments accepted the *Schlussprotocol der Wiener Ministerialkonferenzen*, the Sixty Articles, which remained secret until privately published anonymously in 1843. Only a few of the articles were later given the status of federal decree: Articles 3–14 (creation of a federal court of arbitration) on October 30, 1834; Articles

42–56 (supervision of the universities) and Article 57 (limiting Article 12 of the *Bundesakt* to civil matters), on November 13, 1834. [46]

As with the Six Articles, it was claimed that the Sixty Articles [47] contained nothing new except for the court of arbitration (*Schiedsgericht*) that was never used. In fact, this time the protocol did indeed represent only a restatement of the philosophy underlying decrees adopted since 1830 and were really an extension of the Karlsbad decrees and the Six Articles. The agreement dealt primarily with three topics that had been treated earlier: further limitation of the rights of the *Stände*, censorship, and supervision of the universities. The main goal of the *Schlussprotocol* was to fortify the monarchical principle and, consequently, to emasculate the power of the parliaments.

In particular, the *Stände* were forbidden to discuss federal decrees as they had done in the case of the Six Articles or to interfere with a government's right to issue edicts. The parliament's right to "consent to taxes" was separated from the "right to control expenditures," which was placed solely in the hands of the government. Since the Sixty Articles demanded that the *Stände* first consider the budget before dealing with other matters, those bodies were deprived of the possibility of exerting fiscal pressure to gain reform.

Before a royal official could become or, more importantly, remain a member of the lower Chamber, the sovereign had to give his approval. This reiterated existing practice through which, for example, the Bavarian government could purge its *Landtag* of liberals by appointing them to insignificant government positions. Moreover, the military was now forbidden to take an oath to the state constitutions. It thereby remained dependent on the sovereign and, in theory, outside the constitutional process.

The *Schlussprotocol* sought to limit the press no less than the

Stände. The governments were to use men of "proven disposition and ability" as censors and were to prohibit the inclusion of blank spaces in place of phrases censored. The number of political newspapers was to be limited, and all minutes of the *Stände* and of the law courts were also liable to censorship.

There was to be another article strengthening the Karlsbad press decree and extending its life indefinitely. Bavaria, however, demanded that such an article be limited to six years duration. Since such a limitation would have run counter to the intent of the proposal to "affirm and strengthen" the effectiveness of the existing law, and since Bavaria refused to back down, it was decided to omit the article. [49] The original draft also contained a proposal by which juries would be excluded from competence in political cases, but this too was dropped when Bavaria refused to accept it. [50]

Article 60 of the *Schlussprotocol* bound the governments to observe the agreement as though it were a federal decree and, excepting those articles which were to be published as formal decrees, bound them to maintain the strictest secrecy over the contents. The importance of Article 60 is not to be underrated. Now the Confederation had two sources of law: the published federal constitution and this secret treaty. In essence, this fact serves to underscore the fact that the German Confederation was not a true federal state drawing its power solely from a constitution and allowing for no extraconstitutional arrangements.

Doubts could be raised in law as to the validity of the *Schlussprotocol.* It was designed to extend the authority of the federal Assembly deeper into the affairs of the individual states, and, in fact, it superseded their constitutions, especially in regard to control of the *Stände* and budgetary rights. Such a change in federal legislation and in some state constitutions could legally be arrived at only through a "basic federal law" (*Bundesgrundgesetz*), requiring the unanimous approval of the

Plenum, that is, approval by each member of the Confederation. The Vienna Conference, however, was composed of representatives of only the seventeen members of the *Engerer Rat,* which had no right to cast votes for those states not taking part.

Moreover, the acceptance of the secret protocol contradicted the principle that laws were valid only after publication, for Article 60 attempted to give the agreement the force of a federal decree without publication. No arrangement based on a secret agreement could have the force of a published decree. [51] It is surprising that Bavaria accepted the validity of the Sixty Articles, since one of her main weapons against federal intrusion in her own internal affairs had been the refusal to publish a federal decree or, alternately, to publish it with amendments and reservations. The federal Diet itself had accepted the principle of publication, for what else could explain the repeated discussion of Bavarian actions and the pressure exerted on that state to publish decrees exactly as they had been agreed upon?

The effect of the Sixty Articles was slight. The constitutional states were lax in their enforcement of the agreement, preferring to adjust to the political realities within their states. Few of them were willing to antagonize their subjects or *Stände.* Neither a federal decree nor a secret treaty could crush the representative system where it already existed. The Vienna protocol proved to be a holding action, an attempt to prevent further erosion of the monarchical principle. When the Sixty Articles came to light, they served only to emphasize the fact that the federal Assembly and the state governments that tried to enforce the agreement were conspiratorial, repressive, and reactionary. Measures such as this made it increasingly difficult to visualize the Diet serving as the vehicle for German unification.

The years 1833 and 1834 had seen a crisis for the Confederation. Faced by rebellion, a radical press, and foreign pressures, the Confederation was forced to act rapidly in order to maintain its position. Even Bavaria recognized the dangers of the situation and thus, without surrendering her claims to full sovereignty, cooperated with the other states to work for a resolution of the immediate problem. Although in the long run the measures taken by the *Bundestag* were only of temporary effect, the Confederation had indeed acted, and, for the moment, credibly and successfully enough to bring a state of tranquility back to Germany.

PART III

Completing the System
1835–1848

7

The Interrevolutionary Period

i

Although the federal Diet could be well satisfied with its success against revolutionary ferment, there was still much to be accomplished if peace and order were to be maintained in Germany. However, now the pressures of the last four years had been removed; now the ambassadors could deliberate at a more leisurely pace. "The Diet," Cartwright wrote, "is not now preoccupied with any affair of particular interest." [1] After four years of nearly continuous sessions, the ambassadors once again allowed themselves the luxury of month-long recesses and frequent journeys home. By the end of 1835, even the former practice of a four-month suspension of sessions was restored. Only Münch remained in Frankfurt, largely because he was unwilling to allow the Prussian ambassador to preside due to "the growing influence of Prussia in Germany." [2] This is not to say that Bavarian diplomats neglected to look to Vienna or that the Bavarian monarch had given up all ideas of Bavarian autonomy; but the early successes of the *Zollverein* had strengthened Prussia's position vis-à-vis Austria, and even Bavaria seemed to approach the Prussian orbit. Thus the competition for hegemony, which would lead to the eventual destruction of the German Confederation after 1848, was already beginning to appear.

Nonetheless, the German great powers did agree that the system established in Vienna in 1834 to maintain domestic peace and order was in need of expansion. Accordingly, between 1835 and 1836 the federal Diet issued a series of decrees designed to curb further revolutionary threats from students or traveling journeymen and to protect the public from the corruptive influence of certain authors and knowledge of *Landtag* debates. Without apparent haste each of these potential dangers was carefully examined, discussed, and, through unanimous consent, disposed of through some form of prohibition.

The first of these decrees was concerned with student travel to Switzerland, which, after the failure of the revolutions of 1830, had become a sanctuary for the refugee radicals of Poland, France, and the German states. Democrats, moreover, had founded a university in Zurich that was attracting large numbers of German students. In the face of this, the Diet's Committee on Public Quiet and Order recommended that the individual states prohibit their subjects from attending foreign universities that promoted revolutionary attitudes or associations. [3]

Unfortunately, the Confederation took no action, and students and other young Germans continued to travel to Switzerland in ever greater numbers. The Austrian ambassador was particularly disturbed by this turn of events and argued that common measures were the only way to successfully overcome the revolutionary threat. [4] In the next session, the Committee on Public Quiet and Order reminded the ambassadors that no formal vote had yet taken place in the *Bundestag,* although Bavaria had announced prohibiting its students from going to Zurich. In the meantime, the Committee noted, a large number of students, accompanied by some of the faculty of the University of Zurich, had taken part in a "criminal march" against Savoy, demonstrating that that university was only a rallying point for revolutionary attacks against neighboring states. Since Bern had also founded a university of the same sort as Zurich, the Committee recommended, and the *Bundestag* decreed, that the state governments prevent their students from attending either of those two universities. [5] Not only had the Diet thus given its usual response to a revolutionary threat, but it also continued to acknowledge that the states, not the *Bundestag*, had jurisdiction over the German people. Once again the wording of the decree implied that there were only subjects of the member states, that the concept of a German people would remain as an abstraction.

The *Bundesversammlung* was quite consistent on this point, for, in dealing with the problems of German journeymen traveling outside the Confederation, enforcement of its decree was left to the individual governments. Journeymen, men who had completed their apprenticeship in the medieval guild system but who could not yet qualify as masters, had been encouraged to travel from town to town in order to gain experience and to provide the masters with a source of labor. By the 16th century the system of traveling journeymen had become obligatory, leading to the development of journeymen fraternities and associations that extended throughout the Empire and beyond. At first the princes looked on the journeymen as a means of weakening the power of the guild masters, but then began to see them as a threat to their own powers. Consequently, journeymen organizations were banned by the Empire in 1731, in effect serving only to drive them underground. By the 19th century, increasing governmental interference in guild affairs, the increasing number of journeymen unable to advance in their crafts, the gradual mechanization of production, and the introduction of *Gewerbefreiheit* (freedom of occupation) in some of the German states all served to increase the social tensions inherent in the guild system and suffered especially by the journeymen.

Journeymen associations in Switzerland, as well as in France and in Belgium, were being used by revolutionaries to "corrupt" that "impressionable class" and to use them to further their own revolutionary plans. [6] In their propaganda the radicals emphasized the virtues of the craftsmen, for they believed them to be the only segment of German society that might be revolutionized, while, at the same time, the travels of the German journeymen gave the radicals the opportunity to influence them without the personal danger that they would face in Germany. Consequently, German political refugees gathered in those cities that protected or tolerated them and where they could establish ties to the journeymen who, upon their return to Germany, were to spread the revolutionary doctrines among their colleagues. The Committee of Public Quiet and Order reported that Bern was the center of such activity, and, in spite of assurances to the contrary, an association of several hundred journeymen publicly destroyed the flags of Bavaria, Baden, and Württemberg in that city. Since the Committee believed that it was in the best interest of all the German states to forbid or limit the travel of German journeymen to countries where radical associations were tolerated, it proposed that the *Bundestag* prohibit their travel to Switzerland, France, and Belgium, while leaving to the states the right to grant exceptions, the responsibility for recalling those journeymen already in one of those three lands, and the obligation to impose police supervision of the journeymen and their associations. [7]

The Bavarian ambassador gave strong support to this proposal and noted that since June 1834 Bavarian journeymen had been forbidden to travel to those lands where radical associations existed. But, in order to give the proposed ban the appropriate effectiveness, the Bavarian government wanted those German states that bordered Switzerland, Belgium, and France to refuse to grant visas, passports, or *Wanderbücher* to journeymen planning to travel to those lands. He concluded by noting that unless the governments agreed at least in secret on specific measures to be taken in common, no one should expect success from a generalized construction. [8] This argument served to convince the other ambassadors, and the committee proposal was decreed on January 15, 1835. [9]

Yet the problem of the journeymen went further than the threat of infection from abroad. The *Bundestag* continued to carefully scrutinize this group, which was thought to be the most revolution-prone class in German society. In this context the Saxon ambassador called the Diet's attention to the existence of a journeymen association in almost every guild, and since they were avoiding police supervision, they had wide latitude to commit "excesses" of various forms. These associations (*Gesellenschaften*) and brotherhoods had spread throughout Germany and into neighboring states and attempted to continue those practices which the governments were attempting to extirpate. Since such organizations could also be used for political purposes, he felt that they were dangerous and ought to be banned by the *Bund*. [10]

The Saxon government, however, was concerned with more than the immediate political effects of the journeymen associations, for a question of social justice was also involved. Many crafts demanded that the traveling journeyman produce a license or similar document signed by other, more senior journeymen, in addition to his *Wanderbuch,* before he was eligible for employment or the "present" (*Geschenk*) [11] that was his right. Such abuses had been forbidden in Saxony, the ambassador noted, but as long as they were tolerated in other states, Saxon journeymen would find themselves at a disadvantage since in those states they would be unable to count on the support to which they were entitled, but which would be available to those with the illegal journeyman license. Since the actions taken by the individual states had proven ineffective, Saxony was convinced that the only way to end such abuses and inequities was for the Diet to prohibit both the journeyman license and the existing associations and fraternities.[12] In a later session the Saxon ambassador voiced his government's concern as to whether a traveling journeyman might be denied employment or support, if ill, if he could not identify himself with a journeyman license. There was also the possibility that if licenses were banned, they might simply be replaced by some other illegal proof of identity. Therefore, the *Bundestag* had an obligation to resolve all these questions by decreeing that each traveling journeyman who received legitimate approval for travel from the appropriate authorities would need no other certification. In this way, he concluded, the journeyman would "never lack work or the customary support."[13]

Clearly the Saxon government had missed the point. It correctly diagnosed the symptoms, recognizing that discontent due to the abuses of the journeymen associations was liable to lead to revolutionary actions, but it failed to understand that the jobs that the journeymen needed could not be created by ending these abuses. The day of the journeyman, of the entire guild system, was approaching its end. Since German society was no longer static, an economic system predicated on no change could not accommodate itself to relatively rapid growth and development. But neither the Saxon government, nor the other members of the Confederation, were yet able to comprehend this point, and the federal Diet had become so structured as to prefer traditional approaches such as repression or restoration rather than novelties.

Consequently, the Diet's committee that examined the Saxon proposals acknowledged their importance, for the "revolutionary party" continued its efforts to "entice" the journeymen. The committee also acknowledged that the traditional societies and brotherhoods could easily shelter revolutionary journeymen associations. It therefore concluded that it was in the best interest of the entire Confederation to ban those fraternities and the use of journeyman licenses. But, since those practises were very closely connected with the very existence of the guilds in many states, the committee preferred not to state its opinion until all the governments had given their declarations. [14]

In early 1836 the substitute for the Bavarian ambassador received the instructions necessary to respond to the Saxon proposals. The Bavarian government, he explained, had set for itself the special task of abolishing the old guild system, a task that had become easier since the whole system had been "regenerated" in 1825 and placed under continuous police direction. Moreover, existing Bavarian legislation banned all journeymen associations and licenses. There were therefore sufficient regulations against journeymen abuses, regulations that only needed to be carried out to be successful. Indeed, he argued, a federal decree that would only increase the existing "mass of regulations" seemed to be superfluous. Only if some "deficiency" appeared in the existing legislation should the Diet call for the "required supplement." An "invitation" to the governments concerned would "completely achieve the goal" of abolishing that which in most cases no longer existed without need of a federal decree. The Ten Articles of 1832 had already banned all political associations and only needed to be carried out, whereas a federal decree regulating the police supervision of the crafts would force the revision of the legislation of the individual states, something that was neither "a constitutional occupation" of the *Bundesversammlung* nor "at all a suitable task" for that body. [15]

Bavaria's argument that federal legislation would be either

superfluous or unconstitutional was accepted by enough of the other governments so that no specific proposals for a decree were made nor was a vote taken. Indeed, Mieg, on his return to Frankfurt, took great care to insure the federal Diet's continued inaction in this area since his government reminded him of the importance that it attached to the question. Such general principles taken from the "unique circumstances" within other states, he was told, might come into "collision" with laws and institutions that were "uniquely Bavarian" regarding the organization of the crafts "and other material on that subject." Since this was to be avoided, Mieg was to take every opportunity to sidetrack any proposal for a federal decree in favor of agreements among the individual states.[16]

This remained Bavarian policy until 1840. By then, however, journeymen activities had gotten so out of hand that Bavaria no longer wished to prevent the Diet from considering appropriate remedies. Thus Mieg made no move to prevent the ambassador of the Free Cities from raising the question and noting that the journeymen associations were illegally drawing authority to themselves by setting up their own courts and punishments and by continuing to issue journeyman licenses. In order to "ban and suppress" these abuses, the ambassador asked the *Bundestag* to decree some appropriate action or, at the very least, that each government instruct its ambassador to give an "oral statement" as to what it was doing.[17]

The Bavarian government was not quite aware of the need for action. In mid-October Gise informed his king that it was most urgent that federal action be taken to abolish the "insubordinate" journeymen associations, since their most recent demands made "common intervention most necessary."[18] Ludwig was convinced and appropriate instructions were sent to Mieg,[19] who complied in the next session of the *Bundesversammlung*. However, since several of the ambassadors had not yet received instructions, no mention was made in the protocol of the 23rd session. [20]

Meanwhile, the Saxon government had begun a campaign to prod the German governments into action. In a verbal note the Saxon government reminded Gise that it had proposed banning journeymen associations and their misconduct as early as 1835, but that while a majority of the governments had approved this, the matter could not be concluded due to the opposition of Bavaria, Lippe, and Hamburg, and the silence of other governments. Now, however, the matter had taken a new turn since most of the states were convinced of the persistence of the "pernicious misconduct" of the journeymen. Even Austria had proposed that the governments agree to note in the passport or *Wanderbuch* of an offending journeyman the illegal activity he had been convicted of, to send the offender back to his home state, and to prevent him from finding employment in any other federal state. Saxony supported this in so far as it would achieve the goal "at least in an indirect manner," and hoped that the Bavarian government would "not hesitate to accept it" as well. [21]

Gise quickly informed Saxony that she need have no fears as to Bavaria's position, for Mieg had already been instructed to vote for Münch's suggestions; [22] but it was not until the session of December 3, 1840, that Mieg could report that the *Bundestag* had accepted unanimously the Austrian proposal. [23] Bavaria then quickly published the new decree [24]—a decree that Bavaria and the other governments took quite seriously. Within the next few months Bavaria sent several journeymen to their home states because of illegal associations or "abuses," while Bremen sent some journeymen back to Bavaria on similar grounds. [25]

The German governments again acted only to suppress the manifestation of a problem, doing nothing to deal with the basic reasons for it. Rather than confronting the question of guilds in a period of gradual industrialization, rather than facing the dislocation and discontent that this brought about, the ambassadors in Frankfurt raised only the question of whether the state or the journeymen associations would have ultimate control over the journeymen. All federal decrees went to assure that the authority of the state remained unimpaired. Consequently, the journeymen were to be limited in the supervision of their own affairs and were to be quarantined from the contamination of revolutionary ideas. This was to be done by limiting their travels abroad and by suppressing groups like Young Germany, which attempted to make direct contact with the journeymen abroad or indirectly in Germany through the publication of pamphlets, novels, and other literary works critical of the existing political and social order.

It is in this context, then, that one must approach the Diet's distaste for Young Germany. This group of writers, which included Heinrich Heine and Ludwig Börne, was active in France and Switzerland, where the writers had fled after the failure of the Revolution of 1830. There they contented themselves with publications to incite revolution in Germany and to spread their ideas among the traveling German journeymen—a plan partially thwarted by the Diet's ban on journeyman travel to Switzerland. [26] But to treat this group of writers as an organized political conspiracy in the sense of Young Italy was to mistake their abilities. The name Young Germany was largely a slogan with no fixed meaning except to stress that these writers were new and concerned with contemporary literary forms. [27] This is not to say that Young Germany was free of political activity, for they did make demands that were revolutionary, speaking of abolishing monarchy and the nobility, of leveling all social differences, of destroying the German Confederation, and of replacing it with a unitary democratic republic. [28] They were also close to the *Burschenschaften* and openly applauded the Hambach festival.

But they were rarely in agreement with one another nor did they ever develop a concrete course for political revolution. [29] They were even surprised to find themselves under attack.

Yet after the revolutions of 1830 and the events of the next years, it is understandable that the German governments would be sensitive to any threat of subversion, even if only of a literary nature. In October 1835 Münch raised the subject in the *Bundestag*, and in December that body acted, although, as Cartwright observed, "many persons" thought that it would have been wiser to leave it to the individual governments to "take their own steps" to deal with that group. [30] Nevertheless, the ambassadors decided that since Young Germany had attacked religion in a "most insolent manner," had "demeaned" existing social relationships, and disturbed all "manners and morality," it was necessary to the German governments uniformly to treat their writings as they would abuses of the press [31]—in effect, banning those works.

The Bavarian government was satisfied with the Diet's action. Poems such as Heine's "Song of Praise to King Ludwig," which contained the verse,

He loves the arts and pretty women,
Of whom he has portraits made;
He goes in that painted seraglio,
As art-eunuch on parade [32]

all but guaranteed that Young Germany would find little sympathy in Bavaria. Moreover, the Bavarian government was also pleased that the *Bundestag* had formulated the decree so as to come into conflict with the legislation of no member state. It was to be hoped, Gise wrote to the substitute for the absent Mieg, that this would serve as a precedent for the future, that the Diet would formulate decrees only in the most general terminology, leaving "the manner of fulfillment" to the individual governments "according to the laws of each state."

In this way, the constitutional independence of each state would be protected and the "deplorable collision" between federal decrees and state legislation would be avoided. [33]

The federal decree did, in fact, amount to a ban on the writings of Young Germany. Bavaria and other states had taken the necessary measures and the remaining governments would rapidly do so. If there were to be an influence on public opinion, that influence would be only what the governments wanted it to be. Neither literature nor simple news reporting would be allowed to escape the censor. That an article or poem accurately described a situation or event was of no matter: of prime importance was the maintenance of public peace and order. Clearly, then, anything as potentially unsettling as a novel satirical of a government or the publication of the debates of a *Landtag* had to be prevented if the system of 1834 were to be upheld.

In June 1835 Hannover registered with the *Bundestag* the complaint that some German newspapers were publishing in detail the parliamentary debates of other German states. On the basis of the Six Articles of 1832 and discussions held at the 1834 Vienna Conference, Hannover argued that nothing more might be published by periodicals than that which appeared in the newspapers of the state concerned. [34] The Diet's Press Committee proposed that reports of parliamentary transactions be taken only from official acts and newspapers published in the state concerned. Then, the editor and publisher, each time, were to print the source from which they obtained the reports that they published in their newspaper. [35] After the usual delay necessary for requesting instructions, the ambassadors accepted this proposal, decreeing it with the relative quickness attendant an issue deemed important. [36]

All too often, however, agreeing to a decree in Frankfurt and enforcing it on the district level were not necessarily accomplished with equal ease and rapidity, for the modern unitary state did not yet exist. On June 29 all Bavarian governors were informed of the federal decree of April 28, and were ordered to alert the censors as to their duty. [37] In December, however, the *Allgemeine Zeitung* of Augsburg published in an appendix several reports concerning debates in the Saxon *Landtag* that had not come from "official reports or the censored newspapers of that state." The Bavarian Ministry of the Interior quickly reminded the district governor that such acts went directly against Bavarian law and the federal agreement. He was ordered to "recommend" to the censors that they remain especially alert on that matter. [38]

This proved insufficient, for more Bavarian newspapers began to pick up the story. Instructions were again circulated to the district governors reminding them that the king had sought to protect the "free discussion" of Bavaria's internal affairs and that the government had to observe all the more carefully the sensitivities of the other states and the Confederation as a whole. Since this had already been made known to the censors, the district governors were again to instruct them most carefully and to explain to them that they were to be held responsible for any future lapses. [39] Now that this was clarified, the Bavarian government felt able to respond to Saxony's December 20 complaint by explaining what had been done, that it had been done on Bavarian initiative, and that it demonstrated clearly that Bavaria would not allow such things to take place. [40] The Saxon government was apparently satisfied, for it made no further mention of the matter.

The rigorous censorship of the *Allgemeine Zeitung* was not to last. The Hannoverian government discovered that that newspaper was publishing the debates of its *Landtag* as well as other reports concerning the constitutional crisis brought on by the new monarch. [41] In its response to Hannover's protest, the Bavarian government in effect apologized for the local censor's laxity and explained that "appropriate safeguards" had been taken to prevent a recurrence. [42] Unfortunately, Munich had been too optimistic, for on June 17 another article concerning the Hannoverian constitutional crisis appeared in the *Allgemeine Zeitung*. Because of this and because of the leading role Bavaria was playing in Frankfurt against Hannover's constitutional position, a formal protest was lodged with the federal Diet against Bavaria. [43]

This "unfriendly act" was deeply resented in Munich. Since the Bavarian government had responded "so positively" to Hannover's first complaint, it "was to be expected" that a similar approach would have been followed in this case. Certainly Hannover was aware that "absolutely nothing further" could appear in print about that state unless all legal requirements had been met in Bavaria. Hannover's action, Munich felt, had made a most "disagreeable impression." [44] Still, the district governors were again ordered to enforce the censorship and to call on the editor of the *Allgemeine Zeitung* to refrain from making hostile comments about Hannover. [45] This time the order for rigorous censorship was obeyed. Since Hannover had no further cause for complaint, the *Bundesversammlung* chose to drop the issue.

Once again the Bavarian government had found it necessary to enforce at least the spirit of a federal decree calculated to round out the system established in 1834. Once again, however, that government was able to walk the fine line of sufficient compliance so as to remain cooperative without submission, yet maintain its autonomy without appearing independent. The turn toward the restriction of liberty that the king and his government took after the Revolution of 1830 made it easier for Bavaria to fulfill her federal obligations, since her own legislation came into ever closer harmony with the sentiment of most of the federal decrees. Thus, if reporting *Landtag* discussions were a threat to peace and order in Germany, then they would not be reported.

Yet there was still a very real question of equity involved in the observance of the April 28 federal decree because enforcement, given to the individual states, was carried out in a disparate manner. Thus when a new complaint was leveled against the *Allgemeine Zeitung* for publishing the debates of Baden's parliament, the editor defended himself with the argument that so many other German governments were allowing so many exceptions to the federal decree that unless his newspaper also could publish such reports, the very existence of the newspaper was threatened. [46] This point convinced the Bavarian government to raise the question in Frankfurt. Mieg noted to his colleagues that, although Bavaria was enforcing the decree strictly, other states were not. As a result, the "most grievous disadvantage" would necessarily accrue to the editors of Bavarian newspapers. Under such circumstances, unless all suffered an equal disadvantage, Bavaria could not be expected to continue to uphold that regulation. Therefore, Mieg requested that each state declare through its ambassador in the Diet to what degree it was willing to fulfill the provisions of the decree. [47] This proposal was forwarded to the Press Committee, where it vanished. As a result, Bavaria too relaxed her enforcement of the decree; of all the states in the Confederation, only Austria continued to adhere strictly to the decree's provisions. [48] No other state seemed to take seriously the threat presented to the existence of the *Bund* by the reporting of parliamentary debates. In the long run, they were wrong.

In 1836 the *Bundestag* discovered that there was no way to punish offenses directed solely against the Confederation. To fill this gap it decreed that, since an assault directed against the *Bund* in effect constituted an assault against each member state, any conspiracy or undertaking against the "existence, integrity, security or constitution" of the Confederation was to be treated as "high treason" by the states. [49] This rather straightforward decree provides an interesting insight into the relationship of the Confederation to the states. Although dealing with an offense against the Confederation, such a crime was defined to be directed against the member states who were thus responsible for punishing the offenders. Once again the *Bundestag* acknowledged that it had no right of legislation, that only the states could deal with crimes—that is, breaches of legislation. The Confederation was not a state, and the federal Diet not a legislature. The most that the Confederation could accomplish was to see that a uniform, or at least similar, code of legislation existed in all the member states on certain topics.

Also included in the decree was the promise that extradition for political crimes within Germany would be automatic unless the fugitive were charged with a similar crime by the state to which he had fled or were a subject of that state. In an earlier discussion about extradition, Mieg had insisted upon this last point, for, as he stated, "under no circumstances" would Bavaria extradite one of her own subjects. [50] Mieg, however, was unable to convince his colleagues of the need for greater precision in the definition of extraditable crimes. [51]

Finally, on proposal of the *Präsidium*, the *Bundestag* voted to renew the decree of 1824 that limited publication in newspapers of the Diet's transactions solely to a repetition of what was contained in the public protocols. [52] Thus the system erected in 1834 in response to revolution was completed. All possible exposure to the free flow of ideas was to be denied the German people. Those most susceptible to revolutionary agitation—students and journeymen—were to be kept under careful surveillance and prevented from going to those countries where revolutionary infection was possible. Other Germans were to be spared the dis-ease that open debate on political topics might induce. The Confederation's response to the symptoms of revolution was quite obviously quarantine.

ii

Unexpectedly, the first major threat to the Confederation's stability came not from the revolutionaries but from the states themselves in their reaction to a force that had played no primary political role since the 18th century. Certainly by the beginning of the 19th century religion and religious conflict ceased to be a factor foremost in the minds of most German statesmen. Religion had discontinued its competition with the state for dominance over the individual, recognizing, for the most part, that the claims of state and church were separate and not necessarily in conflict. Contributing to this atmosphere was the tacit understanding that the Reformation was a fact and that within the boundaries of the German Confederation the major Christian confessions could coexist, however uneasily. Even the *Bundesakt* recognized this state of affairs, in Article 16 for it forbade religious discrimination in secular matters.

In Bavaria the issue had been settled, permanently it was thought, by 1818 when religious toleration and confessional parity were given consitutional sanction. At the same time this constitutional edict interpreted the Concordat of 1817 so as to give the state careful supervision over all aspects of the Church. The monarchy did appear to relinquish some of its authoirty in the 1821 Tegernsee Declaration whereby the oath on the Bavarian constitution that all members of the clergy were to take was to be understood as effective only in civil matters. The state, however, continued to base its actions on the constitutional edict and in fact surrendered few important prerogatives.

Ludwig I, although unwilling to abandon his rights over the Catholic Church, did have a deep interest in the Catholic religion. In the first years of his reign he brought the convert Joseph Görres[53] to Munich as professor of history, was closely allied with the Catholic-conservative "Eos" circle, and, in general, tried to revive Catholic piety in his lands. It is in this context that, although for political reasons Ludwig refused to allow the Jesuits the privilege of returning to Bavaria, he did push for the reopening of Bavaria's cloisters.[54] These actions, however, did not find universal approval. In particular, the *Landtag* of 1837 not only challenged the king on budgetary surpluses, [55] but also attempted to ban the use of public funds for reviving monasteries and either to ban or to limit private donations for that purpose. Although a majority of the lower chamber approved this measure, the upper chamber rejected it, allowing the king to continue his policy toward the monasteries.

Given the king's strong position, Bavaria was able to resolve successfully another problem with the Church that would bedevil other states. Since Bavaria now offered legal equality to the different Christian confessions, it was only natural that there would be an increase in the number of mixed marriages. In general the Catholic Church forbade such marriages, although dispensation could be obtained if a pledge to raise the children in the Catholic faith were given. The Protestants, on the other hand, held fast to the constitutional edict that allowed the couple to choose freely the faith in which they would educate their offspring. To prevent this potentially explosive issue from tearing Bavaria's social fabric, the government began negotiations with Rome in September 1830 in response to a papal brief of that year which stressed the Church's disapproval of mixed marriages. The papacy, however, chose rather to enforce its doctrines all the more strenuously and in the papal brief of May 1832, banned clerical participation in mixed marriages if dispensation had not been granted. A personal letter from Ludwig sent to the pope in 1834, coupled with the hint that Bavaria was willing to compel the clergy to obey the constitution, brought about a change of attitude in Rome. Instructions thus were sent to the clergy in Bavaria, permitting them to proceed with a mixed marriage even without an assurance that resultant offspring would have a Catholic upbringing. [56] Since this proved satisfactory to the Bavarian government, the threat of conflict between Church and state ceased.

Prussia was less fortunate. Although it is beyond the scope of this study to examine in detail the so-called *Kölner Wirren*, [57] a brief summary will provide the perspective from which to view the tensions between Munich and Berlin. During the concluding decades of the 18th and the first years of the 19th centuries, the clergy of the three confessions in Prussia tended to treat the question of mixed marriage in a spirit of enlightened toleration. Until 1803 Prussian law decreed that the male children of a mixed marriage should follow the religion of their father, female children that of their mother, although if the parents agreed differently about the religious upbringing of their children, the state would defer. In 1803, with the inclusion of territory with a Catholic majority, the law was altered so that in those lands all children had to follow the religion of their father while the clergy was prohibited from demanding a promise concerning the religious upbringing from the prospective couple. A third approach was used in the Rhineland territories given to Prussia in 1814 in that the existing civil code—stating that children of mixed marriages be raised in their father's religion—was simply continued. [58] To end this anomaly, the decree of 1803 was extended to all Prussian territory in 1825.

Although the Catholic Church was undergoing a religious rejuvenation in the Rhineland, Archbishop Ferdinand Graf Spiegel of Cologne chose to avoid a direct challenge to the power of the state and the Vatican went so far in the spirit of compromise that it recognized the validity of civil marriages in 1830. The death of Pius VIII in that year and of Spiegel in 1835

reversed the Church's conciliatory attitude. The new archbishop, Clemens von Droste-Vischering, refused to allow any
deviation from Church canons, bringing him into direct
confrontation with Prussian civil law. Since the archbishop
would neither comply nor resign, on November 20, 1837, he
was arrested and imprisoned.

This act signaled the beginning of open warfare between
Church and state in Prussia. Only the death of Frederick
William III in 1840 allowed an amicable resolution of the
conflict. The new king, strongly influenced by the Romantics'
perception of the medieval Christian state, saw Church and
state as partners. Consequently, the conflict between the two
institutions had to be resolved, and by 1841 the difficulties
between Rome and Berlin were all but settled. Droste-Vischering was replaced as archbishop in all but name by a
compromise candidate, proposed by Bavaria, and the Prussian
state renounced all authority in the question of mixed
marriages. [59] While the Catholic Church regained many of the
rights of self-control lost over the centuries to the Prussian
state, Frederick William IV succeeded in ending the strife that
threatened to destroy his kingdom.

By the time that Frederick William IV had ascended his
Prussian throne, the controversy had already transcended
Prussian boundaries. In particular, relations between Prussia
and Bavaria rapidly deteriorated so as to threaten the stability
of the entire Confederation. It began with the publication in
January 1838 of the pamphlet *Athanasius*, which was less a
defense of the Catholic Church than a public attack against
Prussia. The author, Joseph Görres, was a Rhineland convert
to Catholicism who, on invitation of Ludwig I, had come to
Munich a decade earlier to accept a professorship at Ludwig-
Maximilian University. From the safety of Munich, Görres was
able to attach religious to political conflicts and in the process
created a movement of political Catholicism that would evolve

into a full-scale political party after 1848.

In April 1838 the group that had gathered around Görres published the *Historische-Politische Blätter*, the first German political Catholic periodical that, although published in Munich, drew contributions from all over the Confederation and made its voice heard even beyond the boundaries of Germany. This, of course, put the Bavarian government into an uncomfortable position. Although Ludwig was on excellent terms with the Prussian court, he felt called upon to defend the Church in Germany, [60] and not only ignored early Prussian complaints against Görres, but gave the Bavarian press free reign to discuss publicly the measures taken by Prussia in Cologne. As a result, Bavarian public opinion quickly turned against Prussia. [61]

If the official *Münchner Politische Zeitung* remained within the limits of good taste, the strongly pro-Catholic *Neue Würzburger Zeitung* under Ernst Zander did not, and the echo from North Germany was no less vigorous. [62] When August Graf von Dönhoff, the Prussian ambassador to Munich, objected, instructions were sent to the Bavarian district governor to personally take charge of the censorship of that newspaper, to suppress all personal attacks and insults against Prussia, but to continue to allow free discussion of the issue. [63]

This did not satisfy the Prussian government, and Dönhoff directed a flood of protests to Gise and the Bavarian government, protests that barely remained within the bounds of civility. [64] These personal attacks resulted in an ill-feeling that influenced Bavarian-Prussian relations in the *Bundestag* as late as 1845. [65] Moreover, rather than attempting to resolve the conflict through bilateral discussion and compromise, Dönhoff threatened to take the matter to the federal Diet for resolution. But there were those, like Wrede, in the Bavarian government who were willing to overlook such excesses in favor of compromise. Wrede hoped to convince the king to stop the

Bavarian newspapers from discussing the *Kölner Wirren*, although Ludwig was "not entirely impartial" in this matter and was "seriously inclined" to take the side of the Bavarian press. Moreover, Wrede hoped for moderation in Berlin, although Dönhoff seemed to expect some form of satisfaction (*Genugtuung*) from Bavaria. Above all, Wrede wanted to keep the matter away from the *Bundestag*. [66] This desire was also shared by Metternich, who, in a letter to the Austrian ambassador in Munich, noted that German public opinion had already become overly excited by events in Cologne and that it would only grow worse if the conflict between Church · and state developed into an open quarrel between German governments. "Where would Germany be," he asked, "if the old conflict between the confessions" were to become "a topic for discussion in the federal Diet?" [67]

On March 11 Prussia demanded that Bavaria suppress the *Neue Würzburger Zeitung* as "satisfaction for the past and a guarantee for the future." [68] Gise responded that this was impossible according to Bavarian law, and, in a carefully worded explanation, he argued that Bavaria had every right to comment on events in Cologne since subsequent papal declarations could not avoid having an impact on Church matters in Bavaria. However, the Bavarian government had no intention of making common cause with the opinion of any journal; rather, Bavaria's comments were to be understood in a sense of friendly esteem. Gise pointed out that it was no secret that the discussions with Prussia were "most undesirable and distasteful" in the way they had been handled. Still, the censor who was to oversee the *Neue Würzburger Zeitung* had been punished, and the punishment and the reasons for it had been made known to the entire governmental council—something that should have given full satisfaction to the Prussian government.

Having established this point, Gise then proceeded to reject any "charge of complicity" with the censors or authorities who were too lax in regulating Bavaria's "legally existing freedom of the press." Moreover, since there were Bavarian journals that had been taking the Prussian viewpoint, the Bavarian press could not be faulted for one-sidedness. Bavaria would continue to support freedom of thought "even if that were directed against herself," but she would also see that the "rules of decency" were not exceeded nor the honor of any government injured. Bavaria, he concluded, had done that to this point, and "she continues to do it now." [69]

By this time the issue had clearly evolved as Metternich had foreseen. Not Church-state conflict, but a quarrel between two German governments over secular matters had taken center stage. Bavaria, Gise wrote, understood that Prussia had a legitimate complaint and objected only to the manner in which it was being presented. Because Prussia had taken her position "falsely," the Bavarian government could not retreat from its own position. At all costs, however, Bavaria wanted to avoid a division between the German princes and thus had limited her defense to "the most necessary" elements. [70] But Prussia was now of a mind to make a formal complaint at the *Bundestag*, an action that Bavaria continued to hope to avoid. If, however, no means could be found to prevent Prussia from going to Frankfurt, then the Bavarian government had its counteractions already prepared in order to demonstrate that Prussia's complaint was without merit. [71]

No one, except perhaps the Prussian government, wanted the matter brought up in a formal session of the federal Diet. Most of the German governments preferred not to risk damaging the federal system and institutions solely for the suppression of one newspaper. And, as Cartwright observed, if Prussia succeeded in obtaining the suppression, Bavaria would probably refuse to comply, and the *Bundestag* would not use force to suppress a newspaper. An "arrangement" of Bavaria's differences with Prussia "without reference" to the Diet was "the more to be wished for," since that would prevent any chance of Bavaria's particularist sentiments from "being manifested upon this occasion."[72] It was for these reasons that Austria chose to mediate, and Münch counseled delay to the Prussian ambassador. Indeed, he was induced to hold back his statement since it contained such "violent language" as to guarantee a break between Bavaria and Prussia.[73]

Meanwhile, although constitutionally unable to suppress the offending newspaper, the Bavarian government was beginning to take action. In a personal letter to Mieg, Ludwig wrote that, if it could be done "without injuring the constitution," he would prohibit Zander from continuing to edit the *Neue Würzburger Zeitung*. At the same time he stressed how much he hoped that the *Bundestag* could be kept out of the matter.[74] Gise then instructed Mieg to explain to his colleagues that it was not the Bavarian government's intention to offend or injure a friendly government "such as Prussia." As evidence, Mieg was to cite Bavaria's "decisively" expressed pronouncements that were supported by carrying out "legally available punishments" against the culpable officials. Vigorous actions, "including dismissals," had been directed against those censors, and appropriate measures had been directed against Zander. Among other things, it was pointed out to the editor that if he were a foreigner, his continued presence in Bavaria "would not be tolerated." Yet, Gise concluded, in spite of all that Bavaria had done, Prussia apparently was still not satisfied and wanted federal intervention. Therefore, if Prussia persisted and succeeded in raising the issue in Frankfurt, Mieg was to make countercomplaints and demand "satisfaction" from Prussia—but this was to be done only in such a way as to demonstrate that Bavaria wanted to maintain good relations with Prussia but felt compelled to defend herself. No avenues were to be closed, so that Prussia could judge fairly what

Bavaria was offering.[75]

The last part of this instruction proved unnecessary because, as Ludwig joyfully wrote Mieg, Zander had been removed as editor of the newspaper.[76] Indeed, below the masthead of issue 151 of the *Neue Würzburger Zeitung* appeared a notice that the paper would no longer appear under Zander's responsibility, for, he wrote, he saw himself "obliged to resign as editor."[77] In this way Bavarian law remained inviolate: the paper had not been suppressed, but rather, the editor had been induced to resign his office. With the constitutional issue so neatly resolved, Bavaria was able to complete those measures necessary to assuage Prussia's injured pride. The errant censor was suspended from all government employment for five years,[78] a note from the Bavarian minister of the interior to the provincal government made clear that both the newspaper and the censor would suffer heavy fines and possibly worse should there be a repetition, [79] and Ludwig personally wrote to the Prussian government explaining that the insult had been done neither with his knowledge nor with his permission. Prussia was placated[80] and instructed her ambassador in Frankfurt not to present his declaration against Bavaria since the government was "completely satisfied" with Bavaria's actions.[81]

What is of particular interest in the whole affair is the attitude taken toward the *Bundesversammlung.* Since that body had the responsibility for resolving conflicts between member states, one might have expected Prussia and Bavaria to welcome its involvement. Instead, most of the members worked resolutely to prevent the Diet from considering the problem in an official manner. Only Prussia, the aggrieved state, wanted to introduce its complaint in Frankfurt, and that, in such a way to force Bavaria openly to give satisfaction to Prussia. It was exactly this potential humiliation of a powerful member and its all but certain rejection that caused the other states to attempt extrainstitutional mediation. All were well aware of the threat to the Confederation that any other course posed. In a period when religious differences were becoming politicized, when German public opinion was making its voice heard, if not yet felt—clearly, this was not the time to test the strength of the only institution that could maintain the status quo. It is true, of course, that the issue had gotten out of hand because of the coupling of religious with political issues in Prussia and because, in defense of its internal prerogatives, the Prussian government had demanded that Bavaria act in a way contrary to her constitution. Bavaria's monarch, although he would never surrender a single constitutional right and would interpret the constitution in his favor as often as possible, still felt obligated to abide by each and every provision in that document. Consequently, it was only after a constitutional bypass could be found that Ludwig felt able to offer Prussia the satisfaction that she deserved. How much easier if the constitution could have been dispensed with.

...
iii

That, at least, was the attitude taken by Hannover's king, who, as events in Cologne were serving to unsettle Germany, not only succeeded in producing a crisis in Hannover, but also managed to shake the entire Confederation. Briefly stated, when Ernst August succeeded to the throne of Hannover in 1837, he considered the constitution that his brother had granted four years earlier to be an impediment to his right of unlimited sovereignty. Accordingly, on November 1, 1837, he issued a patent that abrogated that constitution and replaced it with the more conservative one of 1819. In their well-known protest[82] seven professors of the University of Göttingen condemned their king's illegal behavior, resulting in the dismissal of all seven from the University.

Since there appeared to be no recourse available in Hannover, supporters of the "Göttingen Seven" and others who hoped to have their constitution restored turned to the *Bundestag* for help. That they should do so was perfectly proper since the Diet was justified, even obligated, by Articles 31, 56, and 61 of the *Wiener Schlussakt* to intervene in the constitutional conflict. This was clearly understood not only by the petitioners but also by the Bavarian government, which would spearhead the campaign to force the *Bundestag* to fulfill its obligations.

The first of the petitions directed to Frankfurt came in March 1838 from the magistrates of Osnabrück, acting as a *Wahlkorporation*. This petition, drawn up by Carl Strüve, Osnabrück's mayor, requested the *Bundestag* to reinstate the Hannoverian constitution of 1833 and claimed that the city had the legal right to call on the federal Diet for assistance.[83] Hannover, of course, rejected the arguments that the repeal of the constitution had been done illegitimately, that Osnabrück had a right to appeal to the *Bundesversammlung,* and that the Diet had competence in the matter. The other ambassadors were unsure as to which argument to follow. There was even confusion as to which committee ought to take responsibility for the petition or whether the governments should first be asked for their opinions. Finally, it was decided to follow custom and send both Osnabrück's petition and Hannover's response to the Committee for Complaints (of which Mieg was a member).[84]

As much as the ambassadors detested the thought of intervening in the internal affairs of a larger member state, many did recognize that "the eyes of the whole of Germany" were directed toward the *Bundestag* and the course it would choose,[85] and they realized that that body would be placed in a most unfavorable light if such an important matter were not carefully treated. Mieg observed that the ambassadors representing the constitutional states appeared to wish to move with extreme caution due to "an increasing respect" for their own *Stände.*[86]

The Bavarian government was already well aware of the "inherent importance" of the problem for the constitutional states. Still, Gise preferred to move cautiously and weigh all factors before Bavaria could declare her position. He recognized that Hannover was pushing for the Diet to act rapidly so that there would be no time to fully consider Osnabrück's petition. It would be far better, he felt, if the normal procedures of the *Bundestag* were followed so as to avoid all precipitous acts.[87] Gise's caution was predicated on the fear that Bavaria would find herself isolated if she moved too quickly. Bavarian ambassadors were accordingly instructed to sound out the other constitutional governments to see whether a joint statement might be presented in Frankfurt. At this point, however, Württemberg was reluctant to form any specific position until the Committee for Complaints could study all sides of the issue and produce its report. And Metternich, too, was working to keep the *Bundesversammlung* from even dealing with the topic.[88]

Gise was still convinced that the constitutional states had to have a unified position. He asserted that there was no doubt that a *Korporation* had the right to complain in constitutional matters, and in the present case this right was all the more secure since Hannover had undercut her own position through an "incredible confusion" of monarchical and constitutional principles.[89] Indeed, the argument that Hannover presented to the Diet was fully superfluous and confused at best. Consequently, the Hannoverian government's later arguments were limited to disputing Isnabrück's right to act in place of a parliament and direct a complaint on parliamentary matters to the *Bundesversammlung.*[90] But this request to reject Osnabrück's petitions and others supporting it served only to prevent the committee from presenting its report, for rules of procedure required that the committee examine Hannover's new declaration and include it in the final report.[91]

Before the committee could release its new report, events in Hannover took a new twist. The *Landtag* elected on the basis of the 1819 constitution voted on June 25 that their king had acted illegally and that Hannover's only valid constitution was the one of 1833. Ernst August's response to a request to hold elections for a new *Landtag* on the basis of that constitution was to prorogue the Lower Chamber. Before it dispersed, however, it voted to request the federal Diet's assistance in restoring the legitimate constitution.[92]

This served to reinforce the conclusions drawn by the Committee for Complaints, which reported that the *Bundestag* was competent to deal with the question, that individuals or corporations such as Osnabrück had the right to complain in constitutional matters when there was no other course of appeal. Yet, instead of then calling on the Diet to act, the committee recommended only that the ambassadors request instructions from their governments.[93] This was done largely because of pressure from Austria. Delay might allow the issue to vanish of its own accord and would at least allow the Austrian government the opportunity to convince the other governments that there was no reason to compel a member to revive a liberal constitution.

Consequently, the issue was no longer whether Ernst August had the right to arbitrarily revoke a valid constitution, nor whether he had acted in a legitimate manner. The *Bundestag* had been detoured and was now concerned only with the question of whether Osnabrück and other petitioners had the right to request federal assistance and, if so, whether the *Bundesversammlung* had the competence necessary to judge the issue. Clearly, Hannover and Austria hoped to contrive a negative response, making all further discussion moot, whereas the constitutional states hoped to move rapidly from these preliminaries to the main question.[94]

On September 6, however, the federal Diet voted nine to six to inform Osnabrück that it lacked the legitimacy necessary to complain to the *Bundestag*.[95] When Mieg protested that his formal request that Hannover explain her actions had not yet been voted upon, a majority joined with Münch's ruling that since Osnabrück's petition had been rejected, Hannover had no further responsibilities vis-à-vis the *Bund*. Mieg, however, refused to accept the rejection of the petition as final and compelled Münch to state that he had no intention of suppressing the matter. Hoping to placate the constitutional states, Münch proposed rewriting the decree so as to include an "expectation" that Hannover would give a further explanation to the Diet as Bavaria wanted. Mieg, however, was still not satisfied with "such a generally expressed expectation," for it left the "further course" of the matter solely in the Hannoverian government's hands. Therefore he proposed that Hannover be given a time limit within which to respond, a recommendation that the Hannoverian ambassador accepted.[96]

A few weeks later, after a series of private discussions with Münch that resulted in some minor modifications,[97] the Hannoverian ambassador presented to the *Bundestag* a short statement, supplemented by a thick packet of documents, reiterating the Hannoverian position. Mieg was thereupon surprised to discover that, rather than sending the statement to the committee, it was to be forwarded directly to the states, thus cutting off the Diet from any future discussion of the matter.[98] With Münch's assistance, Ernst August had undercut a federal decree: rather than replying to the *Bundestag*, which had requested it, his answer was directed to the member states separately. In this way, the decree was effectively nullified without the appearance of open opposition to the Confederation.[99]

And it almost worked. Over the next few days, however, Mieg was able to read Hannover's entire statement and to sound out the reaction of his colleagues. In general the response was taken as "entirely unsatisfactory," and even Münch realized that the matter was not yet settled. [100] The Bavarian government was also convinced that the issue could not be dropped. It accused Ernst August of violating the *Wiener Schlussakt* in that rather than following the provisions contained in the constitution of 1833, he had altered it arbitrarily. Even if he claimed a "substantive legal basis" for his actions, he should have considered that those same rights would be endangered if the letter of the law were not followed. Nothing could have prevented the Hannoverian crown from proclaiming those substantive rights, even if the constitution of 1833 had remained in effect until properly amended. And if irreconcilable differences remained between the government and the *Stände* over the limits of those rights, the federal constitution provided a method for surmounting even this difficulty. The federal decree of October 30, 1834, had anticipated the problem by establishing a court of arbitration (*Schiedsgericht*). Ludwig was convinced that Article 56 of the *Schlussakt*, which allowed the *landständische* constitutions to be altered only in a constitutional manner, gave the *Bundestag* the competence to intervene. Since Hannover was attempting "to abrogate the effectiveness of the Confederation," Mieg was instructed to "foster private understandings" with the ambassadors of the other constitutional states to be able to present a uniform declaration to the Diet. But Mieg was to avoid dealing with the substantive legal relationships that were to be decided either by the Hannoverian king and the "legitimate" parliament or, that failing, by a court of arbitration. The *Bundestag* was to deal only with the method, not the substance, of constitutional alteration. Mieg was also to express Bavaria's concern that the continued legal confusion in Hannover could be used by the revolutionary party as a way of attacking the monarchical principle. [101]

Even while vacationing in Naples, the Bavarian king kept close watch on the Hannoverian constitutional affair. He had agreed to postpone a formal Bavarian statement in Frankfurt at Austria's request,[102] but the hope that the conflict could be resolved without the Diet could not be fulfilled.[103] Although Ernst August had recalled his parliament on March 2, 1839, he felt obliged to prorogue it again as it continued its opposition. Therefore, Ludwig decided that the *Bundestag* was again the only proper forum for action. Mieg was reminded, however, to deal only with the formal question of the Diet's competence and to avoid the appearance of trying to influence the further development of the constitution itself.[104]

This, then, is the key to understanding what the king had in mind. Bavaria remained true to her approach to the Confederation, namely, that although the internal affairs of the members were beyond the federal Diet's competence, those same states had an obligation to fulfill the responsibilities that they voluntarily assumed by accepting the federal constitution. Consequently, what mattered in this case was not the fact that a constitution was altered to be less liberal, but rather the manner in which the alteration took place. Ernst August had violated his federal obligations, and this had to be rectified if the Confederation were to continue to have meaning.

Quiet behind-the-scenes diplomacy ended when Mieg was instructed to give Bavaria's position at the next opportunity. Delay, he was told, benefited only the demagogues, whereas maintaining federal rights in an impartial manner would best serve the monarchical principle and preserve peace in Germany.[105] Accordingly, on April 26, Bavaria, Baden, Württemberg, and Saxony renewed the discussion of federal obligations and rights in the Hannoverian affair. Bavaria's declaration [106] was made directly in Ludwig's name, a course rarely followed, making all the stronger the importance that the king attached to the matter. The British ambassador reported that Ludwig was convinced that "all confidence in the good faith" of the German governments would be destroyed unless a speedy stop were put to Ernst August's unconstitutional behavior. Were the *Bundestag* to accept that violation of its constitution with no response, it would be clear to the German people that all control over the behavior of those princes who wished to undermine their constitutions would be "at an end." [107]

The Hannoverian ambassador made one last effort to postpone discussion of the issue by requesting time for his government to respond so that all arguments might appear simultaneously in the Diet's protocol. Mieg objected and observed that Hannover had had sufficient time and opportunity to produce everything that she considered necessary and that "such continually renewed delays" finally had to cease. It was now time, he believed, for the *Bundesversammlung* to carry out the *Schlussakt*. The majority, however, disagreed and voted instead to send all declarations to committee and to request Hannover to respond within four weeks. [108]

When Hannover let even this time period lapse, the Bavarian government demonstrated both its impatience and its pertinacity by instructing Mieg to consult with his colleagues so that they might be empowered by their governments to act with Bavaria to put the federal decree into effect. [109] Moreover, Mieg was instructed to work with the other ambassadors of like-minded governments to secure the election of a special committee to deal with the Hannoverian constitutional matter. [110]

Finally, on June 27, Hannover gave an extremely lengthy and detailed defense of her actions. Mieg then proposed that a special committee be selected, but he was able to muster only seven votes. The majority again chose to support Austria's proposal that the ambassadors request instructions from their governments, [111] clearly a stratagem for delay. Mieg, who had taken the lead in mobilizing the constitutional states against Hannover, was disgusted. He noted that events had confirmed again the "one-sidedness" that characterized the course of events in the *Bundestag*. Consequently, even if "serious confusion" could be avoided, the "regrettable result" would be a loss of trust in the federal Assembly and "an even greater strengthening" of the revolutionary party in Germany. [112]

Still, although the majority would join with Austria and Prussia in deciding that the *Bundestag* lacked the competence necessary, Bavaria and her allies refused to allow the matter to die before obtaining for it the "discussion and investigation which they consider [ed] to be called for." [113] Then, during the session of August 22, 1839, the important states gave their positions, and, for the first time, Austria openly sided with Hannover. [114] The ultimate resolution of the matter was now clear to all. Even Mieg took great pains to point out that everything he had done took place with the "assurance of the unaltered friendly disposition" that Bavaria felt toward Hannover and Austria and that differences of opinion were only over method, not purpose. [115]

One last hurdle had to be overcome before the Hannoverian constitutional matter could be laid to rest in Frankfurt. It was discovered that Münch had not followed the usual and proper procedure concerning petitions. All petitions addressed to the *Bundesversammlung* were normally sent to the Committee for Complaints and duly noted in the Diet's protocols. Münch, however, had returned to the sender each petition dealing with Hannover with no mention to the ambassadors. When the Saxon ambassador raised the issue, Münch tried to justify his actions by arguing that the petitions contained material "improper for communication" to the *Bundestag*—but he convinced no one. To avoid further embarrassment, Münch then abruptly left the session, but later gave private assurances that all future petitions would be properly treated. Britain's ambassador correctly concluded that if this had been passed over quietly, Austria "would have acquired the power" of allowing only that information to reach the *Bundestag* "as tended to support the political views" of the presiding ambassador. The federal Diet would then have become "a blind agent without influence," [116] acting only at Austrian discretion.

Finally, on September 5, the *Bundestag* decreed that it lacked the competence to involve itself in that "internal state affair," although the decree did express the hope that Hannover's king and *Stände* would meet to delineate their respective rights. Ironically and symbolically, this decree was imparted not to the complainant, but only to the Hannoverian government. [117] Ernst August chose to interpret the decree as a vindication of all that he had done and directed his ambassador to declare his pleasure that the *Bundestag* had acknowledged that he had legitimately replaced the constitution of 1833 with that of 1819. The constitutional states naturally disputed this interpretation, for it would have otherwise appeared as if they were turning away from their own constitutions. The result would have been an exacerbation of the relationship between those governments and their parliaments and subjects. Bavaria in particular wanted to act in common with the other constitutional states to dispute the Hannoverian declaration and to quiet the effects that it had on their subjects. [118]

Yet it is true that the *Bundesversammlung* had set back the cause of constitutionalism in Germany. The decree of September 5 implied that the Diet would ignore Article 56 of the *Schlussakt* in the future and that any ruler could arbitrarily abrogate an already established constitution. Article 56's double edge—neither revolutionary nor unilateral change in a state constitution—was now blunted so as to allow its use by the sovereign, not the populace. While this might be seen as a victory for the policy of Metternich and the reaction, it is better seen as a weakening of the *Bundestag* itself. By denying its own competence in a situation clearly outlined in the federal constitution, the Diet had placed itself in the position either of limiting its own authority or of acting arbitrarily on the basis of no principle. The result in either case is the same: the *Bundesversammlung* had undercut its authority and its foundation. When challenged by an apparently more consistent moral authority in 1848, the weakness induced a decade earlier would prevent the *Bundestag* from offering an effective response. [119]

iv

While the *Bundestag* was undermining its moral foundations in inter-German affairs, it was simultaneously attempting to end particularist jealousies so that the Confederation might at least fulfill its role of maintaining the external security of Germany. Although there was nearly unanimous agreement on the desirability of a fourth federal fortress to be built in South Germany, agreement was lacking on where it should be built and what other fortifications might be necessary to repel a French attack. Money had been set aside from the indemnity that France had paid in 1815 to construct a fortress in South Germany, and in 1818 the federal Military Commission [120] agreed unanimously to use that French indemnity to erect a fortress at Germersheim, in the Bavarian Rhineland. The Commission was unable, however, to agree as to whether Ulm or Rastatt, some fifteen miles southwest of Karlsruhe, should also be fortified as South Germany's principal arsenal. A report to this effect was sent to the federal Diet, which did nothing, [121] thus allowing Bavaria to hold on to the fifteen million francs and to keep the interest that it earned.

By 1834 Bavaria had become convinced of the need to fortify Germersheim and submitted plans to the *Bundestag* for a single fortress on the left bank of the Rhine. Baden, however, protested that her needs required a *tête de pont* on the right bank in connection with the main fortress and, after much discussion, convinced Bavaria of this necessity even though expenses would exceed the fifteen million francs. In April 1835 Bavaria resubmitted building plans "in strict conformity" with Baden's wishes and offered to pay all expenses if a Bavarian officer would be the fortress's sole commander. One year later Baden reversed her position and proposed that Rastatt rather than Germersheim be the fourth federal fortress. Germersheim, it was argued, did nothing to protect Baden, although what was probably meant was that Baden was afraid of a strong permanent Bavarian force on her frontier [122] when it was known that Bavaria wanted to regain the Palatine lands on the right bank of the Rhine lost to Baden in 1815. The other states chose to ignore Baden's protests and in June 1836 accepted in their entirety Bavaria's plans for making Germersheim the fourth federal fortress.

Baden refused to concede defeat and demanded that Germersheim be garrisoned by the troops of both Bavaria and Baden with command alternating between the two states, that Germersheim replace Landau as a federal fortress, and that Landau be treated merely as a Bavarian fortress. Baden's ambassador had discussed his government's demands with Münch, who opposed them, but had not consulted with Bavaria, which in any case would not wish to surrender her favorable conditions in Landau. [123] As a result, Baden was unable to win support among the other states, and Germersheim would indeed become the fourth federal fortress—although this point was not yet clear to all.

The selection of Germersheim as a federal fortress did not, however, complete the defensive perimeter, for Southwest Germany remained exposed to attack. Bavaria's king, who was deeply interested in the defense of Germany, had decided as early as 1834 that a federal fortress on the upper Rhine was necessary since events had invalidated the earlier assumption of Swiss neutrality should France go to war with the German states. Although the revolutions of 1830 had had no direct impact on the Swiss federal government, several of the previously reactionary canton governments were replaced by more liberal ones, and by 1833 most of the cantons had liberal constitutions that guaranteed freedom of the press and popular sovereignty. These cantons then became a refuge for German radicals, who openly urged their hosts to oppose the reactionary German governments. Thus, to complete the lines of defense, Ludwig believed that a fortress should be erected at Donaueschingen, in Baden, some thirty miles east of Freiburg. [124]

Although Baden and Württemberg agreed that a fortress on the upper Rhine was necessary, they chose to propose to the *Bundesversammlung* that it should be erected in Rastatt. Münch noted that the Military Commission had already chosen Ulm to protect Germany's southwestern borders, although it had not yet been decided who ought to build that fortress. Münch did agree, however, that another fortress was necessary and called for instructions to decide between Rastatt and Donaueschingen. [125]

Bavaria was not yet willing to accept as final the decision that Ulm would be fortified because it seemed that the fortress, if erected, would be garrisoned by an Austrian contingent and commanded by an Austrian officer. [126] Moreover, Ludwig felt that the Bavarian fortress at Ingolstadt was much more appropriate to be the principal arsenal of South Germany due to its location, [127] a view strongly disputed by Prussia, which felt that it was too isolated and too expensive to serve in the defense of South Germany. [128]

Finally, after each ambassador had received instructions and delivered his government's argument, the *Bundestag* decreed that the Military Commission should reconsider the question of a South German fortress [129] even though it had been long since apparent that, from a strictly military point of view, Ulm and Donaueschingen ought to be fortified and that Rastatt was superfluous since Germersheim was to be a complete fortress. Perhaps that is why the topic vanished from open discussion, although Baden and Württemberg frequently requested over the next four years that the commission make its report to the *Bundestag*.

Meanwhile, there was a great deal of diplomatic activity between the courts of Munich and Karlsruhe. Bavaria was requesting a portion of Baden's territory on the right bank of the Rhine so that a bridgehead for Germersheim might be constructed. Baden was willing to give up some of her land but made this contingent upon Bavaria's acceptance of the erection of a fourth federal fortress at Rastatt. Bavaria was not yet prepared to accept and wanted to bring the matter to the Diet for resolution. This only served, however, to reawaken the old fear that Bavaria was attempting to regain the right bank Palatinate. Moreover, Bavaria now seemed prepared to join with Austria and allow Ulm rather than any place in Baden to become the fortress designed to guard Southwest Germany. [130] The result was to bring Baden and Württemberg into closer cooperation and to widen the differences between them and Bavaria.

Finally, in realization that twenty-four years had elapsed since the original treaties provided the funds for building fortresses in South Germany, the three South German states agreed to have fortresses constructed both at Ulm and at Rastatt. Unfortunately, while Munich desired to begin with the larger fortress at Ulm, Karlsruhe and Stuttgart argued that work should first begin at Rastatt. [131] Moreover, the Bavarian government now linked the question of the fourth federal fortress to the bridgehead for Germersheim and refused to present its final declaration concerning Rastatt and Ulm to the *Bund* until Baden ceded the necessary right bank territory to Bavaria. As a result, the amount of mutual confidence necessary for the erection of an effective defensive system in South Germany was lacking.[132]

By April 1840, however, these petty jealousies and misgivings were set aside and Bavaria decided to accept Baden's proposals: Ulm would be the major fortress and Rastatt would be developed into a second-class stronghold to strengthen the frontier with Switzerland. The fear that France would try sooner or later to regain the boundaries of the Rhine, which the French press tended to encourage periodically,[133] had become sufficiently ominous to convince the Bavarian government that speed was necessary and that an effective defense could be conducted in this case only on Baden's terms. Thus after twenty-five years of delay and six months more of fruitless negotiations, the German Confederation would finally begin to erect the fortresses necessary for the defense of South Germany.

Only after the South German states had resolved their differences did the *Bundesversammlung* again involve itself. Not until February 1841 did the Diet's Military Affairs Committee finally issue its report. The Military Commission, it noted, had decided that at least two fortresses were needed to properly defend the upper Rhine: a central and principal arsenal and a first-rank federal fortress to defend the border and to join the defense of the upper Rhine with that of the middle Rhine. Since the South German states had already agreed that the former was to be erected at Ulm and the latter at Rastatt, it is no surprise to read that the Military Commission argued for precisely this same arrangement, and the two fortresses were to be constructed simultaneously. The Commission also recommended that the government in whose state the fortresses were to be erected pay only for those buildings to be used by the peacetime garrison, leaving the remaining expenses to the Confederation. The Commission wisely chose to leave to the

Bundestag the political question of the territorial ruler's rights and title to the fortresses. [134] The Military Affairs Committee picked up on this point and proposed that even in peacetime, troops from other states be represented in each of the new fortresses so as to symbolize their special tie to the Confederation. In particular, the committee recommended that elements of the artillery and engineering units in each fortress be supplied by Austria. [135]

Bavaria, Baden, Württemberg, and Hesse jointly expressed their pleasure that federal fortresses were finally to be constructed on the upper Rhine, but they did not accept the idea of paying for buildings needed by the peacetime garrison and questioned the Military Commission's apportioning of troops for those garrisons since they preferred only a minimal number of Austrian troops in each fortress. [136] The South German states were able to convince the others of the justice of their argument, for the decree establishing Ulm and Rastatt as federal fortresses yielded to those states on every point. [137] The only question remaining was how Württemberg and Bavaria would share command of the fortress at Ulm.

The problem arose from the nature and location of that fortress. Although Ulm is situated in Württemberg, the boundary between Württemberg and Bavaria at that point was on the left bank of the Danube River. Thus, although the major fortress was to be built in Württemberg, a bridgehead was to be erected on the Bavarian right bank. Originally, Württemberg had planned to name both the governor and the commander of the fortress and, in time of peace, to leave to Bavaria only the right to garrison the bridgehead. For her part, Bavaria wanted to supply one-half of the garrison for the main fortress and claimed the right to name the military commander. [138]

In February 1842, the two states met in Stuttgart and, with Prussian mediation, were able to agree that Württemberg

would name the governor and Bavaria the military commander and that in peacetime Bavarian troops would garrison
the bridgehead while Württemberg garrisoned the main
fortress, the troops to remain under their own state's officers. In
time of war, this division was to cease. [139] Moreover, they agreed
that the main fortress would be built by Württemberg, the
bridgehead by Bavaria, but that the building was to be
coordinated by a joint commission whose chairmanship would
alternate between the two building directors every four
months. [140] Now that the pride of all states had been properly
assuaged, the construction of those fortresses needed for the
defense of South Germany could commence.

  This result was obviously not one desired by France, against
whom these fortresses were directed. Accordingly, she had
attempted to prevent their erection by diplomatic means and,
that failing, attempted to increase her influence in Bavaria by
offering commercial relief for the Bavarian Rhineland. [141] In
March 1837 negotiations had gotten so far as to allow French
and Bavarian ministers to initial an agreement jointly to build
a railroad from Strasbourg to the Rheinschanz (now Ludwigs-
hafen) with a spur from Strasbourg to Saarbrücken. However,
the Bavarian government was divided over the advisability of
such an agreement. Wrede, for example, believed that provisioning the Rheinkreis industries with French coal was only a
pretext hiding some ulterior motive. He told Münch, who was
passing through Munich, that there were plans to extend that
railroad from the Rheinschanz to Mainz, running between the
fortresses of Landau and Germersheim—something which,
from a military point of view, he looked upon with great
skepticism since he recognized that the French forces stationed
in Strasbourg could thus be moved to attack Mainz within
twelve hours. Wrede was convinced that the Confederation
would have to approve any such plan, since it would "sub-
stantially alter" the German defensive system.

When Münch then remarked in a conversation with Gise that building such a railroad would make the federal fortresses superfluous, Gise responded that Bavaria had no other choice. It was not that Bavaria wanted to follow an anticonfederate course or that the importance of the fortresses for Bavaria and Germany was underestimated. However, as both Gise and the king made clear, not military but economic concerns were primary in this matter. Baden had declared that she would construct a railroad from Kehl, about four miles east of Strasbourg, to Mannheim and then on to Mainz. If built, this railroad would serve to draw away the "entirety of trade" in Bavaria and would lead to the ruin of the Bavarian Rhineland. The king and his minister disagreed only in that Gise saw this as unavoidable, whereas Ludwig remained hopeful. He was aware, however, of "all inconveniences" caused by the Franco-Bavarian negotiations and was willing to renounce any subsequent agreement if he could be certain that Baden would gain no economic advantage. [142] Clearly Ludwig hoped to use the negotiations with France as a device with which to bring direct or indirect pressure on Baden and to force her to forego developing a railroad system in the Rhine valley. Baden, however, looked upon this track not only as a way of developing an important trade route, but also as a means for tying together the territories acquired in 1814. Baden would, in fact, construct her railroad, but Bavaria did not follow through. The initialed agreement did not receive final ratification.

This was not simply some Machiavellian stratagem, for very real economic gains and losses were involved. Yet in the long run, Ludwig's "German-patriotism" triumphed over particularist interests. The Bavarian king, no Francophile to begin with, recognized that France was a potential enemy of the German Confederation. Indeed, France appeared to remain the single greatest threat to peace in Europe, and throughout the 1830s the German states periodically felt that war with

France was imminent. This had provided the pressure to erect federal fortresses in order to present a strong defense posture and perhaps deter a French attack.

v

The most acute of the periodic war scares came in 1840 as a result of Great Power difficulties in the Middle East. Whereas most of the European powers preferred that the integrity of the Ottoman Empire be preserved, France chose to support Mehemet Ali, the Viceroy of Egypt, in his challenge to Turkish suzerainty, for he was seen as a useful ally in North Africa. French officers were accordingly sent to train the Egyptian army, loans were extended to the Viceroy, and, when Mehemet Ali began to exert his independence from Turkish control by marching into the Levant, France persisted in her support. Representatives of Austria, Prussia, Great Britain, and Russia met in London to deal with this threat to stability in the Mediterranean world and in July 1840 agreed to guarantee Turkish integrity and to limit Mehemet Ali's rights exclusively to Egypt.

The Parisian press was outraged and began to make demands for compensation, at the very least the left bank of the Rhine. The government, which had refused to treat with the other powers in London, did not quiet public opinion, choosing instead to accelerate its armaments program, thus giving the impression that it was preparing for a war against the German Confederation (which had played no role in the affair). France claimed that she was increasing her forces only to prepare for all possibilities until the Middle Eastern question was resolved. But, as Münch commented in the *Bundestag*, French armaments exceeded any measured, peaceful stance and had taken on an "immediate aggressive character." Germany, he believed, ought not to remain in a state of defensiveness; rather, the governments were obligated to bring their armies to the necessary state of readiness. [143] The threat of war thus produced an outpouring of popular patriotism and governmental activity. Even Bavaria, whose king preferred to spend more on culture than on arms, began to prepare for war. [144]

There was no war and, as events in the Middle East left Mehemet Ali in possession of only Egypt, it became clear to Louis Philippe that French foreign policy needed alteration. Accordingly, its architect, Adolphe Thiers, resigned in October 1841, and France resumed her earlier, peaceful policies. But the year of tension had had an effect on the Confederation's military stance. Gaps had appeared and steps would have to be taken to correct them.

It had not taken the war scare of 1840, however, to demonstrate that Bavaria was not fulfilling her federal military obligations. There were indications as early as the military conference held in Berlin over the winter 1831–32 that the Bavarian king might not act in concert with the other German states. Prussia and Austria had decided that if there were a war with France, South Germany was to be evacuated. But it should have come as no great surprise to them that Bavaria preferred a strategy that would keep France from entering any part of Germany and therefore proposed that the South German armies be concentrated on the Rhine to prevent the French army at Strasbourg from crossing into Germany. [145]

Such a strategy should have been postulated on a large, well-trained and well-equipped army. But Ludwig's "extreme indifference" toward the army, [146] coupled with his habit of using for cultural projects funds budgeted for the military, left Bavaria with a greatly weakened force. Not even the combined arguments of the crown prince, Prince Carl (the king's brother and a talented and highly respected military leader), Wrede, and the War Ministry were able to influence the king. Ludwig made all final decisions, even the most detailed, himself and rarely left anything to the specialists. [147] Thus the Bavarian army was limited to 12,000 men, three-quarters of whom were furloughed in order to save money. The calling up of these men in 1840 in the face of the French threat caused a great deal of difficulty. Many had assumed that they would never be called to duty and had found other employment. Several had chosen to become priests and two had already been ordained and were wearing Franciscan robes and tonsures as the call came. [148]

In order to guarantee that there would be no repetition in Bavaria or the other states, Münch proposed to the *Bundestag* that the members carry out a reciprocal inspection of those forces to be included in the federal contingents. [149] This proposal apparently came as something of a surprise to Ludwig, for he complained to Dönhoff that he had hoped that Austria and Prussia would first inform him before bringing such proposals to the federal Assembly. [150] Once he overcame his surprise, however, the Bavarian king was willing to accept the plan formally presented to the Diet in the name of the Military Commission, which not only asked for an immediate inspection of the federal forces, but also established peacetime contingent size, training and practice periods, appropriate state of preparedness for each contingent, and several other detailed conditions. [151] This was decreed in June 1841, [152] and the inspections were successfully completed with dispatch.

However, it was not until August 1843 that the results were formally presented to the *Bundesversammlung*. Clearly all parties were pleased that the inspection had been a success. Each government had demonstrated its "true federative conviction" by cooperating fully in the inspection of those units and fortresses due the *Bund* and in supplying the military experts needed for the inspection of other contingents. [153] And it is an interesting thought to note that the states were cooperating in an area more sensitive than most to particularist feelings and jealousies. It is also an indication that, at least for the moment, the states had foresworn war against one another.

In principle, then, the inspection was more than satisfactory, but some technical problems were discovered among the federal contingents. Consequently, the Military Commission recommended that Bavaria extend to six months from three the period of initial training for recruits, that full-scale practice be held for four weeks each year rather than every other year, and that at least one-sixth of the Bavarian infantry, excluding raw recruits, be kept in continuous service. The Commission made similar detailed recommendations to the other governments supplying active or reserve units and then proposed that the *Bundesversammlung* decree another inspection to take place no later than 1846.[154] With minor modifications the principles and corrections proposed by the Military Commission were accepted as a federal decree in June 1844.[155] Clearly the ambassadors agreed with the sentiment that a strong defense organization was necessary to ensure the respect of the European powers and the continued independence of the Confederation.[156]

vi

The period generally known as the *Vormärz* in German history appeared to be a quiet continuation of principles and trends already established. In Bavaria, Ludwig became increasingly headstrong, listening only to advice that suited his predispositions. His chief advisor, Minister of the Interior Karl von Abel, only continued the policies established in the 1830s, acting in harmony with his king, who often pointed out that the king, not the ministers, ruled in Bavaria. Thus the decree that both Catholic and Protestant soldiers in Bavaria had to kneel before the monstrance[157] and Abel's policy of "clericalizing Bavarian public life"[158] were really only continued manifestations of that piety which Ludwig had expressed during the *Kölner Wirren*. Similarly, Abel's attempt to interpret the Bavarian constitution in a *landständische* manner duplicated the king's view that the constitution represented the maximum that a monarch might concede to his subjects and still remain sovereign. Abel fell only because the carrying out of those policies caused too much strife in the army and in the *Landtag*, and because of his attitude toward Lola Montez. [159]

In Frankfurt, with the exception of military matters, there was little sense of urgency or innovation. It was on the basis of the Six Articles that the Communist League was banned and the governments required to deal with its members as they would those accused of high treason. [160] The *Bundestag* also renewed those provisions of the 60 Articles dealing with censorship and control of education. [161] Ironically, the *Bundesversammlung* also accorded musical and dramatic works protection against unauthorized reproduction for ten years after their creation [162] and extended lifelong copyright privileges throughout the Confederation to all literary works. [163] The only unique decree accepted by the federal Assembly in the *Vormärz* was a total ban on the slave trade throughout the Confederation, [164] although slavery did not exist in the German states.

The last opportunity for the Diet to voluntarily moderate the system was offered in late 1847 when discussions began concerning a revision of the 1819 press law. The question was raised whether that law ought to be expanded and completed, or whether to accept Prussia's proposal that each state be free to end prior censorship and introduce freedom of the press under guarantee that abuse of such freedom would be punished. [165] Although a majority of the states favored this approach, Austria and Hannover blocked a resolution of the question until it was too late to have a positive effect in Germany.

Thus, although there had been some growth in the federal structure, the German Confederation had remained true to its founding principles: the members, not the *Bundestag*, remained sovereign. Through 1847 the *Bundesversammlung* had continued to build on the system first erected by 1820 and elaborated by 1834 on the assumption that there would be no fundamental changes in German life. More often than not the ambassadors in Frankfurt interpreted new challenges within the traditional framework and responded in what had become the traditional manner. They forgot or ignored those more popular forces which appeared during the *Kölner Wirren* and the threat of war with France. Rather, they assumed that popular opinion could be controlled as in the past, and, although the German governments were preoccupied with the threat of revolution, they took for granted that this too would be overcome.

8
1848
i

News that Louis Philippe had been forced from the French throne struck Germany with a force even greater than that produced by the Revolution of 1830. Within a month most of the German governments had toppled: the conservative, aristocratic ministries were replaced by middle-class cabinets, and, in some cases, the reigning monarch was forced from office. These events would, of course, be reflected in the personnel and ultimately the form of the *Bundestag* in Frankfurt, although in the beginning that body felt strong enough to try to direct the revolution.

When the news from France arrived in Frankfurt, the *Bundesversammlung* quickly elected a committee to study the events in France, to evaluate the impact of that revolution on Germany, and to propose an appropriate course of action.[1] The seriousness with which this threat was taken is indicated by the remarkable speed shown by the Political Committee, for within 24 hours it was able to present its first report. It recognized the "far-reaching agitation of the public spirit" and, in language most unusual for what would become a federal proclamation, called upon the German people to remain calm. Only through the "cooperation" of the princes and the people and the maintenance of "harmony" among all the German peoples could Germany's domestic and external security be kept. Only on the basis of "harmony and cooperation" could Germany maintain her strength and the "security of person and property." Thus the "German *Bundestag*" called upon all Germans "in the name of the whole fatherland" to keep order.[2]

This proclamation was more than an appeal for calm, however. In its report the committee also noted that only the federal Diet, as the "common central organ of all the German governments," could provide the "reference point" around which to rally a defense of Germany. The *Bundestag* was thus the sole legal organ for German national and political unity. In other words, the Political Committee assumed, and the Diet believed, that the *Bundesversammlung* still held moral authority among all levels of the German people and that it was the appropriate body to provide Germany with the moral leadership so necessary in a turbulent period. There was even some discussion of an obligation for federal contingents to intervene in France or, at the very least, in Italy.

Although Bavaria's king recognized that France was providing a dangerous example for other revolutionaries to follow, he instructed Karl von Gasser, since August 1847 Bavaria's talented ambassador to the *Bund* (and who had previously served as *Legationsrat* in Vienna and ambassador in Athens), to oppose all armed intervention abroad. Since the attempt to restore the French king in 1792 had only strengthened the republican movement, surely a similar attempt in 1848 could "only produce the same effect." Ludwig was convinced that the only reasonable course was to confine all agitators to their homelands and to refuse to tolerate any involvements abroad. As long as France remained peaceful, Germany was to pursue a policy of peace. However, the German

206   BAVARIA IN THE GERMAN CONFEDERATION

armies should be brought to the appropriate stage of preparedness should France choose a more warlike path. While Gasser
was to recommend the king's views to the Diet and to push for an
improvement in the German defensive system, under no circumstances was he to allow the *Bundestag* to involve
Germany in defending Austria's Italian possessions.[3]

It is ironic that as the Bavarian king was instructing Gasser
to press for long-term military preparedness, revolution was
breaking out in Munich. The Lola Montez affair, as well as
the causes and course of the Bavarian revolution, are widely
enough known to make superfluous a retelling in the present
study. Suffice it to say that, as in the other South German
states, the Bavarian monarch was forced to accept what
amounted to a thorough revision of the Bavarian constitution.
At first Ludwig resisted the middle-class demands, but, in
response to the demonstrations and disorders that wracked
Munich, on March 6 he issued a proclamation agreeing in
principle with all that the middle class wanted. He promised to
call the *Landtag* within ten days and to submit to it
proposals for ministerial responsibility, complete freedom of
the press, oral proceedings and open sessions in the administration of justice, and having the army swear an oath to the
constitution.

Yet all these concessions could not counterbalance the
continued moral indignation that Lola Montez's behavior was
causing among the population of the capital city. Order was
not restored by the naming of a liberal cabinet on March 11;
rather, demands for a further democratization of the Bavarian
government could be heard among the more vocal and radical
elements of the crowd. That, of course, was impossible for the
king to grant. The man who was the outstanding example of
king as ruler, who allowed his ministers no authority, who
made all decisions—this man could not reign without ruling.
Thus, as the middle-class revolution progressed in Munich,

Ludwig found himself unable to yield further and chose the only possible solution to his dilemma: on March 20, 1848, Ludwig I abdicated in favor of his eldest son. Maximilian II (1848–64) was able to accept without reservation the "March demands" and within a month put into effect the reforms promised by his father.

Ludwig had abdicated only because of events in Bavaria. He was more or less at one with the majority of Bavarians in his outlook toward Germany. Not only had the March 6 proclamation granted domestic concessions, but it had also indicated that Bavaria was spearheading a drive for the revision of the federal constitution so that the "German nation" would also be represented in Frankfurt. Ludwig firmly believed in the necessity for such measures to strengthen German unity, and the Prussian ambassador in Munich was convinced that the Bavarian foreign minister, Oettingen-Wallerstein, hoped to place Bavaria at the head of all constitutional Germany.[4]

He was correct. On March 7 Wallerstein instructed Gasser to press for reform of the Confederation. Ludwig's March 6 proclamation, he wrote, had emphasized that German unity was to be strengthened through common measures, that a "new strength and national importance" was to be assured "with a representation of the German nation" in the *Bundestag* and that a rapid revision of the federal constitution in accordance with those "legitimate expectations" was to be brought about.[5] Wallerstein then incorrectly interpreted this to mean that the "interests of the whole of Germany must outweigh special interests," that the lives of the individual states could "no longer absorb the whole life" of Germany. Not only was Gasser to push for military preparedness, but there was to be a strengthening of "that spiritual element" which had been produced during the wars of liberation.[6] But the king was not willing to go that far. Wallerstein, in part due to his attitude toward Lola Montez, was dismissed four days later, but Ludwig continued to pursue with vigor the idea of reforming the *Bund*.

By this time the concept of a thorough reform of the Confederation was gaining widespread acceptability. The first step in this direction had already been taken in September 1847, when a group of radical democrats led by Gustav von Struve and Friedrich Hecker met in Offenburg to formulate a common position. Their program,[7] directed not only toward constitutional reform but also social revolution, included the abolition of the extraordinary federal decrees of 1819, 1832, and 1834; popular representation in the *Bundesversammlung*; freedom of speech, press, religion, and assembly; trial by jury; and the abolition of all privilege. A second meeting to take place in Donaueschingen was banned by Baden's government, but the Offenburg Program compelled the German liberals to formulate a program of their own. In October 1847 they met in the Hessian town of Heppenheim, where they called for political rather than social reform, namely, for a national government and assembly (based on the *Zollverein*), as well as freedom of the press, trial by jury, and a limit on the administrative authority of the state.[8] Together the two programs would provide the parameters within which the revolutionaries of 1848 would move. The sole point of fundamental agreement, however, was that the German people should elect a national assembly.

On February 12, 1848, Friedrich Bassermann, a leading South German liberal, rose in the lower chamber of Baden's *Landtag* to appeal for a national parliament—a plea that was echoed two weeks later in the Hessian *Landtag* by Heinrich von Gagern. These requests were directed to the state governments, in effect requesting the princes to provide for popular representation in the *Bundestag*, since there seemed to be no other authority to which to appeal. The March revolution, however, saw the middle-class reformers bypass the princes and seize the initiative themselves. On March 5 fifty-one members of the South-West German liberal and democratic groups met in Heidelberg to prepare for elections for a national parliament. Unable to agree among themselves, they chose a committee of seven to prepare proposals for and to invite representatives of all the German states to a second gathering, the *Vorparlament* (preparatory parliament), which would arrange elections for the German parliament.

Meanwhile, the *Bundestag* was also involving itself in reform. On March 3 it decreed the acceptance and immediate publication of Prussia's 1847 proposals regarding freeing the press from prior censorship. Now the Confederation authorized (but did not compel) each government to introduce freedom of the press into its territories, [9] not that many states had a choice by that date. As the British ambassador noted, the result of the long delay made the decree appear as a "tardy concession wrung from them by the force of circumstances." [10] Even the Prussian ambassador in Munich reported pessimistically that the federal Diet "in its present condition and form" was unable to satisfy "the needs of the moment." It was already "overtaken" from all sides, for Baden and Württemberg had, "under the pressure of circumstances," begun to disregard federal decrees, and "without doubt" the same would happen in Bavaria. [11]

Nevertheless the Political Committee remained confident that the Diet could gain control of the reform movement if it would revise the federal constitution. In its report of March 8 the committee emphasized that the German people had "long since" lost faith in the effectiveness of the Confederation and the *Bundesversammlung* both because the constitution contained things better left to the states while excluding matters "essential to the development and strengthening" of the *Bund* and because the dependence of the ambassadors on governmental instructions precluded an independent role for the Diet. Compounding this problem was the fact that many governments were often not publishing federal decrees "assiduously brought into existence," often not complying with these decrees or making them dependent on the state's own legislation, and occasionally declaring these decrees to be not binding on them. Only those decrees which went against public opinion and for which the state governments preferred not to accept responsibility were published as federal decrees and enforced as such.

The state parliaments, the report continued, had become the vehicle of public opinion because they published their deliberations—an opportunity that the *Bundestag* had lost through its emphasis on secrecy. Since the Confederation had been unable to meet the "requirements of the present," the German people turned ever more to the *Ständeversammlungen*. "Such a Confederation cannot win the sympathy of the German people." For years plans for transforming Germany were prepared "in the parliaments, in open and secret meetings and in the press," and the direction that this transformation was to take had been indicated by the demands first made in Baden. Even recent federal decrees, such as freeing the press from prior censorship, had failed to regain the trust of the German people. Thus, the report concluded, other means had to be sought to protect Germany from "internal dissension and anarchy." If Germany were to remain "united, strong and peaceful," the federal constitution had to be revised "on a broad national basis." The *Bundestag* agreed and instructed the committee to determine how this revision should take place. [12]

On the next day the Diet accepted the Political Committee's recommendation that the old German imperial eagle, with the inscription "German Confederation," be the coat of arms of the Confederation and that black, red, and gold be the federal colors [13]—colors that for decades had been condemned as the symbol of revolution. It was not until March 20, however, that the coat of arms and colors were decreed to be displayed in the federal fortresses, on the uniforms of federal soldiers, and in the seal of all federal authorities. [14]

Of more than symbolic importance was the decree of March 10, which requested that each vote in the Select Council select and send to Frankfurt a man of "public trust" to assist the *Bundesversammlung* in revising the federal constitution. [15] By using the phrase "*Männer des öffentlichen Vertrauens,*" the Political Committee, which recommended that this be decreed, clearly meant that such men were to be drawn exclusively from the successful middle-class reform movement that had supplanted the aristocrats in most of the German governments. Gasser's report of this session noted the extreme importance of this decree and observed that it had sprung from the intention to bring the business of revising the federal constitution "at and in [*an und in*]" the Diet. [16] With this construction Gasser was attempting to deal simultaneously with two subjects. On the one hand, he tried to stress that the *Bundestag* rather than an extralegal collection of radicals would reform the constitution, while on the other hand, he was attempting to suggest that such reform should be carried out in Frankfurt rather than Dresden.

Nevertheless, on March 13 the Diet suspended its decree of March 10 in anticipation of the Dresden Congress to which Austria and Prussia had invited the German governments. [17] This was the outcome of a process that began in November 1847, with a proposal to reform the Confederation from General Joseph von Radowitz to his friend, Frederick William IV, king of Prussia. Between November 1847 and March 1848 Prussia and Austria negotiated a common course of action and on March 10 agreed to invite the German governments to Dresden to discuss federal reform. In this way, the German great powers hoped to achieve reform solely by governmental action, excluding any form of a German national assembly. [18] By this time, this was impossible.

The Bavarian king was unalterably opposed to the Dresden Congress, partly because of the disastrous impression another "congress" would have on popular opinion, and partly because it would contribute further to the Diet's weakness (as in 1819, it was to be bypassed) at a time when strengthening that body "had to be the main task" of the states. The whole question had to be left to the *Bundestag*, which, Ludwig thought, might be strengthened through the addition of "distinguished personalities," [19] but, in any case, discussion over revision of the *Bund* had to be carried out in Frankfurt and in the federal Diet if the Confederation were to regain its position of authority among the German people.

The proposal for a congress in Dresden helped only the reformers and radicals. It blocked the Diet's plans to "anticipate the movements of the democratic party," giving the latter "a decided advantage" since it could offer its plans to the German public [20] with no fear of counterproposals from Frankfurt. Austria and Prussia had miscalculated; there could be no repetition of 1834. On the contrary, as Prussia's ambassador in Munich reported, there was no chance to convince Ludwig to be represented in Dresden, and other states were following Bavaria's lead by declaring that they too would work only through the *Bundesversammlung*. [21]

Indeed, by mid-March, the state governments were in the hands of middle-class ministries that would have nothing to do with attempts to bypass the Diet or to prevent the calling of a German national parliament. These governments, through new instructions to their federal ambassadors, quickly changed the direction that the *Bundestag* was to take. In many cases the new governments and the old ambassadors felt uncomfortable with one another, resulting frequently in the latter's replacement with more trustworthy men. Thus Gasser, the professional diplomat, would be replaced by Friedrich Willich, a radical from the Pfalz and one of the Committee of Seven chosen at Heidelberg to summon the *Vorparlament*.

The Dresden Congress scheduled for March 25 never met. Austria and Prussia, under pressure from revolution at home, conceded that revision of the federal constitution was to come from the *Bundestag* in conjunction with the men of public trust (the Committee of Seventeen) who were again invited to Frankfurt for that purpose. The *Bundestag* also named a committee to facilitate communication between it and the Seventeen in the work of revising the constitution. [22]

Neither the Revision Committee nor the Seventeen suffered from a lack of proposals as to how a newly organized confederation should appear—and these proposals were unable to agree on the fundamental question as to whether Germany should remain a confederation or be reorganized into a unitary state. But as far as the Bavarian king was concerned, the basic building block of Germany remained the sovereign states. In an instruction to Gasser, Ludwig declared that the state constitutions had undergone sufficient alteration and should be preserved as they now existed. "The existing political relationship between throne and people should not be shaken," he wrote, but the strengthening of German unity demanded the erection of a "parliamentary center." Where *Landstände* existed, there one found the source for "national representation." But given the diversity of election laws, each based on its particular constitution and institutions, there could be no uniform federal election regulations. Instead, the choice of representation had to be left to the state parliament, which reflected the conditions of their states. The same was true even if there were no popular representation, and it should be left to the government to determine how it would be represented in a national assembly.

Since most of the German constitutional states had a

two-chamber legislature, Ludwig felt that this form should be maintained in the Confederation. Thus the "National Representation" should also be formed of two chambers: one drawn from the first chamber of the state parliaments, the other from the second chamber. These two chambers would then form a Council (*Collegium*) with the existing *Bundesversammlung*. The relation of the Council to the Diet was to be that which the existing *Landstände* had to their governments: only when the two chambers of the Council agreed on a proposal would it be presented to the *Bundestag*, whereas decrees of the latter were valid only after the Council's agreement. The *Präsidium*, which until then was the sole prerogative of Austria, was to be exercised alternately by the "larger German states" and was to be provided with "suitable" powers. [23]

Through this construction, Ludwig not only strengthened the position of Bavaria in the *Bund* (she was, after all, one of the "larger German states"), but maintained the ultimate authority of the princes at home and in the Confederation. As a rule, only the lower chamber of the state legislatures were elected and often represented the medieval corporations rather than the individual citizen per se. Consequently, monarchs were frequently able to control who would be elected or, as in the case of Bavaria, could prevent members of the opposition from taking their seats. [24] Members of the upper chamber were usually, and ambassadors to the Diet were always, appointed by the sovereign.

Nonetheless, this was a compromise with the concept of a German national assembly. Bavaria, as the new foreign minister and professional diplomat, Clems Graf von Waldkirch, explained to the Prussian ambassador, did not want a revolution as the radicals demanded. But the existing federal constitution was "impossible," and the national assembly had become a question of extreme importance "to the Confederation and the South German thrones." It was especially necessary for the Diet to consider the question and discuss all proposals before the *Volksmänner* of the preparatory parliament met in Frankfurt on March 30. To this effect, Waldkirch believed, both Austria and Prussia had to accept openly the principle of the national assembly. [25]

ii

In the midst of the complicated maneuverings to reform the German Confederation by the *Bundestag* or by an extralegal parliamentary body, a third group attempted to involve itself in the decision-making process. When news of the Parisian revolution reached Germany, the fear of an invasion by French revolutionary armies had been reawakened. Some governments responded by mobilizing their armies, and Württemberg went so far as to invite the Bavarian general staff to a meeting in Stuttgart. [26] As it turned out, the danger was not to come from a French army, but rather from an army of German expatriates in France. Württemberg reported to the Diet that the "German Democratic Club" had voted to send a *Freikorps* of five to six thousand men from Paris to the Upper Rhine to proclaim a republic in Baden, Hesse, and the Bavarian Rhine province. Since the French government refused to act, Württemberg requested that the affected states discuss common defensive measures. [27] Baden too began to worry and, noting that a large number of German workers had recently been dismissed from Alsatian factories, expressed her fear that she would be overrun by them in conjunction with the *Freikorps* marching from Paris. [28]

On recommendation of its Military Affairs Committee, the Diet requested the governments of Württemberg, Baden, and Hesse each to prepare one division to send to any threatened point and to use the national guard to assist in maintaining the peace and order of Germany. Bavaria was requested to take similar measures in her Rhine province and to join with Baden, the Hesses, and Nassau to take suitable measures to prevent any unauthorized armed troop from reaching the assembly of the *Vorparlament* on March 30. [29]

On the next day Baden reported the news that immediate military counteraction was needed to repel an attack by a contingent of Germans and Poles. These were being outfitted in Paris, and within two weeks ten to twelve thousand well-led men would be at the Rhine. Emissaries had already been sent to Zweibrücken and Mannheim to announce a "German Federal Republic." Since it was no longer simply a question of defending against a few thousand workers, but rather one of resistance against a well-organized and commanded army, more federal troops were needed as quickly as possible. The Military Affairs Committee agreed with Baden's assessment, and the *Bundestag* accepted its proposal that the VII (Bavaria) and VIII (Württemberg, Baden, and Hesse) contingents be placed on a war footing. The latter governments were requested to agree on a single commander for the VIII corps, while Bavaria was to name the supreme commander over both contingents. [30] On April 4 Willich announced that Bavaria had chosen Prince Carl as the supreme commander. [31]

Meanwhile, the poet Georg Herwergh had organized a *Freikorp* that crossed into Baden and called on the residents of Mannheim to overthrow their prince. He found support only among the radicals, and when his band met a federal contingent on April 27, the revolutionary force was destroyed and the city of Mannheim garrisoned. [32] Indeed, this was typical of Prince Carl's reports. [33]

By early May federal arms had crushed the rebels, whose leaders were either captured or had fled back into France. By mid-May Prince Carl was willing to disband several of the units under his command and send them back to their home states. [34] By mid-June the Bavarian government was requesting that her army in Baden be replaced by other troops, since the danger had diminished and it was costing Bavaria too much to provision them. [35]

However, the danger had not passed, for the revolutionaries began to regroup, purchase new weapons, and establish depots in several Swiss and Alsatian towns. Furthermore, since they were again distributing pamphlets in Baden, the *Bundestag* requested Bavaria not to recall her armies yet and asked Switzerland to aid in preventing the rebels from using Swiss territory as a sanctuary against Germany. [36] Although the danger was exaggerated, Bavaria complied with the Diet's wishes. The federal army, under Prince Carl's command, proved itself able to defend Germany against this invasion. Unfortunately, these successes would not save the German Confederation. The VII and VIII corps would not be used to reverse the revolution that had taken place in the states nor to prevent the revolution about to take place in Frankfurt. The federal army only succeeded in allowing the revolution to take place in a parliamentary rather than violent manner.

iii

As the federal contingents were defeating the radicals in the field, the *Bundestag* attempted to gain control over the reform movement. Already on March 23 the Free Cities proposed that all extraordinary decrees passed since 1819 [37] be formally repealed. On April 2 the committee considering this proposal argued for its adoption since those decrees owed their existence to "particular circumstances and views" in contradiction to "present conditions." Not only were those decrees "antiquated," but most of the states had repealed them *de facto* if not *de jure*. Thus the question was really one of form rather than content, and the *Bundesversammlung* formally repealed the extraordinary decrees [38] (although, through oversight, it was not until May 29 that the decree prohibiting travel by journeymen to France, Belgium, and Switzerland was repealed[39]).

On April 7 the *Bundestag* repealed another outdated decree. Württemberg had proposed that the Diet's protocols be published, as they had been before 1824, to prevent "erroneous opinions" over the Diet's effectiveness and activities. A committee composed of the ambassadors of Austria, Prussia, Saxony, Baden, and Württemberg was elected to examine the question. [40] In its report (from which Austria dissented) the committee noted that keeping federal proceedings secret served only to limit the teaching about and the number of scholarly publications concerned with the Diet's activities. This was not in the Confederation's interest because publication of discussions and decrees would reveal the motives of both the *Bundestag* and the individual states, thereby correcting "false judgments." Since the development and strengthening of the national spirit could only be promoted if "the central organ of all the German governments" proved its existence by giving some sign of its "life and activity," the committee proposed that all the transactions of the *Bundesversammlung* be published six weeks after signing unless there were a vote to the contrary. [41] Not until fundamental changes had taken place in Germany, however, did the Diet decide to publish its protocols under the same conditions as before the decree of 1824. [42] Thereafter, all discussions and decrees concerning federal reform would be published in their entirety.

Of far greater consequence was the agreement reached between the Diet's Revision Committee and the Committee of Seventeen (to which Bavaria sent no representative until April 7) in their first joint session. In its report to the *Bundestag*, the Revision Committee pointed out that there were only two ways in which a constitution could be brought into existence: either by agreement among the governments and imposed by federal decree, or by agreement between the governments and the German people. Both committees agreed that, since "under present circumstances" an imposed constitution would be impossible, only the second course could give a guarantee of its continuance. Thus, on committee proposal, the *Bundestag* decreed and immediately published in the newspapers that it, with the men of public trust, had already begun to work on the draft of a new constitution. In furtherance "of this important matter," the governments were requested to order elections for national representatives who were to come "to the seat of the *Bundesversammlung*" in order to help in the creation of a constitution between the governments and the people. Each state, the decree read, was to elect one representative for every 70,000 inhabitants. [43]

On the next day the *Vorparlament*, 574 present or former legislators invited by the Committee of Seven, met in Frank-furt—bringing to 3 the number of political groups concerned with the constitutional future of Germany. Each was jealous of the other, but the *Bundestag* and the Committee of Seventeen usually cooperated to try to prevent the *Vorparlament* from becoming dominant. With the assistance of the Seventeen, the Diet was not only able to maintain its traditional legitimate authority, but was also able to "pose as the proper representative of the German national constitutional reform." [44]

Naturally the *Vorparlament* would dispute any such claims, and as early as April 2 attempted to seize the initiative. It decreed that it was dissatisfied with the election law decreed by the *Bundestag* and demanded that changes in it be made. [45] The Revision Committee, to which this demand had been for-warded, argued for acceptance of the changes since the governments had already given the initiative for creating a draft constitution to the Seventeen and, by accepting the decree of March 30, had decided that it was necessary for the German people to give their approval. Since the "only reasonable way" was for an elected "popular constituent assembly" to have placed before it for its approval the draft of a new federal constitution drawn up by the *Bundestag* and its committees, the Diet accordingly decreed that all independent adult German males had the right to vote, that all German property holders might be elected, that all returning political refugees could vote and be elected, and that each state elect one representative for every 50,000 inhabitants. [46]

Such a decree would have been inconceivable as little as five weeks earlier. No one would have thought then that the princes would, in effect, ask their subjects to act in partnership in shaping a new German constitution. But the decrees of March 30 and April 7 meant that this work would indeed be done by the governments and the representatives of the German people. And although the decrees left to the governments the exact method by which elections would be carried out, elections for a national representation would be held. For the first time the German people, or at least the middle classes, were legally involved in shaping the political future of Germany.

In these and all other decrees, however, the *Bundestag* emphasized that the National Assembly was only to aid in the revision of the already existing federal constitution; it would not accept the fact that revolution had already effectively abrogated that constitution. Both the federal Diet and the state governments accepted the role of a national representation in revising the constitution; at no time could they accept the claim that this was a national parliament with the right unilaterally to create a constitution. The *Bundestag* and the states that it represented had to stress continuity in order to justify a continued role in the reform process. The revolution needed no such justification.

The democrats attempted to use the *Vorparlament* as a tool to further the cause of revolution. Struve and Hecker, the leaders of the Offenburg meeting, proposed a fifteen-point program [47] that would have produced social revolution as well as constitutional reform. Moreover, Struve wanted the *Vorparlament* to remain in session and act as a legislature until the National Assembly could be elected and proposed that an "executive committee" be elected to act as a provisional government for Germany. Had this plan been accepted, the *Vorparlament* alone would have determined the form and direction that the future national government was to take.

The liberal majority, however, was not willing to abdicate to the radicals and, after the Diet accepted their revisions in the election law, rejected the proposal that the *Vorparlament* remain in session. In the spirit of compromise and caution, however, the liberals agreed that a Committee of Fifty should remain until the national assembly was able to convene. [48] The Fifty, which excluded the radical left, were to act as watchdogs over the *Bundesversammlung* to see that it did nothing in opposition to the best interests of the German nation. But, by implication, the *Vorparlament* accepted the Diet's continued existence as a right, while the *Bundestag* anticipated the *Vorparlament* by repealing the extraordinary decrees and by informing that body on April 2 that all the ambassadors involved in the enactment of the extraordinary decrees had resigned or were about to do so.

Having fulfilled its mission of preparing elections for the national parliament, and having no remaining function, the *Vorparlament* disbanded, leaving the Committee of Fifty to watch over the Diet until the elections were held and the National Assembly could begin its deliberations. The committe's importance was increased by the fact that the *Bundestag* and the governments were forced eventually to deal directly with it, thereby granting the Fifty a legitimacy above that derived from the *Vorparlament*.[49] At first, however, the *Bundestag* attempted to deal with the *Vorparlament* and the Fifty only through intermediaries, thereby denying the very legitimacy that they desired. Thus, when the Fifty demanded that the *Bundestag* declare immediately the degree to which it agreed with the *Vorparlament's* election demands, the Diet simply forwarded a copy of its April 7 decree. When the Committee of Fifty invited the Diet to absorb the Seventeen and begin direct communications with it, the ambassadors informed the Fifty that they would continue to consider their views and wishes and that while the arrangement between the Diet and the Seventeen had proven mutually satisfactory, under some conditions the two would deliberate directly with one another.[50] This was, of course, not what the Fifty had demanded, since no mention was made of communicating directly with them. In this way the *Bundesversammlung*, although granting a modicum of legitimacy to the Fifty, was able to hold off full, formal recognition.

As a rule, the Diet treated the Fifty's demands as "proposals of the people" and would co-opt them by decreeing and publishing as their own what the Fifty wanted before they could fully formulate and publish them themselves. This gave the *Bundestag* the appearance of continued independence and activity while leading to ever more bitter disputes between the two bodies.[51] But for as long as the federal Diet decreed what the Fifty, and later the National Assembly, wanted, by implication the *Bundestag* remained the sole source of legitimate authority. By maintaining the pretense that it was accepting only their recommendations, the *Bundestag* could make the claim that these recommendations had no force in law until they were sanctioned by federal decree. It was only when the *Bundestag* dropped this argument and appeared to obey the revolutionary bodies that it lost its claim to preeminence. Once this occurred, the German Confederation was doomed.

Still, the federal Diet had one chance remaining to seize the initiative: to draw up a new constitution and thereby reform the Confederation before the National Assembly could hold its first session. But it was in the Committee of Seventeen that most of the activity for reforming the federal constitution was taking place. The committee's lively discussions were held in secret, away from the Revision Committee, in fear that the Diet might somehow regain its preeminence and control the process for creating a new constitution. By a narrow majority the Seventeen approved Friedrich Dahlmann's[52] draft and authorized its immediate publication so as to present the *Bundestag* with a fait accompli.[53] The proposed constitution, however, which would have created a strong central government with a two-chamber legislature and a hereditary emperor with true executive authority, met with strong opposition in the committee from Bavaria and Austria and, after a great deal of criticism, was pigeonholed by the *Bundestag.*

The most vociferous objections to the Dahlmann draft dealt with the form and powers of the executive. Indeed, most of the discussion in the Diet or its Revision Committee was concerned precisely with the question of executive authority. Whereas the Holy Roman Empire had had an emperor at its head, the German Confederation had been created without an executive authority because, in 1815, it was thought preferable to allow the states to carry out federal decrees.[54] As early as February 1848, however, Heinrich von Gagern had called for the establishment of a federal executive authority, and on April 12 the Committee of Seventeen made a formal proposal to this effect to the *Bundestag.*

On April 18 Baden's ambassador proposed that the *Bund* establish an executive authority until constitutional revision was completed. Austria and Prussia were each to name one member, while the remaining states would select the last member from three candidates proposed by Bavaria. Although its primary function was to carry out the Diet's decrees, Baden wanted to invest the executive authority with the right of independent action in matters of lesser importance or in cases where a swift decision was needed.[55] The proposal was sent to the Revision Committee for study. The committee also received a decree from the Fifty, suggesting that the *Bundesversamlung* set up a three-headed executive authority drawn from among the members of the Seventeen and the federal Diet.[56] Clearly, Germany was again to have some form of executive body.

Meanwhile, the Bavarian government was putting into final form its king's idea of a constitution for Germany and thus became the first state to present a draft for a complete national constitution.[57] Rejecting Dahlmann's draft because it would "mediatize the princes," Bavaria proposed the establishment of a federal German state that would create a united German nation while allowing the rights and interests of the individual states to be maintained. Rather than establishing a two-chamber legislature as Dahlmann had envisaged, Bavaria proposed that a *Reichstag* be erected parallel with the National Assembly. Whereas the latter would represent the German people, the *Reichstag*, whose members were to be fully dependent on their governments' instructions, would represent the German states. Whether or not this arrangement differed fundamentally from the idea of the *Bundestag* as the upper chamber of a national parliament, Bavaria's proposal for an executive was in sharp contrast to that which Dahlmann envisaged. Rather than a single hereditary emperor, Bavaria wanted an organ composed of one representative each from North, South, and East Germany acting either concurrently or alternatively.

At the heart of Bavaria's proposal lay an idea dear to the new king's heart: *Trias.* As with the proposal made by Württemberg's minister, Wangenheim, some three decades earlier, Maximilian II considered Bavaria the natural leader of the small- and middle-sized German states and hoped that Bavaria would play the same role in South Germany as Prussia was playing in the North. As the third German power, Bavaria would then increase her political importance while acting as a balance to Austria and Prussia in the new Germany. Thus, what Aretin and Lerchenfeld had dismissed as utopian in the 1820s was now offered as official Bavarian policy and even found a positive response in Baden and a few of the North German courts. [58] It did not, however, receive the support necessary for serious consideration in Frankfurt, and, consequently, Bavaria's proposed constitution was quietly shelved.

On May 3 the Revision Committee reported its conviction that a federal executive authority was needed to enable the *Bundestag* to communicate rapidly with both the state governments and the National Assembly. It was clear, the committee believed, that such an authority could not be composed solely of the Diet's ambassadors, just as it was certain that the two German great powers would have to be represented on that body. There was, however, disagreement as to how to complete the membership of that body. Although a majority on the committee preferred a three-member board, there was also a proposal that the executive be composed of six, based on the federal military contingents, [59] in order to allow the smaller states a voice. The majority, however, felt that more than three members would make the executive too weak and argued that the interests of the smaller states would be covered as well by their selection of the third of a three-member board. Therefore, since both the Seventeen and the Fifty had already recognized the need for a federal executive authority, the *Bundestag* accepted its committee's proposal that the governments agree to include three more special ambassadors in the *Bundestag* to act as an executive authority. Bavaria was to select three men from three different states, one of whom would be elected by a majority of the votes cast by the fourth through the seventeenth votes of the *Plenum*. [60] Despite protests from the Fifty, [61] the Diet asserted that it had acted both properly and within its duly constituted authority. Bavaria even went so far as to nominate the three candidates,[62] while Prussia proposed the diplomat Karl Freiherr von Usedom as its representative. But since Austria refused to respond, the *Bundesversammlung* lost the advantage that the hiatus between the preparatory parliament's adjournment and the first session of the National Assembly had given it. The Diet would not be able to face the representatives of the German people with an executive authority after all.

On May 18 the German Constituent National Assembly convened in the Church of St. Paul, which had been prepared for the delegates at the Confederation's expense.[63] The delegates were greeted with great joy and high hopes, for it seemed that the (often contradictory) dreams of the German patriots and liberals would finally be realized. The result, as well as the composition, discussions, and divisions, is too well documented to warrant repetition here. The process by which an executive authority was constructed, however, is of relevance for the present study, for once this was accomplished, the German Confederation ceased to exist.

The Committee of Fifty terminated its activities when the National Assembly began its first session, but the seventeen "men of public trust" were not dissolved until June 5, when, on their own request, the *Bundestag* relieved them of their responsibilities.[64] Now only the federal Diet and the National Assembly remained as the sources of legitimate[65] power in Germany.

As was to be expected, neither body was fully comfortable with the other, but neither could either body dispense with the other without appearing antinational or revolutionary, respectively. Clearly some way had to be found out of this impasse, and the answer was provided by the creation of an executive authority.

There were three formulations that drew most of the serious discussion. The executive might be headed by one person or by three and, if the latter fashion were accepted, then they might be chosen along the lines of the May 3 decree or be composed of three princes. Karl Freiherr von Closen, who had replaced the ineffectual Willich on May 1, was instructed to join with Austria and Prussia in accepting the Austrian Archduke Johann if, as expected, the National Assembly decreed that the German Confederation's executive authority were to be placed in the hands of one man. [66]

The National Assembly began the process on June 3 when it selected a committee to evaluate all proposals and return its recommendation. The committee report, presented June 17, very closely approximated Bavaria's suggestion that the provisional executive authority be composed of three men chosen by the states and approved by the National Assembly. This "federal board of directors" would act as Germany's highest authority, although it was to have no involvement in the creation of a constitution. [67] Rather than gaining the majority's support, however, the report only touched off a debate that lasted for more than a week.

The Bavarian government reflected the uncertainty felt by many in an instruction to Closen that noted that it would be a decided advantage if the Bavarian plan for a three-member directory were accepted. If, as Closen apparently had reported on June 18, the executive were to be composed of three princes, Bavaria would accept Prince Carl as one of them. If, on the other hand, it were to be composed of three statesmen, the Bavarian government proposed Heinrich von Gagern, to satisfy the National Assembly, Karl Fürst Leiningen, to please Baden (since most of his estates lay in that land, although he was a member of the upper chambers of both Baden and Bavaria), and Gustav von Lerchenfeld, since the third candidate should be a Bavarian. The Bavarian government, it concluded, now looked less favorably on a single executive because "for a *single* favorable opportunity, countless unfavorable ones have presented themselves." [68]

Yet it was to the single executive that the National Assembly turned. After rejecting the Bavarian plan, the delegates seemed to lean toward accepting Prince William of Prussia, Prince Carl of Bavaria, and Archduke Johann of Austria as a triumvirate, but the debate soon shifted to other possible combinations. Finally, Heinrich von Gagern proposed that the National Assembly elect an imperial regent (*Reichsverweser*) as the German provisional executive authority. By accepting Gagern's proposal on June 28, the delegates were exerting the authority of the National Assembly at the expense of the Diet, for they were setting aside the federal decree of May 3. Moreover, in the resolution declaring the establishment of the *Reichsverweser*, the National Assembly included a clause abolishing the *Bundestag* at that moment when the provisional executive authority came into being. [69] But when, on June 29, the National Assembly overwhelmingly elected Archduke Johann as imperial regent, the *Bundesversammlung*, in a most unusual evening session, decreed its best wishes and support. [70] Still, the Bavarian government realized the "urgency and absolute necessity" for some organ to allow uninterrupted communication between the individual states and the *Reichsverweser* and, "where necessary," the National Assembly. Closen was therefore instructed to create such an arrangement with the other ambassadors to the Diet. [71] The states clearly were looking to other means to preserve their authority and autonomy.

iv

Only the formalities remained before the *Bundesversammlung* would cease to function. On July 12 the presiding ambassador reported that the *Reichsverweser* had appeared before the National Assembly and that he had been invited to come to the Diet in order that the "constitutional powers and responsibilities" that the *Bundestag* exercised in the name of the states might be transferred to him. After a brief pause, the archduke, accompanied by the *Bundestag* delegation that had invited him, entered the chamber and was "festively received" by the ambassadors and the Military Commission. In his concluding address to the Diet and the *Reichsverweser*, the presiding ambassador neatly avoided crediting the National Assembly with the authority necessary for dissolving the Diet. Instead, he recited a long list of the powers given the Diet by the state governments and then, in the name of those governments, delegated those constitutional powers to the imperial regent. [72] In this way, it has been correctly argued, [73] the *Bundestag* tried to protect the continuity of Germany's constitutional and legal development. By supplementing the rights granted to the imperial regent by the National Assembly with its own federal powers, the *Bundestag* was in essence claiming the right of the states to be involved in the creation of a new German constitution. At the same time, by declaring its "present activity to be concluded," the impression was left that the Diet had not been dissolved as the June 28 resolution demanded, but rather, that its activities had only been suspended, leaving the possibility open that the states might once again reactivate that body.

With the assurance of the personal admiration that the ambassadors felt for the *Reichsverweser*, the *Bundesversammlung* ceased to exist. The re-creation of Germany was now in the hands of the revolution.

9

Conclusion

It was not a simple renewal when Austria reconvened the federal Diet in 1851. Rather than continuing to be a vehicle allowing the German governments to work with one another more or less harmoniously, the *Bundesversammlung* became an arena within which the two German great powers dueled for hegemony over Germany. And although Bavaria continued to proclaim her autonomy, she became, in fact, little more than an Austrian satellite by the time the *Bundestag* was again dissolved in 1866.

None of this, however, was foreseen or foreseeable when the Confederation was established to deal with the transformation wrought upon inter-German relations by the French Revolution and Napoleon. During the period after Napoleon's final defeat, Bavaria attempted to use the *Bundestag* as a device to further her own goals and, at the very least, to maintain each iota of her independence. Conversely, the federal Diet spent a great deal of effort challenging Bavaria's particularist ways. After its formative years, however, the *Bund* assumed a relatively lethargic character, allowing the contest between

Bavarian autonomy and federal authority to all but cease. This dispute had by no means been resolved, but rather, it seemed to lose importance as an immediate issue and faded quietly into the background. As long as the Confederation was not forced to react to some significant stimulus, no conflict between Bavaria and the *Bund* would manifest itself. Neither side desired a clash of principle, and there would be none so long as the Confederation was not called upon to act: the *Bundesver-, sammlung* rarely initiated actions, although it claimed the power to do so. As a rule it reacted, moving only when events forced it to. When Germany was calm the members of the Confederation preferred to keep the federal Diet's activities to a minimum, avoiding all actions that might tend to bring an evolution of the federal constitution toward a more centralized governmental form.

All this was indicative of the fact that the Confederation never had a life of its own separate from the component member states. The federal Assembly lacked that certain spark which might have transformed a permanent congress of ambassadors into the independent legislature of a sovereign state. Working within the federal constitutional framework, it proved unable to transcend its bounds and take the actions necessary to unify the parts of Germany into a whole and create a true nation-state. This was in no small measure due to Bavarian obstinance in defending her "rights of sovereignty" against federal encroachment. From 1815 on Bavaria labored to prevent the Confederation from expanding its influence at the expense of the member states, or, in particular, at Bavarian expense.

It is apparent that Bavaria took the German Confederation seriously, albeit often in a negative sense. King Ludwig I himself, both as crown prince and king, read and annotated many ambassadorial reports from the federal Diet and placed a high degree of importance on events that took place in that body. As a rule, Bavarian ambassadors were skilled diplomats who were instructed to work in conjunction with like-minded ambassadors or, if need be, alone to preserve the autonomy of the individual states, or, more accurately, to preserve Bavarian independence. Under the particularist banner of state sovereignty the Bavarian government and ambassadors labored to undermine each federal decree that might be interpreted as expanding federal authority.

It is in light of the above that Bavarian noncompliance with and nonpublication of the press laws of 1819 and 1824 must be understood. The Karlsbad decrees were published but were vitiated by an appended reservation that limited their effectiveness to the extent that existing Bavarian law would allow. The act of renewal in 1824 was simply not published. In other words, Bavaria argued that her laws and constitution took precedence over those of the Confederation. It is this thesis that underlay the consistent Bavarian opposition to federal acts that touched her sovereign rights. Although Bavaria chose not to state the issue in these terms—indeed her ambassadors were instructed to avoid such terminology in order to mute the inevitable reaction in Frankfurt—this attitude is the key to Bavaria's activities vis-à-vis the Confederation. By avoiding any reference to the superiority of Bavarian over federal law, the Bavarian government hoped to avoid a confrontation with the federal Diet over the *Wiener Schlussakt*, which explicitly subjected states to federal law. In this effort Bavaria was generally successful: attention was rarely drawn to the relevant articles, and Bavaria was never forced to admit the fundamental illegality of her position. The interminable discussions over Landau, the long and ultimately unsuccessful struggle against the majority in the *Bundestag* over title to that fortress; the ultimately successful dispute over Princess Berkeley's pension and the attendant question of responsibility for liabilities incurred within territories acquired by Bavaria;

the continual rejection of federal press decrees: all testify to Bavaria's deep-seated conviction that her independence and autonomy, that is, her laws, took precedence over everything else.

This drive to preserve Bavarian independence, however, was not developed into a theory of states' rights to be extended to all federal states. Although there were times when Bavaria seemed to champion the independence of all states from federal authority, as a rule the Bavarian government was primarily concerned only with Bavaria. Thus the anomalous situation arose wherein Bavaria rejected federal interference with her press law while voting with the majority to nullify a similar law in Baden on the grounds that it was incompatible with federal law. Moreover, even when it seemed to be in her best interests to work with other German states to strengthen their, and her, independence from Austria, Prussia, and the Confederation, Bavaria chose to advance selfish claims that precluded all hope of cooperation. She refused to support the economic union that the Darmstadt and Stuttgart Conferences tried to achieve, and she opposed the political cooperation implicit in Württemberg's Trias policy, although Maximilian II had no qualms about Trias in a form that stressed Bavarian parity with Austria and Prussia. It seems that Bavaria would not concede to others the rights she claimed as her own.

There was, however, a change in direction in Bavarian policy regarding the Confederation after 1830. The shock of the July Revolution and the reverberations that it produced in Germany led the Bavarian government to increase its cooperation with the federal Diet's efforts to restore order and stability. King Ludwig I had been greatly disturbed by the outbreak of revolutionary disturbances and at one point went so far as to instruct his ambassador in Frankfurt to request a federal press law. For domestic political reasons the king was forced to rescind this instruction, yet he did impose restrictions on the Bavarian press and the *Landtag*. The formerly liberal-appearing monarch gradually turned toward the more conservative elements in German and Bavarian politics.

Nevertheless, there was no reversal of Bavarian attitude regarding her independence; where possible the Bavarian government attempted to anticipate the federal Assembly and to act first, thereby removing all excuse for federal interference in Bavarian affairs. The foremost concern of the Bavarian government remained Bavarian sovereignty.

> There was little interest in giving the Confederation authoritative influence. The defense of independence, the avoidance of all federal interference in the affairs of the states remained the primary goal of Bavarian policy. [1]

Ludwig himself wanted no federal state of Germany but a harmonious federation of sovereign states in which Bavaria would be able to pursue her own interests. Only when a matter touching Bavarian interests affected the whole Confederation did Bavaria consider working with, but not surrendering her rights to, the federal Diet.

Bavaria, moreover, would not permit Austria and Prussia to determine the role and direction of the Confederation. Ideally, she hoped that the members would decide together how the Confederation should react to a given situation.

> Bavaria and the constitutional states have been unwilling to recognize in the Diet the arbitrary right of interfering beyond a given point in their internal affairs, and Austria will not be mending matters by carrying through the Diet by a simple majority a string of resolutions to increase that arbitrary power which those states already view with jealousy. If she does resort to such a course, the dissenting states will assuredly not feel themselves bound by articles to which they refused to accede.... The Diet therefore will not find affairs advanced one iota by the adoption of any

measures to which Bavaria and the other constitutional states are not parties; on the contrary the difficulties of its actual position will only be aggravated. [2]

Without Bavarian agreement on major matters, the federal Diet would only have found itself further weakened and divided. For this reason it became increasingly clear, especially after 1830, that Bavarian interests and prejudices had to be taken into account in Frankfurt.

By 1834 it appeared as if a working accommodation had been reached between Bavaria and the Confederation. Bavarian autonomy seemed assured, for the federal constitution would evolve no further. Simultaneously, Bavaria increased her cooperation with other German states in order to help fulfill the stated purpose of the Confederation: the maintenance of the external and internal order and tranquillity.

From this point on the *Bundestag* spend its efforts completing and fulfilling the repressive system established in 1834. In general, Bavaria cooperated with the Confederation against the revolutionary threat presented by students and traveling journeymen and against the contamination contained in the ideas of Young Germany and parliamentary debates. Yet there were times, as in the case of the *Kölner Wirren* or the Hannoverian constitutional conflict, when a majority of the states actively worked to prevent federal involvement, even if that meant the sacrifice of principle to expediency. Only in the defense of Germany against attack from abroad could all parties, after particularist jealousies were allayed, work in harmony.

Bavaria had been able to work within the federal constitution once all attempts to make the federal Diet the center of power in Germany had ceased. There was little chance that this would happen, especially after Austria, in the face of stiff opposition, ceased trying to transform the *Bundestag* into an instrument for carrying out her own policies or using the Confederation as a vehicle for achieving German unification under Austrian hegemony. The Confederation, moreover, had proven itself to be a more divisive than unifying force for the people of the German states; it alienated much of the politically conscious population with its attempts to repress the liberal press under the guise of preventing revolution.

> There seems to be a fatality attending all the measures which the Diet devises for the well-being of the German nation, which renders it impossible for any one act to emanate from the Assembly without carrying with it some antidote to counteract the beneficial results which might otherwise be derived from it. [3]

The Revolution of 1848 saw Bavaria and the other constitutional states advocate a thorough reform of the federal constitution while maintaining the basic structure of the Confederation. Once the middle classes had replaced the aristocratic ministries with liberals, the *Bundestag* joined in the movement for reform, going so far as to attempt to seize leadership of the movement. However, the system that had worked so well through 1847 had also undermined the Diet's credibility with the German people, and both the Confederation and the states found themselves not in control but struggling simply to maintain their viability and existence. Finally the *Bundesversammlung* had to admit defeat, suspended its activities, and left the rebuilding of Germany to the National Assembly.

Yet when all is said and done the German Confederation did serve a useful function for the German governments. Since it was the openly announced goal of the Confederation to protect and maintain the monarchical principle, each state desiring federal assistance against internal revolutionary outbreaks could expect to receive it and could also expect federal support against forced liberalization of its constitution. Moreover, although the states remained largely autonomous, this due largely to Bavarian actions, the Confederation provided an effective buffer for the states against foreign pressures. Finally, if the German Confederation served no other purpose, it did provide the framework within which the member states could consult with one another in the pursuit of common goals and the resolution of common problems. Although the Confederation would not provide the means for creating a German state, the governments, through regular sessions of the *Bundesversammlung*, became accustomed to working with one another. This provided one slender thread to the later union of the German sovereigns in the Bismarckian *Reich*.

Notes

Introduction

1. M. Doeberl, *Entwicklungsgeschichte Bayerns,* ed. Max Spindler, 3 vols. (Munich, 1912-31), 2: 449; Karl O. Aretin, "Die deutsche Politik Bayerns in der Zeit des staatlichen Entwicklung der Deutschen Bundes, 1814-1820" (Ph. D. diss., Ludwig-Maximilian Universität, Munich, 1954), passim.

2. Aretin, "Die deutsche . . .," p. 12.

3. See chap. 3.

4. "Bundesakt," Article 2 in Ernst R. Huber, *Dokumente zur deutschen Verfassungsgeschichte,* 3 vols. (Stuttgart, 1961–66), 1:75–81. (Hereafter cited as Huber, *Dokumente.*)

5. Commonly found was the presidial statement that although a majority had approved a proposition, those abstaining would be given time to obtain instructions by holding the minutes open until then.

6. This also explains why, when Bavaria felt her vital interests to be threatened, she requested that the matter be dealt with in plenary session.

7. See chap. 3.

8. See Huber, *Dokumente,* 1:150.

9. Wolfgang Zorn, *Kleine Wirtschafts- und Sozialgeschichte Bayerns, 1806-1933* (Munich-Pasing, 1962), p. 87.

10. Doeberl, *Entwicklungsgeschichte Bayerns,* 2:596.

11. Wilhelm Schreiber, *Geschichte Bayerns in Verbindung mit der deutschen Geschichte,* 2 vols. (Freiburg, 1889-91), 2: 439-40; Lothar Sachs, *Die Entwicklungsgeschichte des Bayerischen Landtags in den ersten drei Jahrzehnten nach der Verfassungsgebung, 1818-1848* (Würzburg, 1914), pp. 32-33.

12. Ernst R. Huber, *Deutsche Verfassungsgeschichte seit 1789,* 4 vols. (Stuttgart, 1960-69), 1:363. (Hereafter cited as Huber, *DVG.*)

13. Huber, *DVG,* 1:367.

14. Crown Prince Ludwig to Lerchenfeld, May 10, 1820, in Max Frh von Lerchenfeld, *Aus den Papieren des k. b. Staatsministers Maximilian Frh von Lerchenfeld* (Nördlingen, 1887), p. 303.

15. Huber, *DVG,* 1:738.

16. Doeberl, *Entwicklungsgeschichte Bayerns,* 2:466-67.

17. Report Lamb # 5, June 11, 1820, Public Records Office (hereafter cited as PRO), London, FO/30/20.

18. Karl Biedermann, *Fünfundzwanzig Jahre deutsche Geschichte, 1815-1840,* 2 vols. (Breslaw, 1890), 1:344.

19. Report Lamb #7, June 20, 1820, PRO FO/30/20.

20. See especially Article 32.

21. Lerchenfeld, *Aus den Papieren,* p. 141.

22. Leopold Ilse, *Geschichte der deutschen Bundesversammlung, insbesondere ihrer Verhaltens zu den deutschen National-Interessen,* 3 vols. (Marburg, 1861-62), 2:413.

23. This in itself was double edged for, by implication, a constitution could be altered neither by revolution nor by an arbitrary act of the sovereign or of the federal Assembly.

24. Richard Meier, "Die Regelung der inneren Verhältnisse des deutschen Bundes" (Ph.D. diss., Ludwig-Maximilian Universität, Munich, 1952), pp. 27-28.

25. Report Lerchenfeld, February 20, 1831, Bayerisches Geheime Staatsarchiv, Deutscher Bund (hereafter cited as GSA, DB) 1351. Italics in original.

26. Report Aretin, December 14, 1821, Bayerisches Geheime Staatsarchiv, K Grün (hereafter cited as GSA, KG) 2/1.

27. Ernst R. Huber, "Bundesexekution und Bundesintervention. Ein Beitrag zur Frage des Verassungsschutzes im Deutschen Bund," *Archiv des oeffentlichen Rechts* 79 (1953):1.

28. Huber, *DVG,* 1:631-33.

29. Huber, "Bundesexekution und Bundesintervention," p. 1.

30. *Exekutions-Ordnung* of August 3, 1820, in Huber, *Dokumente,* 1:105-07.

Chapter 1

1. Karl Fischer, *Die Nation und der Bundestag* (Leipzig, 1880), p. 10.

2. Report Cathcart #6, January 31, 1826, PRO FO/30/26.

3. Report Cathcart #17, July 13, 1823, PRO FO/30/23.

4. Ibid.

5. Private report Milbanke, February 8, 1827, PRO FO/30/27.

6. Each German was granted the right to own land in any state, to migrate freely, and to enter the army or civil service of any German state.

7. *Protocolle der deutschen Bundesversammlung* (hereafter cited as *PBV*), 51 vols. (Frankfurt/Main, 1816-66), August 19, 1824, 9, 25th session, *Separat-Protocol.*

8. Armansperg to Lerchenfeld, March 16, 1830, Privat Archiv der Familie Lerchenfeld, Max Frh von Lerchenfeld 1823-33; Correspondenz mit Zentner, Armansperg, Wrede.

9. Heinrich von Treitschke, *The History of Germany in the Nineteenth Century,* trans. Eden and Cedar Paul, 7 vols. (New York, 1916–19), 4:458.

10. Wrede to Metternich, April 1, 1832, in Viktor Bibl, *Metternich in neuer Erleuchtung und sein geheimer Briefwechsel mit dem bayerischen staatsminister Wrede* (Vienna, 1928), p. 300.

11. Von Küster to King Frederick William III, November 15, 1825, in "Gesandtschaftsberichte aus München, 1814–1848: Abteilung III. Die Berichte der preussischen Gesandten," vols. 39–43 of *Schriftenreihe zur Bayerischen Landesgeschichte,* ed. Anton Chroust (Munich, 1949–51), 40, #245.

12. Instruction to Dönhoff, November 22, 1833, in Chroust, ed., Abt. III, 40, #454.

13. Beidermann, *Fünfundzwanzig Jahre,* 2:118.

14. Report Aretin, December 12, 1820, GSA,DB 1340.

15. Report Aretin, March 15, 1822, GSA,DB 1342.

16. *PBV,* May 21, 1822, 7, 17th session, *Beilage.*

17. Ibid.

18. Report of Aretin, July 1, 1820, GSA,DB 1339.

19. *PVB,* May 21, 1822, 7, 17th session, *Beilage.*

20. Instruction to Pfeffel, November 14, 1822, GSA,KG 21/J8.

21. Instruction to Lerchenfeld, January 8, 1831, GSA,KG 21/J8.

22. Ibid.

23. Biedermann, *Fünfundzwanzig Jahre,* 2:118–19.

24. Report Pfeffel, June 27, 1823, GSA,DB 1342.

25. Report Pfeffel, July 2, 1824, GSA,DB 1344.

26. Report Lerchenfeld, May 16, 1828, GSA,DB 1348.

27. Ibid.

Chapter 2

1. Trauttmansdorff to Metternich, April 3, 1821, in Chroust, ed., Abt. II, 33, #265.

2. Lerchenfeld to Ludwig, December 31, 1822, Lerchenfeld, *Aus den Papieren,* p. 344.

3. Lerchenfeld to Ludwig, January 3, 1823, in Lerchenfeld, *Aus den Papieren,* p. 346.

4. Aretin, "Die deutsche . . .," p. 31.

5. Metternich to Neumann, January 25, 1820, in *Aus Metternichs nachgelassenen Papieren,* ed. Richard Metternich-Winneburg, 8 vols. (Vienna, 1881–84), 3, #468.

6. Gentz to Metternich, August 1, 1820 in Metternich-Winneburg, ed., 3, #479.

7. Ibid.

8. Wolff to Metternich, November 1, 1820, in Chroust, ed., Abt. II, 33, #248.

9. Report Lamb #24, December 14, 1820, PRO FO/30/20.

10. Report Lamb #28, December 28, 1820, PRO FO/30/20.

11. Wolff to Metternich, March 30, 1821, in Chroust, ed., Abt. II, 33, #259.

12. Zastrow to Frederick William III, January 15, 1823, in Chroust, ed., Abt. III, 39, #191.

13. Theodore S. Hamerow, *Restoration, Revolution, Reaction: Economics and Politics in Germany, 1815-1871* (Princeton, N.J., 1958), p. 75.

14. Ludwig K. Aegidi, *Aus der Vorzeit des Zollvereins. Beitrag zur deutschen Geschichte* (Hamburg, 1865), p. 59.

15. Aretin to Maximilian I, October 30, 1819, in W. von Eisenhart-Rothe and A. Ritthaler, *Vorgeschichte und Bergründung des deutschen Zollvereins, 1815-1834,* 3 vols. (Berlin, 1934), 1:353.

16. Lerchenfeld to Rechberg, August 22, 1823, in Eisenhart-Rothe and Ritthaler, 1:451.

17. Instruction to Zentner, November 12, 1819, in Eisenhart-Rothe and Ritthaler, 1:355-56.

18. Agreement and Punctuation are printed in Aegidi, *Aus der Vorzeit,* pp. 99-101. The other signatories were Hesse-Darmstadt, Saxony, Sachsen-Weimar, Nassau, and Reuss.

19. Foreign Ministry to Finance Ministry, September 26, 1823, in M. Doeberl, "Bayern und die wirtschaftliche Einigung Deutschlands," *Abhandlung der königlich bayerischen Akademie der Wissenschaft,* 39 (1915):68-71.

20. Protocol der Bayerische Ministerialsitzung, October 14, 1824, in Eisenhart-Rothe and Ritthaler, 1:462-64.

21. William I to Ludwig I, December 23, 1826, in Doeberl, "Bayern und . . . Deutschland," pp. 71-72.

22. Ludwig I to William I, December 29, 1826, in Doeberl, "Bayern und . . . Deutschland," pp. 72-73.

23. Doeberl, "Bayern und . . . Deutschland," p. 29.

24. Bavaria claimed that Sponheim was to go to her on the death of the reigning Grand Duke of Baden, on the basis of an 1819 treaty concerning the succession to the territory. The matter was eventually settled in Baden's favor. For the full and complex story, see Liselotte von Hoermann, "Der bayerisch-badische Gebietsstreit, 1825-1832," *Historische Studien* 336 (Berlin, 1938).

25. Lerchenfeld, among others, found Wangenheim's *Triaspolitik* to be too utopian to merit support.

26. Huber, *DVG,* 1:757.

27. Report Lamb#5, May 3, 1823, PRO FO/30/23.

28. Printed in Ilse, *Geschichte der deutschen Bundesversammlung,* 2:576-97, Appendix II.

29. Ibid.

30. Report Lamb#1, April 11, 1823, PRO FO/30/23.

31. Trauttmansdorff to Metternich, May 15, 1823, in Chroust, ed., Abt. II, 33, #353.

32. *PBV,* May 30, 1823, 8, 14th session, §92.

33. Ibid.

34. Report Lamb #10, June 13, 1823, PRO FO/30/23.

35. Metternich to Gentz, June 30, 1824, in Metternich-Winneburg, ed., 4, #704.

36. Metternich to Kaiser Franz, July 28, 1824, in Metternich-Winneburg, ed., 4, #721.

37. Instruction to Pfeffel, June 26, 1824, GSA,DB 1871.
38. "Protocol über die . . . Besprechung der Herr Staats Minister . . .," July 29, 1824, GSA,DB 1871.
39. *PVB*, August 16, 1824, 9, 24th session, §131.
40. Huber, *DVG,* 1:766.
41. Report Cathcart #29, June 16, 1826, PRO FO/30/26.
42. Schreiber, *Geschichte Bayerns,* 2:455–56.
43. Trauttmansdorff to Metternich, January 1, 1826, in Chroust, ed., Abt. II, 33, #448.
44. Otto Westphal, "System und Wandlung der auswärtigen Politk Bayerns in den ersten Jahren Ludwigs I," in *Staat und Volkstum: Neue Studien zur baierischen und deutschen Geschichte und Volkskunde. Festgabe für Karl Alexander von Müller* (Diessen vor München, 1933), p. 359.

Chapter 3

1. See Introduction.
2. *PVB*, June 16, 1817, 2, 35th session, §231.
3. The term *Austrägal* was derived from *austragen:* to decide or settle. Huber, DVG, 1:628.
4. Ph. Friedrich von Leonhardi, *Das Austrägalverfahren des Deutschen Bundes,* 2 vols. (Frankfurt/Main 1838–45), 1:91.
5. Report Aretin, August 4, 1820, GSA,KG 1/5.
6. Report Aretin, December 22, 1820, GSA,KG 1/5.
7. *PBV*, August 4, 1831, 16, 24th session, §155.
8. Dated July 17, 1792. *PBV*, June 21, 1827, 12, 18th session, *Separat Protocol.*
9. Report Pfeffel, September 12, 1825, GSA,KG 10/7.
10. "An die hohe Bundesversammlung. Dritte Erinnerungsgesuch des Bevollmächtigten der . . . Prinzessen Berkeley," Appendix to Lerchenfeld's report of May 6, 1826, GSA,DB 1827.
11. *PBV*, June 21, 1827, 12, 18th session, *Separat Protocol.*
12. Instruction to Lerchenfeld, March 2, 1827, GSA,KG 10/7.
13. *PBV,* June 21, 1827, 12, 18th session, §69.
14. *PBV*, July 17, 1830, 15, 14th session, *Oeffentliches Protocol.*
15. Instruction to Lerchenfeld, September 29, 1830, GSA,KG 10/7.
16. Instruction to Mieg, April 16, 1835, GSA,KG 10/7.
17. Instruction to Mieg, June 7, 1839, GSA,KG 10/7.
18. *PBV*, July 17, 1845, 30, 25th session, §265.
19. *PBV*, July 24, 1845, 30, 26th session, §282.
20. *PBV*, March 15, 1827, 11, 8th session, *Separat Protocol.*
21. *PBV*, May 21, 1827, 11, 16th session, *Separat Protocol.* I.
22. "Beschreibung der teutschen Bundefestung Landau," October 2, 1821, Bayerisches Kriegsarchiv, A XXXI Bund 204.

23. *PBV*, November 11, 1830, 15, 37th session, §286.

24. Bayerisches Kriegsarchiv, A XXXI Bund 201.

25. Report Aretin, August 11, 1820, GSA,DB 1340.

26. *PBV*, October 5, 1820, 5, Plenary Session.

27. *PBV*, August 19, 1824, 9, 25th session, *Separat Protocol.*

28. Trauttmansdorff to Metternich, January 11, 1825, in Chroust, ed., Abt. II, 33, #395.

29. Algemeines Staatsarchiv (hereafter cited ASA), Staatsrat 70, February 19, 1825.

30. ASA, Staatsrat 74, April 15, 1825.

31. Ibid.

32. *PBV*, April 12, 1825, 10, 9th session, *Separat Protocol.*

33. *PBV*, May 13, 1825, 10, 12th session *Separat Protocol* I.

34. Mainz and Luxemburg were maintained through yearly contributions from the states as determined by decree. Bavaria, since she was carrying Landau's full costs, was not assessed for the other fortresses.

35. *PBV*, July 28, 1825, 10, 19th session, *Separat Protocol.*

36. Thürheim to King Ludwig I, December 10, 1825, Geheimes Hausarchiv, ARO 30.

37. ASA, Staatsrat 89, Beilage 1, December 19, 1825. Italics in original.

38. ASA, Staatsrat 89, Beilage 2, December 19, 1825.

39. Cyprey to Damas, January 20, 1826, in Chroust, ed., Abt. I, 19, #222.

40. *PBV*, July 17, 1828, 13, 19th session, §124.

41. *PBV*, November 11, 1830, 15, 37th session, §286.

42. *PBV*, December 14, 1830, 15, 42d session § 320.

43. On March 3, 1831, the Diet decreed that of the 6291-man wartime garrison on Landau, 2291 were to come from the seven smallest federal states instead of from Baden. This was satisfactory to the governments of both Bavaria and Baden. PBV, March 3, 1831, 16:7, session §53.

44. Report Addington #2, May 15, 1828, PRO FO/30/28.

45. Report Addington #9, June 24, 1828, PRO FO/30/28.

46. Treitschke, *The History of Germany,* 4:86.

Chapter 4

1. Report Lerchenfeld, August 19, 1830, GSA,DB 1617.

2. Hanno Böck, *Karl Philipp Fürst von Wrede als politischer Berater König Ludwig I. von Bayern, 1825-38* (Munich, 1968), p. 144.

3. Spiegel to Metternich, August 27, 1830, in Chroust, ed., Abt. II, 36, #603.

4. "Berichte über den Zustand in Frankreich," GSA,DB 1617.

5. *PBV,* September 9, 1830, 15, 26th session, §204.

6. Report Cathcart #21, February 19, 1832, PRO FO/30/37.

7. Instruction to Lerchenfeld, March 1, 1830, GSA,KG 14/19.

8. King Ludwig to Lerchenfeld, September 27, 1830, in Lerchenfeld, *Aus den Papieren*, pp. 423-24.

9. Lerchenfeld to King Ludwig, October 6, 1830, ibid., pp. 424-25. Bavarian censorship was limited solely to periodicals treating foreign affairs.

10. King Ludwig to Lerchenfeld, October 24, 1830, ibid., p. 431.

11. King Ludwig to Lerchenfeld, November 26, 1830, ibid., p. 434.

12. Treitschke, *The History of Germany,* 5:292. Cf. Huber, *DVG,* 2:32 and Doeberl, *Entwicklungsgeschichte Bayerns,* 3:100.

13. Huber, *DVG,* 2:32-33.

14. Spiegel to Metternich, February 4, 1831, in Chroust, ed., Abt. II, 36, #625.

15. Anton, Doll, "Philipp Jakob Siebenpfeiffer/Johann Georg August Wirth," in *Das Hambacherfest, 27. Mai 1832: Männern und Ideen,* ed. Kurt Baumann (Speyer, 1957), p. 27.

16. Joh. Richard Mucke, *Die politischen Bewegungen in Deutschland von 1830 bis 1835,* 2 vols. (Leipzig, 1875), 1:62; Huber, *DVG,* 2:32-33.

17. Huber, *DVG,* 1:371.

18. *Registratur* of September 18, 1830, GSA,DB 1631; Bibl, *Metternich in neur Erleuchtung,* pp. 103-5.

19. Report Lerchenfeld, September 24, 1830, GSA,DB 1631.

20. Bibl, *Metternich in neur Erleuchtung,* pp. 108-10.

21. *PBV,* September 30, 1830, 15, 29th session, §227.

22. Report Lerchenfeld, October 1, 1830, GSA,DB 1631; *PBV,* October 1, 1830, 15, 30th session, §233.

23. Instruction to Lerchenfeld, October 4, 1830, GSA,DB 1631.

24. ASA, Staatsrat 108, *Beilage,* October 5, 1830.

25. *Protocolle des Ministerialrathes,* October 6, 1830, ASA, Staatsrat 108.

26. Instruction to Lerchenfeld, October 6, 1830, GSA,DB 1631.

27. *PBV,* October 7, 1830, 15, 31st session, §238.

28. Report Lerchenfeld, October 8, 1830, GSA,DB 1631.

29. *PBV,* October 7, 1830, 15, 31st session, §238.

30. Report Lerchenfeld, October 9, 1830, GSA,DB 1631.

31. Instruction to Lerchenfeld, October 9, 1830, GSA,DB 1831.

32. Spiegel to Metternich, October 11, 1830, in Chroust, ed., Abt. II, 36:280, n2.

33. Instruction to Lerchenfeld, October 12, 1830, GSA,DB 1631.

34. Instruction to Lerchenfeld, October 13, 1830, GSA,DB 1631.

35. Wolzogen to Bernstorff, October 14, 1830, in Chroust, ed., Abt. III, 40, #371.

36. *PBV,* October 14, 1830, 15, 32d session, §249. These troops had never been sent; only the frontier garrisons had been strengthened.

37. *PBV,* October 21, 1830, 15, 34th session, §258.

38. Ibid.

39. Lerchenfeld to Armansperg, October 22, 1830, in Lerchenfeld, *Aus den Papieren,* pp. 429-30.

40. Instruction to Lerchenfeld, November 12, 1830, GSA,KG 8/8.

41. Instruction to Lerchenfeld, October 15, 1830, GSA, KG 8/8.

42. *PBV*, November 18, 1830, 15, 38th session, §291.

43. Huber, *DVG*, 2:117-18.

44. *PBV*, September 9, 1831, 16, 9th session, *Separat-Protocol* I.

45. On March 18, 1831.

46. On August 30, 1831. Huber, *DVG*, 2:120.

47. *PBV*, September 9, 1831, 16, 9th session *Separat-Protocol* I.

48. Treitschke, *The History of Germany*, 5:377-85; Huber, *DVG*, 2:120-24. See chapter 7.

49. Biedermann, *Fünfundzwanzig Jahre*, 2:97. In 1864 the Confederation sent its ambassador to the London Conference meeting to deal with the question of Schleswig-Holstein.

Chapter 5

1. Metternich to Apponyi, November 15, 1831, in Metternich-Winneburg, ed., 5, #1013.

2. *PBV*, October 27, 1831, 16, 36th session, §239.

3. Spiegel to Metternich, December 2, 1831, in Chroust, ed., Abt. II, 36, #674.

4. Memo of the Interior Ministry, December 20, 1831, GSA, DB 1630.

5. Ministerialrath to Ludwig I, February 2, 1832, GSA,DB 1630.

6. Report Lerchenfeld, February 29, 1832, GSA,DB 1630.

7. Report Cathcart #143, November 23, 1831, PRO FO/30/35.

8. *PBV*, November 19, 1831, 16, 39th session, *Separat Protocol* #1.

9. *PBV*, December 7, 1831, 16, 42d session, §301.

10. Gise to Ludwig I, January 10, 1832, GSA,DB 1872.

11. Gise to Ludwig I, January 12, 1832, GSA,DB 1872.

12. Gise to Ludwig I, February 9, 1832, GSA,DB 1872.

13. Gise to Ludwig I, February 10, 1832, GSA,DB 1872.

14. Instruction to Lerchenfeld, February 12, 1832, GSA,DB 1872.

15. Gise to Ludwig I, February 14, 1832, GSA,DB 1872.

16. *PBV*, February 20, 1832, 17, 7th session, §48.

17. Ibid.

18. *Die Verhandlungen der Bundesversammlung von den revolutionären Bewegungen des Jahres 1830 bis zu den geheimen Wiener Ministerial-Conferenzen* (Heidelberg, 1846), p. 159.

19. Report from Württemberg Minister Schmitz-Grollenberg to Gise, February 20, 1832, GSA,DB 1872.

20. Lerchenfeld to Ludwig I, February 29, 1832, in Lerchenfeld, *Aus den Papieren*, pp. 441-42.

21. Instruction to Lerchenfeld, March 1, 1832, GSA,DB 1873.

22. *PBV*, March 2, 1832, 17, 9th session, §67.

23. *PBV*, March 8, 1832, 17, 10th session, §80.

24. Spiegel to Metternich, March 6, 1832, in Chroust, ed., Abt. II, 36, #690.

25. Schönberg to Metternich, March 8, 1832, in Chroust, ed., Abt. II, 36, #691.
26. Gise to Ludwig I, March 9, 1832, GSA,DB 1873.
27. Schönberg to Metternich, March 13, 1832, in Chroust, ed., Abt. II, 36, #694.
28. Circular to Bavarian ambassadors, March 16, 1832, GSA, DB 1873.
29. Metternich to Spiegel, March 26, 1832, GSA,DB 1873.
30. Report Cathcart #33, March 19, 1832, PRO FO/30/37.
31. Ibid.
32. Royal decree, March 31, 1832, GSA,DB 1873.
33. Report Lerchenfeld, April 12, 1832, GSA,DB 1874.
34. Report Cartwright #48, May 25, 1832, PRO FO/30/38.
35. Oettingen-Wallerstein to Gise, May 9, 1832, GSA,DB 1874.
36. Gise to Lerchenfeld, May 30, 1832, GSA,DB 1874.
37. *PBV,* February 9, 1832, 17, 6th session, §38.
38. Instruction to Lerchenfeld, February 18, 1832, GSA,DB 1881.
39. *PBV,* April 26, 1832, 17, 14th session, §119.
40. *PBV,* July 5, 1832, 17, 24th session, §230.
41. Report Cartwright #94, July 29, 1832, PRO FO/30/39.
42. Huber, *DVG.* 2:43.
43. Instruction to Lerchenfeld, April 12, 1832, GSA,KG 8/8.
44. Huber, *DVG,* 2:135-36.
45. *PBV,* March 8, 1832, 17, 10th session, §81.
46. Huber, *DVG,* 2:141.
47. Karl Heigel, *Ludwig I. König von Bayern* (Leipzig, 1872), passim; Kurt von Raumer, "Das Hambacher Fest," in *Staat und Volkstum,* passim.
48. Baumann, ed., *Das Hambacherfest,* p. 323.
49. Report Lerchenfeld, June 3, 1832, GSA,DB 1632.
50. See *PBV,* June 14, 1832, 17, 21st session, *Separat Protocol* II and *Beilage.*
51. Instruction to Lerchenfeld, June 7, 1832, GSA,KG 11/10.
52. Metternich to Gise, June 8, 1832, in Metternich-Winneburg, ed., 5, #1088.
53. Wrede to Metternich, June 16, 1832, in Bibl, *Metternich in neuer Erleuchtung,* p. 333.
54. *PBV,* June 7, 1832, 17, 20th session, *Separat Protocol.*
55. Huber, *DVG,* 2:162-63.
56. Report Sercey, June 24, 1832, in Chroust, ed., Abt. I, 21, #575.
57. Instruction to Lerchenfeld, June 1832, GSA,KG 8/8.
58. *PBV,* June 28, 1832, 17, 22d session, *Oeffentliches Protocol.*
59. Metternich to Apponyi, August 4, 1832, in Metternich-Winneburg, ed., 5, #1093.
60. The Six Articles are printed in Huber, *Dokumente* 1:119-20.
61. *PBV,* July 5, 1832, 17, 24th session, §231.
62. Gise to Lerchenfeld, July 15, 1832, GSA,KG 10/12.
63. *PBV,* August 9, 1832, 17, 29th session, §288.
64. Report Sercey, September 14, 1832, in Chroust, ed., Abt. I, 21, #586.
65. Weissenberg to Metternich, September 19, 1832, in Chroust, ed., Abt. II, 36, #731.
66. Instruction to Lerchenfeld, September 21, 1832, GSA,KG 8/10.
67. Great Britain had no ties to the Confederation because of Hannover, for un-

like the kings of the Netherlands and Denmark, she had no ambassador in the federal Assembly.

68. See chapter 6. The Russian note, unlike those from France and Great Britain, received the thanks of the federal Diet.

69. Report Cartwright #127, October 11, 1832, PRO FO/30/40.

70. Chroust, ed., Abt. II, 36, pp. 483-84, n2.

71. Huber, *DVG,* 2:159-60.

72. *PBV,* November 8, 1832, 17, 42d session, §485.

Chapter 6

1. Huber, *DVG,* 2:165.

2. Treitschke, *The History of Germany,* 5:364-65; Huber, *DVG,* 2:165-66.

3. *PBV,* April 4, 1833, 18, 13th session, §130.

4. *PBV,* April 9, 1833, 18, 14th session, §133.

5. *PBV,* April 12, 1833, 18, 16th session, § 148.

6. Ernst R. Huber, "Bundesexekution und Bundesintervention," 79:16.

7. Lerchenfeld had been recalled to his former post of finance minister.

8. Instruction to Mieg, July 6, 1833, GSA,KG 21/J8.

9. *PBV,* June 20, 1833, 18, 26th session, §258.

10. Instruction to Mieg. July 6, 1833, GSA,KG 21/J8.

11. *PBV,* September 19, 1833, 18, 40th session, §417.

12. Huber, *DVG,* 2:174, nn8, 10.

13. Gise to Ludwig I, November 14, 1883, GSA,DB 1702.

14. Instruction to Mieg, November 28, 1833, GSA,DB 1702.

15. *PBV,* April 3, 1834, 19, 13th session, §164.

16. *PBV,* April 24, 1834, 19, 16th session, §204.

17. *PBV,* May 1, 1834, 19, 17th session, §221, 223.

18. Friedrich von Weech, *Correspondencen und Actenstücke zur Geschichte der Ministerial-conferenz von Carlsbad und Wien in dem Jahren 1819, 1820, und 1834* (Leipzig, 1865), pp. 258-59. Nothing ever came of these proposals.

19. *PBV,* May 12, 1834, 19, 19th session, §245.

20. *PBV,* May 22, 1834, 19, 20th session, §261.

21. Instruction to Trott, May 24, 1834, GSA,DB 1703.

22. *PBV,* May 28, 1834, 19, 21st session, §274.

23. *PBV,* June 3, 1834, 19, 22d session, §276, *Beilage* 1.

24. Nikolas Dommermuth, *Das angebliche europäische Garantierecht über den Deutschen Bund von 1815 bis 1866* (Frankfurt/Main, 1928), pp. 58-59.

25. Dönhoff to Frederick William III, May 31, 1834, in Chroust, ed., Abt. III, 40, #471.

26. Gise to Mieg, June 12, 1834, GSA,DB 1703.

27. *PBV*, September 18, 1834, 19, 34th session, §454.

28. *PBV*, June 12, 1834, 19, 23d session, §287.

29. See chapter 4.

30. *PBV*, February 26, 1834, 19, 8th session, §95.

31. Printed in *PBV*, March 20, 1834, 19, 11th session *Separat Protocol*.

32. Instruction to Mieg, March 13, 1834, GSA,KG 4/1.

33. Instruction to Mieg, March 21, 1834, GSA,KG 4/1.

34. Dommermuth, *Das angebliche,* pp. 62–63; Nagler to Münch, September 20, 1834; Haus-Hof-und Staatsarchiv, Deutsche Akton 34.

35. *PBV*, September 18, 1834, 19, 34th session, §455.

36. Ibid.

37. This argument is derived especially from Huber, *DVG*, 1:675–79, 681.

38. *PBV*, September 1, 1842, 27, 24th session, §264.

39. Weech, *Correspondencen und Actenstücke*, p. 130–31.

40. Ibid., pp. 131–34.

41. Huber, *DVG*, 2:178; Treitschke, *The History of Germany*, 5:414.

42. Bibl, *Metternich in neuer Erleuchtung*, p. 211.

43. Weech, *Correspondencen und Actenstücke*, p. 139.

44. Metternich to Wrede, March 17, 1834, in Bibl, *Metternich in neuer Erleuchtung*, p. 416.

45. Metternich to Wrede, May 1, 1834, in Bibl, *Metternich in neuer Erleuchtung*, p. 424.

46. Huber, *DVG*, 2:180.

47. Printed in Huber, *Dokumente*, 1:123–35.

48. Huber, *DVG*, 2:181.

49. Huber, *Dokumente*, 1:128, n35.

50. Ibid., p. 129, n37.

51. The basis for much of the preceding discussion is in Huber, *DVG*, 2:178–80.

Chapter 7

1. Report Cartwright #12, February 22, 1835, PRO FO/30/55.

2. Report Cartwright #73, October 9, 1835, PRO FO/30/57.

3. *PBV*, April 27, 1833, 18, 20th session, §181.

4. *PBV*, August 28, 1834, 19, 32d session, §423.

5. *PBV*, September 11, 1834, 19, 33d session, §442.

6. *PBV*, August 28, 1834, 19, 32d session, §423.

7. *PBV*, September 11, 1834, 19, 33d session, §441.

8. *PBV*, January 3, 1835, 20, 1st session, §11.

9. *PBV*, January 15, 1835, 20, 3d session, §36.

10. *PBV*, August 27, 1835, 20, 20th session, §324.

11. If there were no position available in a town, a newly arrived journeyman received sufficient money from a fund established by the journeymen or guilds of each to allow that journeyman to support himself in his travel to the next. Lujo Brentano, *On the History and Development of Guilds and the Origin of Trade-Unions* (New York, 1969), p. cliii.

12. *PBV*, August 27, 1835, 20, 20th session §324.

13. *PBV*, October 29, 1835, 20, 26th session, §417.

14. *PBV*, September 10, 1835, 20, 22d session, §365.

15. Instruction to substitute ambassador, January 29, 1836, Bayerisches Geheimen Staatsarchiv, Gesandschaft Frankfurt (hereafter cited as GSA,GF), III-66; and *PBV*, March 17, 1836, 21, 1st session, §11.

16. Instruction to Mieg, March 7, 1837, GSA,GF III-66.

17. *PBV*, August 27, 1840, 25, 17th session, §217.

18. Gise to Ludwig, October 12, 1840, GSA,DB 1672.

19. Instruction to Mieg, October 13, 1840, GSA,GF III-66.

20. Report Mieg, October 22, 1840, GSA,DB 1672.

21. Verbal note Könneritz to Gise, October 31, 1840, GSA,DB 1672.

22. Gise to Könneritz, November 5, 1840, GSA,DB 1672.

23. Report Mieg, December 3, 1840, GSA,DB 1672. The decree is in *PBV*, December 3, 1840, 25, 27th session, §310.

24. January 14, 1841, in Instruction to Mieg, January 20, 1841, GSA,GF III-66.

25. Instruction to Lerchenfeld, November 25, 1841, GSA,DB 1672.

26. Carl von Kaltenborn, *Geschichte der deutschen Bundesverhältnisse und Einheitsbestrebungen, von 1806 bis 1856* (Berlin, 1857), 1:445.

27. Helmut Koopmann, *Das Junge Deutschland, Analyse seines Selbstständnisses* (Stuttgart, 1970), p. 7. There was indeed a revolutionary secret society named *Young Germany* founded as part of Mazzini's Young Europe movement, but it was in no way identical to the literary movement of that name.

28. Huber, *DVG*, 2:130.

29. Koopmann, *Das Junge Deutschland*, pp. 29–30.

30. Report Cartwright #3, January 16, 1836, PRO FO/30/60.

31. *PBV*, December 10, 1835, 20, 31st session, §515.

32. "Er liebt die Kunst,/und die schönsten Frauen,/Die lässt er porträtieren;/Er geht in diesem gemahlten Serail/Als Kunst Eunuch spazieren." Jost Hermand, ed., *Der deutsche Vormärz, Texte und Dockumentation* (Stuttgart, 1967), pp. 91–92.

33. Instruction to Trott, December 19, 1835, GSA,GF II-47.

34. *PBV*, June 25, 1835, 20, 16th session, *Registratur II*.

35. *PBV*, October 1, 1835, 20, 25th session, §401.

36. *PBV*, April 28, 1836, 21, 3d session, §70.

37. Lithograph included in Instruction to *Bundestag* ambassador, June 29, 1836, GSA,GF I-89.

38. Lithograph dd. December 17, included in Instruction to *Bundestag* ambassador, December 23, 1836, GSA,GF I-89.

39. Dated January 9, 1837, in Instruction to *Bundestag* ambassador, January 18, 1837, GSA,GF I-89.

40. Note to the Saxon Foreign Minister dd. January 29, 1837, in Instruction to *Bundestag* ambassador, January 29, 1837, GSA,GF I-89.

41. See below, chap. 7.

42. Note to Hannoverian Foreign Minister in Instruction to Mieg, June 11, 1838, GSA,GF I-89.

43. Report Mieg, June 22, 1838, GSA,GF I-89.

44. Instruction to Mieg, June 27, 1838, GSA,GF I-89.

45. Interior Ministry to *Kreis* government July 1, 1838, in Instruction to Mieg, July 4, 1838, GSA,GF I-89.

46. Instruction to Mieg, April 22, 1839, GSA,GF I-89.

47. *PBV*, May 2, 1839, 22, 6th session §82.

48. Instruction to Lerchenfeld, May 21, 1842, GSA,GF I-89.

49. *PBV*, August 18, 1836, 21, 16th session §226.

50. *PBV*, November 5, 1835, 20, 27th session §437.

51. *PBV*, August 18, 1836, 21, 16th session §226.

52. *PBV,* June 21, 1838, 23, 12th session §155.

53. See below, chap. 7.

54. Franz Schnabel, *Deutsche Geschichte in neunzehnten Jahrhundert*, 2 vols. (Freiburg in the Breisgau, 1929–36), 4:99–100.

55. Royal policy was to propose a budget with overestimated outlays and understated income. The surplus that this and a further curtailment of expenditures brought about could, in the king's view, be spent as he saw fit—especially in the realm of art and architecture. This was challenged by the *Landtag*, which claimed that it had the right not only to approve the budget but also to alter it on a line-by-line basis. The *Landtag* was supported in this claim by the royal ministers—resulting in Wallerstein's dismissal and replacement by Abel. The problem was finally resolved in 1843 when the *Landtag* gave retroactive sanction to previous uses of budgetary surpluses on condition that all future surpluses be applied toward the state's income. Doeberl, *Entwicklungsgeschichte Bayerns*, 3:123; Huber *DVG*, 2:436–37; Max Spindler, ed., *Handbuch der Bayerischen Geschichte*, 4 vols. (Munich, 1967–75), 4, pt. 1:189–90, 206.

56. Spindler, ed., *Handbuch*, 4, pt. 1:194–95.

57. See among others, Huber, *DVG*, 2:185–281, and Schnabel, *Deutsche Geschichte in neunzehnten Jahrhundert*, 4:97–164.

58. Huber, *DVG*, 2:912.

59. See Huber, *DVG*, 2:259, for provisions of the Convention of September 1841.

60. Spindler, ed., *Handbuch*, 4, pt. 1:195.

61. Colloredo to Metternich December 28, 1837, in Chroust, ed., Abt. II, 37, #884.

62. Spindler, ed., *Handbuch*, 4, pt. 1:199–200.

63. Colloredo to Metternich, January 11, 1838, in Chroust, ed., Abt. II, 37, #887.

64. See for example, Colloredo to Metternich, February 8, 1838, in Chroust, ed., Abt. II, 37, #890, and Dönhoff to Gise, March 2, 1838, GSA,GF III-40.

65. See for example, Senfft to Metternich, January 27, 1845, in Chroust, ed., Abt. II, 37, #1097.

66. Colloredo to Metternich, March 7, 1838, in Chroust, ed., Abt. II, 37:18, n1.

67. Metternich to Colloredo, March 11, 1838, in Chroust, ed., Abt. II, 37 #899.

68. Report Cartwright #36, May 22, 1838, PRO FO/30/68.

69. Gise to Dönhoff, March 11, 1838, GSA,GF III-40.

70. Gise to Lerchenfeld, March 15, 1838, in Chroust, ed., Abt. II, 37:22, n1.

71. Instruction to Mieg, April 25, 1838, GSA,GF III-40.

72. Report Cartwright #36, May 22, 1838, PRO FO/30/68.

73. Report Molyneux #4, June 5, 1838, PRO FO/30/69.

74. Ludwig to Mieg, May 28, 1838, GSA,GF III-40.

75. Instruction to Mieg, May 24, 1838, GSA,GF III-40.

76. Ludwig to Mieg, June 1, 1838, GSA,GF III-40.

77. "Neue Würzburger Zeitung" #151, June 1, 1838, GSA,GF III-40.

78. Report Molyneux #10, June 30, 1838, PRO FO/30/69.

79. Ministry of the Interior to Untermainkreis government, June 8, 1838, GSA,GF III-40.

80. See Prussian Foreign Minister von Werther to the Bavarian ambassador in Berlin Luxberg, June 17, 1838, GSA,GF III-40; Trauttmansdorff to Metternich June 18, 1838, in Chroust, ed., Abt. II, 37:42, n3.

81. Report Molyneux #10, June 30, 1838 PRO FO/30/69.

82. In Huber, *Dokumente*, 1:253–55.

83. For the full constitutional justification see Huber, *DVG*, 2:110–11.

84. Report Meig, March 23, 1838, GSA,DB 1357.

85. Report Mieg, April 4, 1838, GSA, DB 1357.

86. Ibid.

87. Gise to Mieg, April 27, 1838, GSA,GF I-97.

88. Report of Bavarian ambassador in Stuttgart, April 26, 1838, in Instruction to Mieg, May 5, 1838, GSA, GF I-97.

89. Gise to Mieg, May 14, 1838, GSA,GF I-97.

90. *PBV*, May 25, 1838, 23, 9th session, §125.

91. Report Mieg, May 25, 1838, GSA,DB 1357.

92. Huber, *DVG*, 2:109.

93. *PBV*, July 12, 1838, 23, 15th session, §180.

94. Votes of Bavaria, Baden, and Württemberg. *PBV*, August 30, 1838, 23, 22d session, §253.

95. *PBV*, September 6, 1838, 23, 23d session, §265.

96. Report Mieg, September 7, 1838, GSA,DB 1357.

97. Report Mieg, November 29, 1838, GSA,DB 1357.

98. Report Mieg, November 30, 1838, GSA,DB 1357; *PBV*, November 29, 1838, 23, 34th session, §373.

99. Huber, *DVG*, 2:111.

100. Report Mieg, December 10, 1838, GSA,DB 1357.

101. Instruction to Mieg, December 12, 1838, GSA,GF I-97.

102. Instruction to Mieg, February 19, 1839, GSA,GF I-97.
103. Instruction to Mieg, March 22, 1839, GSA,GF I-97.
104. Ibid.
105. Instruction to Mieg, April 18, 1839, GSA,GF I-97.
106. *PBV*, April 26, 1839, 24, 5th session, §69.
107. Report Abercromby #32, April 29, 1839, PRO FO/30/72.
108. *PBV*, April 26, 1839, 24, 5th session, §69; Report Mieg, April 26, 1839, GSA,DB 1358.
109. Instruction to Mieg, June 14, 1839, GSA,GF I-97.
110. Instruction to Mieg, June 18, 1839, GSA,GF I-97.
111. *PBV*, June 27, 1839, 24, 12th session, §161.
112. Report Mieg, June 27, 1839, GSA,DB 1358.
113. Report Abercromby #69, July 7, 1838, PRO FO/30/73.
114. *PBV*, August 22, 1839, 24, 17th session, §227.
115. Instruction to Mieg, August 30, 1839, GSA,GF I-97.
116. Report Abercromby #86, August 28, 1839, PRO FO/30/74.
117. *PBV*, September 5, 1839, 24, 19th session, §256.
118. Instruction to Mieg, Septembr 19, 1839, GSA,GF I-97.
119. By way of postscript, in 1840 Ernst August recalled the prorogued *Landtag*, which, all other avenues of legal opposition being closed, accepted a new constitution similar to, but a bit more liberal than, that of 1819.
120. The Military Commission was composed of one senior officer from each of the six military commands (Austria, Prussia, Bavaria, VIII, IX, and X military commands) and is not to be confused with the Diet's Military Affairs Committee composed solely of ambassadors.
121. Instruction to Mieg, December 14, 1834, GSA,GF VIII-103.
122. Report Cartwright #55, August 1, 1836, PRO FO/30/62.
123. Report Cartwright #73, October 1, 1836, PRO FO/30/63.
124. Instruction to Völderndorff in Instruction to Mieg, December 14, 1834, GSA,GF VIII-103.
125. *PBV*, June 22, 1837, 22, 17th session, §199.
126. Report Cartwright #6, September 12, 1837, PRO FO/30/66.
127. Instruction to Völderndorff in Instruction to Mieg, December 14, 1834, GSA,GF VIII-103.
128. Dönhoff to Frederick William III, July 12, 1837, in Chroust, ed., Abt. III, 40, #582.
129. *PBV*, September 21, 1837, 22, 26th session, §295.
130. Report Dönhoff, October 28, 1838, in Chroust, ed., Abt. III, 41, #652.
131. Kast to Metternich, October 23, 1839, in Chroust, ed., Abt. II, 37, #940.
132. Dönhoff to Werther, June 24, 1840, in Chroust, Abt. III, 41, #698.
133. Report Molyneux #23, April 11, 1840, PRO FO/30/76.
134. *PBV*, February 18, 1841, 26, 4th session, *Separat Protocol*.
135. Ibid.
136. Ibid.

137. *PBV*, March 26, 1841, 26, 7th session, *Separat Protocol.*

138. Dönhoff to Frederick William IV, January 26, 1841, in Chroust, ed., Abt. III, 41, #731

139. *PBV*, April 28, 1842, 27, 10th session, *Separat Protocol.*

140. *PBV,* March 10, 1842, 27, 7th session, *Separat Protocol.*

141. Report Dönhoff, May 29, 1837, in Chroust, ed., Abt. III, 40, #574.

142. Münch to Metternich, June 4, 1837, in Chroust, ed., Abt. II, 36, #862.

143. *PBV*, March 13, 1841, 26, 6th session, *Separat Protocol* 1.

144. Ibid; Canitz to Werther, October 22, 1840, in Chroust, ed., Abt. III, 41, #718; Colloredo to Metternich, March 21, 1841, in Chroust, ed., Abt. II, 37, #990.

145. Spiegel to Metternich, March 24, 1833, in Chroust, ed., Abt. III, 36, #754.

146. Dönhoff to Frederick William III, March 10, 1838, in Chroust, ed., Abt. III, 41, #613.

147. Dönhoff, to Frederick William IV, January 26, 1841, in Chroust, ed., Abt. III, 41, #731.

148. Colloredo to Metternich, November 18, 1840, in Chroust, ed., Abt. II, 37, #971.

149. *PBV*, March 13, 1841, 26, 6th session, *Separat Protocol.*

150. Dönhoff to Frederick William IV, April 5, 1841, in Chroust, ed., Abt. III, 41, #743.

151. *PBV*, May 13, 1841, 26, 13th session, *Separat Protocol.*

152. *PBV*, June 24, 1841, 26, 17th session, *Separat Protocol.*

153. *PBV*, August 10, 1843, 28, 25th session, §255.

154. Ibid.

155. *PBV*, June 27, 1844, 29, 21st session, §194.

156. *PBV*, June 20, 1844, 29, 20th session, §186.

157. This was the so-called *"Kniebeugungsfrage"* that so troubled the Prussian ambassador in Munich (Chroust, ed., Abt. III, 41–42, passim). It was decreed in 1839 and rescinded in December 1845, after loud and long protest from Bavaria's Protestants.

158. Huber, *DVG*, 2:437.

159. See chap. 8.

160. *PBV*, August 6, 1846, 31, 23d session, §210.

161. *PBV*, July 29, 1841, 26, 22d session, §243 and *Registratur.*

162. *PBV*, April 22, 1841, 26, 10th session, §130.

163. *PBV*, June 19, 1845, 30, 21st session, §228.

164. *PBV*, June 19, 1845, 30, 21st session, §227.

165. *PBV*, September 9, 1847, 32, 28th session, §268 and *Beilage* 3.

Chapter 8

1. The Political Committee was composed of the ambassadors of Bavaria, Prussia, Saxony, Baden, and Holstein. *PBV*, February 29, 1848, 33, 9th session, §103.

2. *PBV*, March 1, 1848, 33, 10th session, §108.

3. Instruction to Gasser, February 29, 1848, in M. Doeberl, *Bayern und Deutschland. Bayern und die Deutsche Frage in der Epoche des Frankfurter Parlaments* (Munich, 1922), pp. 203–5.

4. Bernstorff to Frederick William IV, March 6, 1848, in Chroust, ed., Abt. III, 42, #1035.

5. Doeberl, *Bayern und Deutschland*, p. 12.

6. Ibid.

7. Huber, *Dokumente*, 1:261–62.

8. Huber, *Dokumente*, 1:262–64.

9. *PBV*, March 3, 1848, 33, 12th session, §119; Foreign Ministry to Max II, April 9, 1848, GSA,DB 1367.

10. Report Orme #13, March 3, 1848, PRO FO/30/104.

11. Bernstorff to Frederick William IV, March 5, 1848, in Chroust, ed., Abt. III, 42, #1034.

12. *PBV*, March 8, 1848, 33, 15th session, §133.

13. *PBV*, March 9, 1848, 33, 16th session, §137.

14. *PBV*, March 20, 1848, 33, 21st session, 161.

15. *PBV*, March 10, 1848, 33, 17th session, §140.

16. Report Gasser, March 18, 1848, GSA,DB 1385.

17. *PBV*, March 13, 1848, 33, 18th session, §142.

18. Huber, *DVG*, 2:589.

19. Brenner to Metternich, March 12, 1848, in Chroust, ed., Abt. II, 37, #1286; Bernstorff to Frederick William IV, March 12, 1848, in Chroust, ed., Abt. III, 42, #1041.

20. Report Orme #25, March 18, 1848, PRO FO/30/106.

21. Bernstorff to Canitz, March 15, 1848, in Chroust, Abt. III, 42: 425, n2.

22. *PBV*, March 29, 1848, 33, 25th session, §198.

23. Instruction to Gasser, March 16, 1848, in Doeberl, *Bayern und Deutschland*, pp. 207–8.

24. It was a simple process by which a person was given or kept in a governmental position, then refused a "vacation" to attend the *Landtag* session.

25. Bernstorff to Frederick William IV, March 18, 1848, in Chroust, ed., Abt. III, 42, #1045.

26. Bernstorff to Frederick William IV, March 2, 1848, in Chroust, ed., Abt. III, 42, #1027.

27. *PBV*, March 23, 1848, 33, 22d session, §170.

28. *PBV*, March 25, 1848, 33, 23d session, §182.

29. *PBV*, March 25, 1848, 33, 23d session, §188.

30. *PBV*, March 26, 1848, 33, 24th session, §191.

31. *PBV*, April 4, 1848, 33, 28th session, §219.

32. Report of Prince Carl in *PBV*, May 1, 1848, 33, 44th session, *Separat Protocol* 1.

33. For details of the campaign, see *PBV*, May 1, 1848, 33, 44th session, *Separat Protocol* 2 and May 4, 1848, 33, 47th session, *Separat Protocol* 1.

34. *PBV*, May 17, 1848, 33, 54th session, §518.
35. *PBV*, June 25, 1848, 33, 66th session, §655.
36. *PBV*, June 30, 1848, 33, 68th session, §681.
37. These included the Karlsbad decrees of 1819, the 1832 ban on petitions, and the decrees of October 21, 1830; June 28 and July 5, 1832; June 30, 1833; and June 21, 1834.
38. *PBV*, April 2, 1848, 33, 27th session, §214.
39. *PBV*, May 29, 1848, 33, 58th session, §565.
40. *PBV*, March 26, 1847, 32, 9th session, §88.
41. *PBV*, September 9, 1847, 32, 28th session, §269.
42. *PBV*, April 7, 1848, 33, 29th session, §237.
43. *PBV*, March 30, 1848, 33, 26th session, §209.
44. Huber, *DVG*, 2:598.
45. *PBV*, April 2, 1848, 33, 27th session, §215.
46. *PBV*, April 7, 1848, 33, 29th session, §238.
47. Huber, *Dokumente*, 1:269-71.
48. Huber, *Dokumente*, 1:271-73.
49. Kaltenborn, *Geschichte der deutschen Bundesverhältnisse*, 2:48.
50. *PBV*, April 10, 1848, 33, 30th session, §254.
51. Kaltenborn, *Geschichte der deutschen Bundesverhältnisse*, 2:49.
52. Dahlmann, representing Prussia, had been one of the Göttingen Seven; see chap. 7.
53. Veit Valentin, *Geschichte der deutschen Revolution von 1848-49*, 2 vols. (Berlin, 1930-31), 1:518.
54. This was, of course, not purely voluntary, for a mechanism had been established to compel a recalcitrant state to comply; see Introduction.
55. *PBV*, April 18, 1848, 33, 37th session, §297.
56. *PBV*, April 29, 1848, 33, 43d session, §364.
57. What follows is derived largely from Valentin, *Geschichte der deutschen Revolution*, 1:518-20; Doeberl, *Bayern und Deutschland*, pp. 34-51; Doeberl, *Entwicklungsgeschichte Bayerns*, 3:197-201; Kaltenborn, *Geschichte der deutschen Bundesverhältnisse*, 2:62-63.
58. Valentin, I, 520.
59. Austria (I–III corps), Prussia, (IV–VI), and Bavaria (VII) would each provide one member, while the states providing each of the remaining three contingents would name the remaining three members.
60. *PBV*, May 3, 1848, 33, 46th session, §406.
61. Especially that of May 5, in *PBV*, May 8, 1848, 33, 49th session, §435.
62. Karl Mathy of Baden, Saxony's Foreign Minister Ludwig von der Pfordten, and Bavaria's Joseph Graf von Armansperg. Ministerial Council to Max II, May 16, 1848, GSA,DB 1131.
63. *PBV*, April 14, 1848, 33, 34th session, §279.
64. *PBV*, June 5, 1848, 33, 61st session, §601.
65. The legitimacy of the National Assembly had been established by the federal decree calling for elections, while that of the *Bundesversammlung* had not yet been rescinded.

66. Instruction to Closen, June 9, 1848, GSA, GF I-8.
67. Bray to Max II, June 20, 1848, GSA,DB 1131.
68. Instruction to Closen, June 21, 1848, GSA,DB 1131.
69. Huber, *Dokumente*, 1:276–77.
70. *PBV*, June 19, 1848, 33, 67th session.
71. Instruction to Closen, July 11, 1848, GSA,GF I-8.
72. *PBV*, July 12, 1848, 33, Plenar Session.
73. Huber, *DVG*, 2:632–33, which provides the basis for what follows.

Chapter 9

1. Max Frh von Lerchenfeld, *Aus den Papieren des k. b. Staatministers Maximilian Frh von Lerchenfeld* (Nördlingen, 1887), p. 175.
2. Report Cartwright #73, June 25, 1832, PRO FO/30/38.
3. Report Cartwright #98, July 4, 1833, PRO FO/30/44.

Bibliography

1. Archival Materials

Bayerisches Hauptstaatsarchiv, München.
Abteilung I: Allgemeines Staatsarchiv. Staatsrat 60,70, 74–76, 89, 95, 136, 138.

Abteilung II: Geheimes Staatsarchiv. Deutscher Bund MA II 1131–32, 1201–2, 1209, 1219–20, 1228–29, 1277 (a-d), 1316–18, 1326, 1339–67, 1378, 1385, 1521–23, 1617, 1630–36, 1655 (a-c), 1672, 1702–4, 1718, 1871–75, 1877, 1881, 1962.

Abteilung II: Geheimes Staatsarchiv. K Grün (Gesandtschaft Frankfurt/Main) 1/5, 2/1–7, 3/1–6, 4/1, 7/5, 8/8–10, 10/7, 10/12, 11/3, 11/10, 14/19, 15/A6, 17/B8, 21/J8.

Abteilung II: Geheimes Staatsarchiv. Gesandtschaft Frankfurt I-8, 89, 97; II-46–61, 66–68; III-40, 66; VIII-103.

Abteilung III: Geheimes Hausarchiv. II A 15, ARO 27, ARO 30.

Abteilung IV: Kriegsarchiv. A XXXI 201, 204, 219.

Bayerisches Landtagsarchiv, München. *Protocolle,* vols. 1–153.

Fürst Oettingen-Wallerstein'sches Archiv, Wallerstein über Donauwörth. VII 2a 1b 11.

Haus- Hof- und Staatsarchiv, Wien.
Deutsche Akten 34, 36, 66, 74, 93, 147.
Frankfurt (Bundestag und Stadt) 38, 54, 58.

Lerchenfeld, Privat-Archiv der Familie von. Bundestagspapiere 1826–33.

————. Correspondenz mit König Ludwig I, 1828–41.

————. Max Frh von Lerchenfeld 1828–33; Bundestag; Correspondenz mit Zentner, Armensperg, Wrede.

————. Denkschriften und Bruchstücke, innere Verwaltung und Verfassung von Baiern, betr.

————. Correspondenzen des Max Frh von Lerchenfeld mit dem Kronprinzen Ludwig von Baiern, 1810–1825.

Public Records Office, London. FO/30 20–35, 37–40, 42–45, 49–52, 55–109.

2. Published Documents

Chroust, Anton, ed. "Gesandtschaftsberichte aus München, 1814–1848: Abteilung I. Die Berichte der französischen Gesandten (1816–1843)." Schriftenreihe zur Bayerischen Landesgeschichte. Vols. 18–24. Munich, 1935–37.

————. "Gesandtschaftsberichte aus München, 1814–1848: Abteilung II. Die Berichte der oesterreichischen Gesandten." Schriftenreihe zur Bayerischen Landesgeschichte. Vols. 33, 36–38. Munich, 1939–42.

————. "Gesandtschaftsberichte aus München, 1814–1848: Abteilung III. Die Berichte der preussischen Gesandten." Schriftenreihe zur Bayerischen Landesgeschichte. Vols. 39–43. Munich, 1949–51.

Eisenhart-Rothe, W. von, and Ritthaler, A. Vorgeschichte und Begründung des deutschen Zollvereins, 1815–1834. 3 vols. Berlin, 1934.

Hermand, Jost, ed. Der deutsche Vormärz. Texte und Dokumentation. Stuttgart, 1967.

Huber, Ernst R. Dokumente zur deutschen Verfassungsgeschichte. 3 vols. Stuttgart, 1961–66.

Klüber, Johann K., and Welcker, C., eds. Wichtige Urkunde für den Rechtszustand der deutschen Nation mit eigenhändigen Anmerkungen. Mannheim, 1844.

Lerchenfeld, Max Frh von, ed. Aus den Papieren des k. b. Staatsminister Maximilian Freiherrn von Lerchenfeld. Nördlingen, 1887.

Metternich-Winneburg, Richard, ed. *Aus Metternichs nachgelassenen Papieren.* 8 vols. Vienna, 1881–84.

Meyer, Philipp von, ed. *Staats-acten fuer Geschichte und oeffentliches Recht des Deutschen Nation.* 2d ed. 2 vols. Frankfurt/Main, 1833–40.

Protocolle der Deutschen Bundesversammlung. 51 vols. Frankfurt/Main, 1816–66.

Die Verhandlungen der Bundesversammlung von den revolutionären Bewegungen des Jahres 1830 bis zu den geheimen Wiener Ministerial-Conferenzen. Heidelberg, 1846.

3. Contemporary Publications

Erichson, George [Friedrich Lindner]. *Manuscript aus Süd-Deutschland.* 2 ed. London, 1821.

Die Gegenwart: Eine encyklopädische Darstellung der neuesten Zeitgeschichte für alle Stände. 2 vols. Leipzig, 1848–49.

Gruben Franz Frh. von. *Die deutschen Bundes-Staaten am Vorabend der Konferenzen zu Wien.* Munich, 1834.

Ilse, Leopold F. *Geschichte der deuschen Bundesversammlung, insbesondere ihrer Verhaltens zu den deutschen National-Interessen,* 3 vols. Marburg, 1861–62.

_____. *Geschichte der politischen Untersuchungen welche durch die neben der Bundesversammlung errichteten Commission der Central-Untersuchungs-Commission zu Mainz und der Bundes-Zentral-Behörde zu Frankfurt in den Jahren 1819 bis 1827 und 1833 bis 1842 geführt sind.* Frankfurt/Main, 1860.

Kaltenborn, Carl von. *Geschichte der deutschen Bundesverhältnisse und Einheitsbestrebungen von 1806 bis 1856.* 2 vols. in 1. Berlin, 1857.

Kombst, Gustaf. *Der deutsche Bundestag gegen Ende des Jahres 1832.* Strassburg, 1836.

Leonhardi, Gustav Frh von. *Geschichte Baierns unter König Max Joseph I.* Berlin, 1854.

Leonhardi, Ph. Friedrich von. *Das Austrägalverfahren des Deutschen Bundes.* 2 vols. Frankfurt/Main, 1838–45.

Nauwerk, Karl. *Die Thätigkeit der deutschen Bundesversammlung oder die wesentlichen Verhandlungen und Beschlüsse des Bundestages, 1815–46.* 4 vols. Berlin, 1845–46.

[Rauschenplatt]. *Die geheime Beschlüsse der Wiener Kabinets-Konferenzen vom Jahre 1834.* Strassburg, 1844.

Schaumann, Adolf F. *Geschichte der Bildung des Deutschen Bundes auf dem Wiener Congresse.* (Historisches Taschenbuch, 3. Folge.) Leipzig, 1850.

Struve, Gustav von. *Erster Versuch auf dem Felde des deutschen Bundesrechts, betreffend die Verfassungsmässige Erledigung der Streitigkeiten zwischen deutschen Bundesgliedern.* Bremen, 1830.

Weech, Friedrich von. *Correspondencen und Actenstücke zur Geschichte der Ministerialconferenz von Carlsbad und Wien in dem Jahren 1819, 1820, und 1834.* Leipzig, 1865.

Wirth, Joh. G. *Die politische Reform Deutschlands. Noch ein dringendes Wort an die deutschen Volksfreunde.* Strassburg, 1832.

[————]. *Das Recht des deutschen Volkes und die Beschlüsse des Frankfurter Bundestages von 28. Juni 1832.* N.p., 1832.

4. General Works

Aegidi, Ludwig, K. *Aus der Vorzeit des Zollvereins. Beitrag zur deutschen Geschichte.* Hamburg, 1865.

Albrecht, Curt. *Die Triaspolitik des Frh Karl August von Wangenheim.* Stuttgart, 1914.

Artz, Friederick. *Reaction and Revolution: 1814–1832.* New York, 1963.

Bechtel, Heinrich. *Wirtschafts- und Sozialgeschichte Deutschlands.* Munich, 1967.

Bibl, Viktor. *Metternich in neuer Erleuchtung und sein geheimer Briefwechsel mit dem bayerischen Staatsminister Wrede.* Vienna, 1928.

Biedermann, Karl. *Fünfundzwanzig Jahre deutsche Geschichte, 1815–1840.* 2 vols. Breslaw, 1890.

Bitterauf, Theodor. "Die Zensur der politischen Zeitungen in Bayern, 1799–1825." *Riezler Festschrift: Beiträge zur bayerischen Geschichte,* pp. 305–51. Gotha, 1913.

————. *Bayern als Königreich, 1806–1906.* Munich, 1906.

Böck, Hanno. *Karl Philipp Fürst von Wrede als politischer Berater König Ludwig I. von Bayern, 1825–38.* Munich, 1968.

Brentano, Lujo. *On the History and Development of Guilds and the Origin of Trade-Unions.* 1870. Reprint. New York, 1969.

Doeberl, M. "Bayern und die wirtschaftliche Einigung Deutschlands." *Abhandlung der Königlich Bayerischen Akademie der Wissenschaft* 39:1–117 (Munich, 1915).

————. *Bayern und Deutschland. Bayern und die Deutsche Frage in der Epoche des Frankfurter Parlaments.* Munich, 1922

————. *Ein Jahrhundert bayerischen Verfassungslebens.* 2d ed. Munich, 1918.

————. *Entwicklungsgeschichte Bayerns.* Edited by Max Spindler. 3 vols. Munich, 1912–31.

Doll, Anton. "Philipp Jakob Siebenpfeiffer/Johann Georg August Wirth." In *Das Hambacherfest, 27. Mai 1832: Männern und Ideen,* edited by Kurt Baumann, pp. 7–94. Speyer, 1957.

Dommermuth, Nikolas. *Das angebliche europäische Garantierecht über den Deutschen Bund von 1815 bis 1866.* Frankfurt/Main, 1928.

Fischer, Karl. *Die Nation und der Bundestag.* Leipzig, 1880.

Fischer, Wolfam. *Handwerksrecht und Handwerkswirtschaft um 1800.* Berlin, 1955.

Gerber, Harry. "Der Frankfurter Wachenstrum vom 3. April 1833. Neue Beiträge zu seinem Verlauf und seiner behördlichen Untersuchung." *Quellen und Darstellungen zur Geschichte der Burschenschaft und der deutschen Einheitsbewegung.* Berlin, 1934.

Hamerow, Theodore. *Restoration, Revolution, Reaction: Economics and Politics in Germany, 1815–1871.* Princeton, N.J., 1958.

Heffter, Heinrich. *Die deutsche Selbstverwaltung im 19. Jahrhundert: Geschichte der Ideen und Institutionen.* Stuttgart, 1950.

Heigel, Karl. *Ludwig I. König von Bayern.* Leipzig, 1872.

Henderson, W. O. *The Zollverein.* 1st U.S. ed. Chicago, 1959.

Hoermann, Liselotte. "Der bayerisch-badisch Gebietsstreit, 1825–1832." *Historiche Studien* 336 (Berlin, 1938).

Holborn, Hajo. *A History of Modern Germany.* 3 vols. New York, 1964–69.

Huber, Ernst R. *Deutsche Verfassungsgeschichte seit 1789.* 4 vols. Stuttgart, 1960–69.

Kahn, Richard. *Untersuchungen zur Entstehungsgeschichte des Konstitutionalismus in Bayern.* Mannheim, 1915.

Koopmann, Helmut. *Das Junge Deutschland. Analyse seines Selbstständnisses.* Stuttgart, 1970.

Lamprecht, Karl. *Deutsche Geschichte.* 3d ed. Berlin, 1913.

Lütge, Friedrich. *Deutsche Sozial- und Wirtschaftsgeschichte. Ein Ueberblick.* 2d ed. Berlin and Göttingen, 1960.

Mann, Golo. *The History of Germany since 1789.* Translated by Marian Jackson. New York, 1968.

Menn, Walter. *Zur Vorgeschichte des deutschen Zollvereins.* Greifswald, 1930.

Merk, Wilhelm. *Verfassungsschutz.* Stuttgart, 1935.

Mucke, Joh. Richard. *Die politischen Bewegungen in Deutschland von 1830 bis 1835.* 2 vols. Leipzig, 1875.

Passant, E. J. *A Short History of Germany, 1815-1945.* Cambridge, 1959.

Pinson, Koppel S. *Modern Germany: Its History and Civilization.* 2d ed. New York, 1966.

Price, Arnold M. *The Evolution of the Zollverein.* Ann Arbor, Mich., 1949.

Raumer, Kurt von. "Das Hambacher Fest." *Staat und Volkstum: Neue Studien zur baierischen und deutschen Geschichte und Volkskunde. Festgabe für Karl Alexander von Müller,* pp. 207-17. Diessen vor München, 1933.

Renner, Helmut. "Fürst Karl von Wrede." *Das Hambacherfest, 27. Mai 1832: Männer und Ideen,* pp. 305-24. Speyer, 1957.

Sachs, Lothar. *Die Entwicklungsgeschichte des bayerischen Landtags in den ersten drei Jahrzehnten nach der Verfassungsgebung, 1818-48.* Würzburg, 1914.

Sagarra, Eda. *Tradition and Revolution: German Literature and Society, 1830-1890.* New York, 1971.

Sartorius von Waltershausen, August. *Deutsche Wirtschaftsgeschichte, 1815-1914.* 2d ed. Jena, 1923.

Schieder, Theodor. "Partikularismus und nationales Bewusstsein im Denken des Vormärz." In *Staat und Gesellschaft im deutschen Vormärz,* edited by Werner Conze, pp. 9-38. Stuttgart, 1962.

Schnabel, Franz. *Deutsche Geschichte im neunzehnten Jahrhundert.* 4 vols. Freiburg in the Breisgau, 1929-36.

Schreiber, Wilhelm. *Geschichte Bayerns in Verbindung mit der deutschen Geschichte.* 2 vols. Freiburg, 1889–91.

Schrörs, Heinrich. *Die Kölner Wirren (1837). Studien zu ihrer Geschichte.* Berlin and Bonn, 1927.

Spindler, Max, ed. *Briefwechsel zwischen Ludwig I. von Bayern und Eduard von Schenk, 1823–1841.* Munich, 1930.

————. *Erbe und Verpflichtung. Aufsätze und Vorträge zur bayerischen Geschichte,* edited by Andreas Kraus. Munich, 1966.

————, ed. *Handbuch der Bayerischen Geschichte.* 4 vols. Munich, 1967–75.

————. "Das Kabinett unter König Ludwig I." *Staat und Volkstum: Neue Studien zur baierischen und deutschen Geschichte und Volkskunde. Festgabe für Karl Alexander von Müller,* pp. 318–30. Diessen vor München, 1933.

Treitschke, Heinrich von. *The History of Germany in the Nineteenth Century.* Translated by Eden and Cedar Paul. 7 vols. New York, 1916–19.

Valentin, Veit. *Geschichte der deutschen Revolution von 1848–49.* 2 vols. Berlin, 1930–31.

Weber, W. *Der deutsche Zollverein. Geschichte seiner Entstehung und Entwicklung.* 2d, expanded ed. Leipzig, 1871.

Webster, Charles. *The Foreign Policy of Palmerston.* 2 vols. London, 1951.

Westphal, Otto. "System und Wandlung der auswärtigen Politik Bayerns in den ersten Jahren Ludwigs I." *Staat und Volkstum: Neue Studien zur baierischen und deutschen Geschichte und Volkskunde. Festgabe für Karl Alexander von Müller,* pp. 355–66. Diessen vor München, 1933.

Zorn, Wolfgang. "Gesellschaft und Staat im Bayern des Vormärz. In *Staat und Gesellschaft im deutschen Vormärz,* edited by Werner Conze, pp. 113–42. Stuttgart, 1962.

————. *Kleine Wirtschafts- und Sozialgeschichte Bayerns, 1806–1933.* Munich-Pasing, 1962.

5. Periodical Literature

Heigel, Karl Theodor. "Das Hambacher Fest vom 27. Mai 1832. *Historische Zeitschrift* 111 (1913):54–88.

Huber, Ernst R. "Bundesexekution und Bundesintervention. Ein Beitrag zur Frage des Verfassungsschutzes im Deutschen Bund." *Archiv des oeffentlichen Rechts* 79 (1953):1–57.

Jenal, Emil. "Der Kampf gegen die jungdeutsche Literatur." *Zeitschrift für deutsche Philologie* 58 (1933):165–95.

Müller, Karl Alexander von. "Probleme der neuesten bayerischen Geschichte." *Historische Zeitschrift* 118 (1917):222–49.

Wrede, Oskar Fürst von. "Aus der Wirksamkeit des Feldmarschalls Fürst von Wrede als Minister und Reichsrat." *Zeitschrift für bayerische Landesgeschichte* 5 (1932):51–88.

6. Unpublished Dissertations

Aretin, Karl O. Frh von. "Die deutsche Politik Bayerns in der Zeit der staatlichen Entwicklung des Deutschen Bundes, 1814–1820." Ph.D. dissertation, Ludwig-Maximilian Universität, Munich, 1954.

Meier, Richard. "Die Regelung der inneren Verhältnisse des Deutschen Bundes durch die Bundesversammlung." Ph.D. dissertation, Ludwig-Maximilian Universität, Munich, 1952.

Index